D0058145

NULLIFICATION

NULLIFICATION

How to Resist Federal Tyranny in the 21st Century

THOMAS E. WOODS, JR.

Cataloging-in-Publication data on file with the Library of Congress

ISBN 978-1-59698-149-2

Published in the United States by
Regnery Publishing, Inc.
One Massachusetts Avenue, NW
Washington, DC 20001
www.regnery.com

Manufactured in the United States of America

10 9 8 7 6 5 4 3 2 1

Books are available in quantity for promotional or premium use. Write to Director of Special Sales, Regnery Publishing, Inc., One Massachusetts Avenue NW, Washington, DC 20001, for information on discounts and terms or call (202) 216-0600.

Distributed to the trade by:
Perseus Distribution
387 Park Avenue South
New York, NY 10016

To our daughters,
Regina, Veronica, Amy, and Elizabeth

CONTENTS

PART I: THE CRISIS NOW

PART II: ELEVEN ESSENTIAL DOCUMENTS

Part I

The Crisis Now

CHAPTER 1

The Return of a Forbidden Idea

WHEN HOUSE SPEAKER NANCY PELOSI was asked by a reporter in 2009 where in the Constitution she found the authority to impose a health insurance mandate on Americans, she laughed and replied, "Are you serious? Are you serious?" The reporter answered that indeed he was. The Speaker just shook her head, and then took another question.

Pelosi's press spokesman clarified the Speaker's non-answer by explaining that this was "not a serious question."[1]

Senator Pat Leahy was asked the same thing—where in the Constitution is the federal government granted the authority to do this? His answer: "There's no question there's authority. Nobody questions that."[2] He had no idea, in other words.

Senator Mark Warner, in turn, came out with this gem of constitutional insight: "There is no place in the Constitution that talks about you ought to have the right to get a telephone, but we have made those choices as a country over the years."[3] Got that? *So what* if the Constitution says nothing about granting the federal government the power to force Americans to buy approved health insurance packages? The Constitution also says nothing about allowing American citizens to buy a telephone, eat at Taco Bell, or have children, and we do those things, don't we?

The difference that managed to escape Senator Warner is that in a free society *people* do not require constitutional authority to act. Government does.

The controversy over health care reflects a much broader and deeper constitutional void in American life. Some fifteen years ago, a Supreme Court Justice asked the United States Solicitor General (the government's lawyer for Supreme Court cases) if he could name an activity or program that, in his view, would fall outside the bounds of what the Constitution authorized the federal government to do. He could not.[4]

This contempt for constitutional limitations on the federal government is bipartisan and long-standing. Unsurprisingly, when the Constitution is thought of not as the strict limitation on government that its original supporters sold it as, but as something so compendiously broad as almost to defy limitation, government will continue to grow. Some federal activities have begun to alarm even those who have historically cheered government growth as a progressive force. Yet nothing has been able to stop it. Even Ronald Reagan, for all his charisma and rhetorical prowess, was able only to *slow the growth* of certain categories of federal spending.[5] In 1994, the Republican Party won control of both houses of Congress in a historic off-year election victory. Government would at last be shrunk, politicians assured us.

Sure it would.

More and more Americans concerned about ongoing and apparently unstoppable government growth are beginning to wonder if some other strategy should be pursued, the exclusively electoral one having been such a failure. In the face of decades of broken promises and precious few victories against the seemingly inexorable federal advance, the pretty speeches of the plastic men are starting to ring a little hollow.

This is the spirit in which the Jeffersonian remedy of state interposition or nullification is once again being pursued. As we shall see in chapter 2, it was Thomas Jefferson, in his draft of the Kentucky Resolutions of 1798, who introduced the term "nullification" into American political discourse. And as we'll see in chapter 4, Jefferson was merely building upon an existing line of political thought dating back to Virginia's ratifying convention and even into the colonial period. Consequently, an idea that may strike us as radical today was well within the mainstream of Virginian political thought when Jefferson introduced it.

Nullification begins with the axiomatic point that a federal law that violates the Constitution is no law at all. It is void and of no effect. Nullification simply pushes this uncontroversial point a step further: if a law is unconstitutional and therefore void and of no effect, it is up to the states, the parties to the federal compact, to declare it so and thus refuse to enforce it. It would be foolish and vain to wait for the federal government or a branch thereof to condemn its own law. Nullification provides a shield between the people of a state and an unconstitutional law from the federal government.

The central point behind nullification is that the federal government cannot be permitted to hold a monopoly on constitutional interpretation. If the federal government has the exclusive right to judge the extent of its own powers, warned James Madison and Thomas Jefferson in 1798, it will continue to grow—regardless of elections, the separation of powers, and other much-touted limits on government power. A constitution is, after all, only a piece of paper. It cannot enforce itself. Checks and balances among the executive, legislative, and judicial branches, a prominent feature of the Constitution, provide little guarantee of limited government, since these three federal branches can simply unite against the independence of the states and the reserved rights of the people. That is precisely what Jefferson warned William Branch Giles was already happening in 1825: "It is but too evident, that the three ruling branches of [the Federal government] are in combination to strip their colleagues, the State authorities, of the powers reserved by them, and to exercise themselves all functions foreign and domestic."[6] Much more important than the feeble restraint of "checks and balances" is the ability of the states to interpose to prevent the enforcement of unconstitutional laws. That is a *real* check on federal power.

It is not clear what the alternative to Jefferson's remedy of nullification might be. Unconstitutional laws have indeed been passed, in very great abundance, so the question he poses about what to do in such a situation is not merely academic. Should people gather petitions, asking those who drafted the objectionable law to change their minds? Good luck with that. They could instead appeal to the courts. Although it would be nice if the courts were to grant us relief, what if they do not? The federal courts have, for all intents and purposes, ceased to police the federal government. We cannot be expected to believe that the matter is settled, and an odious law to be complied with, merely because a handful of politically well-connected lawyers whom we are urged to treat with superstitious awe have solemnly informed us that all is well.

It is not difficult to find support in history for the general principle that an unconstitutional law is void. Alexander Hamilton contended in Federalist #78 that "there is no position which depends on clearer principles, than that every act of a delegated authority contrary to the tenor of the commission under which it is exercised, is *void*. No legislative act, therefore, contrary to the constitution, can be *valid*. To deny this, would be to affirm that the deputy is greater than his principal; that the servant is above his master; that the representatives of the people are superior to the people themselves; that men, acting by virtue of powers, may do not only what their powers do not authorize, but what they forbid."

This principle should be beyond debate. The controversy arises when we consider how and by whom an unconstitutional law should be *declared* void (and thus not enforced). It was Hamilton's view that the courts would put things right. But what if they didn't? And since the federal courts are themselves a branch of the federal government, how can the people be expected to consider them impartial arbiters? The Supreme Court itself, after all, although usually pointed to as the monopolistic and infallible judge of the constitutionality of the federal government's actions, *is itself a branch of the federal government*. So in a dispute between the states and the federal government, the resolution is to come from . . . the federal government? Jefferson refused to accept that answer. Under that arrangement, the states would inexorably be eclipsed by the federal government. It was impossible for Jefferson to believe that the states would have agreed to a system that assured their unjust subordination.

Spencer Roane, a Virginia judge who would have been appointed Chief Justice of the United States by Thomas Jefferson had John Adams not chosen John Marshall in the waning hours of his presidency, noted that if the federal judiciary were to arbitrate such a dispute between itself and the states, it would be presiding over its own case, a clear absurdity:

> It has, however, been supposed by some that... the right of the State governments to protest against, or to resist encroachments on their authority is taken away, and transferred to the Federal judiciary, whose power extends to all cases arising under the Constitution; that the Supreme Court is the umpire to decide between the States on the one side, and the United States on the other, in all questions touching the constitutionality of laws, or acts of the Executive. There are many cases which can never be brought before that tribunal, and I do humbly conceive that *the States never could have committed an act of such egregious folly as to agree that their umpire should be altogether appointed and paid by the other party*. The Supreme Court may be a perfectly impartial tribunal to decide between two States, but cannot be considered in that point of view when the contest lies between the United States and one of its members.... The Supreme Court is but a department of the general government. A department is not competent to do that to which the whole government is inadequate.... They cannot do it unless we tread underfoot the principle which forbids a party to decide his own cause.[7]

Joseph Desha, governor of Kentucky, identified the very same problem in 1825:

> When the general government encroaches upon the rights of the State, is it a safe principle to admit that a portion of the encroaching power shall have the right to determine finally whether an encroachment has been made or not? In fact, most of the encroachments made by the general government flow through the Supreme Court itself, the very tribunal which claims to be the final arbiter of all such disputes. What chance for justice have the States when the usurpers of their rights are made their judges? Just as much as individuals when judged by their oppressors.

Desha concluded that it is "believed to be the right, as it may hereafter become the duty of the State governments, to protect themselves from encroachments, and their citizens from oppression, by refusing obedience" to "unconstitutional mandates."[8]

Once we accept the underlying premise that an unconstitutional law is *ipso facto* void, it is not a long way to Jefferson's commonsense conclusion that someone ought to protect the people from the enforcement of such a law, and that the state governments, each one speaking only for itself, are the logical choice to do so.[9]

All over the country today, state legislators are introducing measures by which their states would refuse to enforce federal laws that violate the Constitution. Two dozen states nullified the REAL ID Act of 2005, legislation which aroused the opposition of both fiscal conservatives, who resented another unfunded federal mandate imposed on the states, and civil libertarians, who raised privacy concerns against the legislation's proposed standardization and centralization of identification procedures. Resistance was so widespread that although the law is still on the books, the federal government has, in effect, given up trying to enforce it. This makes for an excellent example of how nullification can work—the states' resistance to some federal action is perceived as being so fierce and determined that Washington backs off, deciding that a particular struggle isn't worth pursuing. A new piece of legislation, the so-called PASS ID Act, is now under consideration at the federal level, but the states are likely to grant it a similar reception.

Another example of a state challenge to federal power is the Sheriffs First initiative, whereby, with a few exceptions, it would be a state crime for a federal law enforcement official to make an arrest or engage in a search or seizure without first receiving permission from the local sheriff.[10] Locally elected sheriffs, who have some semblance of accountability to the people, might thereby be able to prevent some of the inevitable abuses that have accompanied the increasing centralization of law enforcement in the United States. Anyone concerned for the protection of civil liberties must find great appeal in this movement.

One of the most successful examples of modern-day nullification involves the medicinal use of marijuana, which is illegal under federal law. As of this printing, fourteen states are openly resisting the federal government's policy.

California's Angel Raich suffers from an astonishing range of afflictions, including fibromyalgia, seizures, nausea, and an inoperable brain tumor. Scoliosis, endometriosis, and temporomandibular joint dysfunction put her in constant pain. She loses a pound a day as a result of a mysterious wasting syndrome.

Cannabis alone has granted her any relief worth speaking of, without burdening her with intolerable side effects, and has arrested her weight loss. Her physician testified in court that she would die without it.

California's Compassionate Use Act of 1996, passed into law in the wake of a popular referendum in defiance of the federal prohibition, allowed her to have recourse to the one treatment that could help her. When a series of raids by federal agents in 2002 led to a wave of arrests, Angel Raich and fellow sufferer Diane Monson sought an injunction against further raids by the federal government. Although they lost in district court, a panel of the U.S. Circuit Court of Appeals for the Ninth Circuit came down in their favor and forbade federal agents from seizing the women's marijuana. The Justice Department, in turn, appealed the case, which would go before the Supreme Court as *Gonzales* v. *Raich* (2005).

The Justice Department pointed to the Constitution's commerce clause to justify the federal prohibition on the use of marijuana even for medical purposes.[11] The presence of medical marijuana in one state, it was argued, could have spillover effects on other states. Even though the marijuana was grown in one state, was never transported out of that state, was never sold at all, and was immediately consumed in that state, the Justice Department wanted it to be treated as interstate commerce and therefore subject to federal regulation. It was the typical absurdity for which commerce-clause jurisprudence has become notorious. As usual, the Court's liberals, Stephen Breyer and Ruth Bader Ginsburg, took the nationalist position against the states. It was the much-maligned conservative, Clarence Thomas, who composed the most withering critique of the Court's decision and the inane jurisprudence that informed it. "One searches the Court's opinion in vain for any hint of what aspect of American life is reserved to the States," Thomas wrote.[12] The Court ruled against Angel Raich, and declared that medical marijuana suppliers and users could be prosecuted even when the states had legislated to the contrary.

Had the Supreme Court been correct about the alleged spillover effects of medical marijuana from one state into another, we should expect some of those state governments to have filed amicus briefs in support of the federal government's position. To the contrary, Alabama, Louisiana, and Mississippi, three southern states known for their conservatism, filed amicus briefs *in support of Angel Raich*. They opposed California's policy on medical marijuana, they said, but they were much more strongly opposed to a federal government so oblivious to restraints on its power that it would actually disallow California's policy.[13]

In 2007, Angel Raich renewed her litigation before the Ninth Circuit, with an even more grotesque result. The circuit court conceded the seriousness of her condition, and noted that if she did not have recourse to the liberties the California Compassionate Use Act made available to her she would be forced to endure "intolerable pain, including severe chronic pain in her face and jaw muscles due to temporomandibular joint dysfunction and bruxism, severe chronic pain and chronic burning from fibromyalgia that forces her to be flat on her back for days, excruciating pain from non-epileptic seizures, heavy bleeding and severely painful menstrual periods due to a uterine fibroid tumor, and acute weight loss resulting possibly in death due to a life-threatening wasting disorder." The Ninth Circuit admitted

Raich did "not appear to have any legal alternative to marijuana use."[14] But that was just too bad. "Federal law does not recognize a fundamental right to use medical marijuana prescribed by a licensed physician to alleviate excruciating pain and human suffering."[15]

Now consider: the federal government defied the states' resistance efforts, launching a series of raids on medical marijuana patients and dispensaries. The Supreme Court ruled against the states. And yet the use of medical marijuana goes on as if none of this ever occurred. There are as many as one thousand functioning dispensaries in Los Angeles County alone, each of which operates in direct defiance of the federal will.[16]

Medical marijuana is not a cause that is losing momentum. If anything, its supporters are becoming more confrontational and identifying their cause more consistently as a constitutional struggle with the federal government. In socially conservative Kansas, the movement is proceeding apace. House Bill 2610 declares, "The legislature of the state of Kansas declares that this act is enacted pursuant to the police power of the state to protect the health of its citizens *that is reserved to the state of Kansas and its people under the 10th amendment to the United States Constitution*."[17] According to New York's Assembly Bill A09016 and Senate Bill S4041B, "This legislation is an appropriate exercise of the state's legislative power to protect the health of its people under article 17 of the state constitution *and the tenth amendment of the United States Constitution*."[18] The Tenth Amendment, discussed further in chapter 2, clarifies that the federal government possesses only the powers delegated to it in the Constitution, and guarantees the states the power to govern themselves in all other areas.

Nullification is being contemplated in many other areas of American life as well—and not just in health care (an issue to be discussed in chapter 5).

In early 2010, Wyoming state representative Allen Jaggi introduced House Bill 95, the Firearms Freedom Act. The Act seeks to rein in the federal government's assumed power to regulate anything it chooses on the spurious grounds of "interstate commerce." It declares that "specified firearms that are manufactured, sold, purchased, possessed and used exclusively within Wyoming shall be exempt from federal regulation, including registration requirements." Thus, Wyoming guns with no interstate dimension cannot be regulated under any honest reading of the commerce clause.[19] This statement of common sense doubtless sounds shocking and uppity to the modern ear, accustomed as it is to accepting federal usurpations as unchangeable facts of life. Tennessee, Montana, and South Dakota have enacted similar legislation into law. Nearly two dozen other states are considering doing the same. South Carolina's legislature is considering a law (House Bill 4509) that would nullify federal gun registration requirements regardless of where the guns are manufactured. Proposed legislation in New Hampshire and Wyoming even includes penalties for federal agents attempting to enforce unconstitutional regulation. As the Framers of the Constitution intended, these matters properly belong to the states and the people, not the federal government.

An effort that bears more than a family resemblance to nullification, concerned as it is with the reserved powers of the states, is called Bring the Guard Home. It seeks to restore the traditional powers of the state governors over their own National Guard units.[20] Bring the Guard Home argues that the

National Guard, the successor to the militias of an earlier time, may be deployed by the president only for the constitutional purposes of repelling invasions or insurrections, or executing the law.[21] Such a role for the National Guard is consistent with the popular portrayal of the citizen soldier who assists his own community and his own country.

The Bring the Guard Home movement boasts a diverse array of supporters, including liberals, conservatives, libertarians, military families, and active-duty servicemen. Proposed legislation to reassert traditional state authority over the Guard has twice received favorable coverage on WorldNetDaily.com, a popular conservative website.[22] The libertarian Tenth Amendment Center has proposed legislation even more straightforward and powerful than what Bring the Guard Home itself has suggested. According to its model legislation,

> The governor shall withhold or withdraw approval of the transfer of the National Guard to federal control in the absence of: a) A military invasion of the United States, or b) An insurrection, or c) A calling forth of the Guard by the federal government in a manner provided by Congress to execute the laws of the Union, provided that said laws were made in pursuance of the delegated powers in the Constitution of the United States, or d) A formal declaration of war from Congress.[23]

The Tenth Amendment Center became especially active on the issue in the wake of an executive order from Barack Obama in early 2010 that established a new Council of Governors that would review "such matters as involving the National Guard of the various states; homeland defense, civil support; synchronization and integration of state and federal military activities in the United States; and other matters of mutual interest pertaining to National Guard, homeland defense, and civil support activities."[24] In light of this vague mandate, supporters of the National Guard's traditional role found it opportune to try to introduce into the various state legislatures clarifying measures regarding the proper role of, and authority over, the National Guard.

Objections have been raised against nullification, to be sure, and we shall address them, implicitly or explicitly, throughout this book. But one misplaced criticism ought to be answered right away: that nullification violates the Constitution's supremacy clause, which says the Constitution and laws in pursuance thereof shall be the supreme law of the land.[25] This argument merely begs the question. The supremacy clause says the Constitution and *laws in pursuance thereof* shall be the supreme law of the land. In other words, the Constitution and *constitutional laws* shall be the supreme law of the land. *That's precisely the issue*: a nullifying state holds that the law in question is unconstitutional and *not* "in pursuance thereof." The supremacy clause does not say *unconstitutional laws* shall be the supreme law of the land. William Harper, by turns judge, U.S. senator, and state representative, understood the matter correctly back in 1830 when he noted that "the clause declaring that the Constitution and the laws made in pursuance of it, shall be the supreme law, would, of itself, conclude nothing. The question would still recur—who shall judge *whether the laws are made in pursuance of it*."[26]

This need not be a traditional left-right issue. Before the Left decided that the bureaucratization of all of life, administered by a remote central government, was the ideal social arrangement, some on the Left considered such a system repulsive and inhumane. Kirkpatrick Sale, for instance, argued in his book *Human Scale* that so much of modern life, its political dimension included, had grown dysfunctional simply by virtue of having *grown*. Everything was simply much too big, its scale grotesquely out of proportion to what a humane existence would appear to demand.[27]

Some of this earlier decentralist spirit is still alive in community-supported agriculture, the defense of farmers' markets against federal incursions, and the "small is beautiful" outlook in general—causes associated in the public mind with, but by no means confined to, the Left. It is this spirit that would find nullification and what came to be known as the Principles of '98—described in detail in the next chapter—congenial, and it is in this spirit that today's burgeoning nullification movement has made inroads among the Left. Yes, Vermont and Kansas may use nullification, which the Kentucky Resolutions of 1799 described as the states' "rightful remedy" against unconstitutional federal power grabs, for different purposes. Vermont may object to one unconstitutional law and Kansas another. Heaven knows there are plenty to choose from. But for those who do not feel compelled to mold every last community in America into their own image, and prefer instead to live and let live and mind their own business, this is quite all right. We might actually wind up with the diverse collection of self-governing communities the ratifiers of the Constitution thought they were protecting.

Unfortunately, only a tiny remnant of this school of thought remains on the Left. For the most part, we are faced with what I call the imperial Left—which, not content to let a hundred flowers bloom, seeks to impose a federally administered uniformity upon states and communities, in defiance of decentralism and localism, to say nothing of the spirit and practice of the original American republic. Proposing nullification around such people is like holding a crucifix before Dracula.

Now I do not doubt that many readers, exposed to this idea for the first time, will initially be skeptical, even dismissive. All I ask is that you give serious consideration to Jefferson's side of things, which I have reproduced as faithfully as I can in the pages that follow. I hope to persuade you that the case for nullification is a strong one—logically, constitutionally, historically, and morally.

To my surprise, a significant number of Americans are already sympathetic to nullification, without necessarily having heard of the idea before or weighed the arguments for and against. According to a February 2010 Rasmussen Reports poll, 59 percent of likely voters believe the states should have the right to opt out of federal government programs of which they disapprove. Just 25 percent disagree, while another 15 percent are not sure.[28] This is not exactly the same thing as nullification, which involves the refusal to enforce *unconstitutional* laws, not simply laws the states do not like. But these numbers are significant all the same.

This initial sympathy for nullification may be a product of the public's inchoate sense that Washington, D.C., is where the least responsive level of government, significantly worse than its state and local counterparts, is to be found. The bank bailouts of 2008 are an instructive example: with constituent calls running fifty-to-one—or higher—against the bailout package, Congress eventually approved it anyway. Instead of concluding that the people had spoken, political figures simply rewrote the bill until enough pressure groups got their bribes. This much worse bill was then pushed through the House of Representatives. Democracy in action.

There is likewise a sense that matters of great importance are rushed through Congress on the spurious grounds that desperate times call for reckless measures. Whatever the merits of these measures, items ranging from the North American Free Trade Agreement and the World Trade Organization to the bailout of the Mexican peso, the PATRIOT Act, the Wall Street bailouts, and the fiscal stimulus bill of 2009—to name only a few—were imposed on the country without sufficient deliberation and (perish the thought!) likely with interests other than the public good in mind.

Some of this lack of responsiveness, in turn, is attributable to how few representatives per capita we now have, as a result of how large the country has grown. When the Constitution was ratified, there were three million Americans. When the first Congress convened in 1790, there was one member of the House of Representatives for every 30,000 people (which translated into one per 5,000 voting citizens). The size of the House was capped at 435 members in 1920, when the U.S. population was at 90 million. By 2010 the population was nearly 309 million. That's one representative per 710,345 people. Had this ratio been observed in 1790, there would have been about four people in the House of Representatives. Were the old ratio observed today, there would be 10,300 members in the House.[29] What, on such a scale, could political representation amount to? If political representation ever really meant anything, it surely doesn't today. Governments are notoriously difficult to control, even under the best of conditions. Are we surprised when a government on this scale, so remote from popular control and oversight, routinely acts in such open defiance of public opinion?

To be sure, nullification is not a perfect remedy. It cannot solve all our problems. Like nearly any principle, it can be abused. But we are grown-ups. We understand that no political arrangement is without shortcomings, even serious ones. Whenever we try to wrestle with the issue of political power, the greatest and most dangerous monopoly in history, we are inevitably faced with imperfect choices. All we can do is ask some basic questions and be content to draw some general conclusions. Is liberty more likely to be preserved under one monopoly jurisdiction or through the competition of many jurisdictions? Where have the worst outrages against human dignity occurred: in decentralized polities or in the centralized states of the nineteenth and twentieth centuries? In which arrangement is some modicum of popular control more likely to be preserved? Would the world not have been better off had Germany remained a decentralized collection of states? Are we to believe that the American system makes none but the lamest and most ineffectual provision for the states to protect themselves against catastrophic decisions by the central power? These questions are never answered, because in our stunted political discourse, they are never asked.

As we shall see in this book, generations of Jeffersonians described nullification as the "rightful remedy" when the federal government exercised unauthorized powers. Yes, it throws a monkey wrench into the federal works. That's precisely the point. Some will bemoan the states' interference with the wheels of government in Washington. Why, this will be disorderly! But these are the sentiments we have heard and will always hear, until the end of time, from those who favor power over liberty. As one proponent of nullification observed, "It is impossible to propose *any* limitation on the authority of governments, without encountering, from the supporters of power, this very objection of feebleness and anarchy."[30]

Notice, further, what these critics do *not* consider disorderly: the ongoing and evidently ceaseless exercise of unconstitutional powers by the federal government. The alleged chaos that would result should the states follow Jefferson's advice and defend themselves against unconstitutional expansions of federal power is where they pretend to detect such great danger. As usual, Jefferson had the correct reply to "the supporters of power." "I would rather be exposed to the inconveniences attending too much liberty," he said, "than to those attending too small a degree of it."[31]

Our Founding Fathers took a deliberate stance against the centralizing trends that were already at work in the eighteenth century and which would explode in the nineteenth and twentieth. Americans admired the Dutch federation, which was organized as a federative polity, and which became something of an anomaly amid the trend toward centralized states, of which the French Revolution would give the world such a notable example.[32] We have allowed this unique inheritance to be undermined and destroyed, such that the United States, once a federative polity, has become just another modern unitary state like France or Germany. We have been taught to celebrate this betrayal of our Founding Fathers. We have cheered what we ought to have mourned.

CHAPTER 2

The Problem and the "Rightful Remedy"

IN MODERN AMERICA, the Constitution has become The Great Unmentionable. Where the federal government derives constitutional authorization for its various activities is hardly ever considered or discussed. The maverick journalist who does pose the forbidden question is laughed at or ignored. On the rare occasion in which a federal official deigns to answer, the response is nearly always an awkward and inane reference to one of three constitutional clauses we shall examine in the first part of this chapter, none of which grants the power whose exercise the official is trying to defend. When the Constitution was ratified, the people were assured that it established a government of limited powers (primarily related to foreign policy and the regulation of interstate commerce), that the states retained all powers not delegated to the new government, and that the federal government could exercise no additional powers without their consent, given in the form of constitutional amendments. This is not a peculiarly conservative or libertarian reading of the historical record. This *is* the historical record.

The three constitutional clauses that have most frequently been exploited on behalf of expansions of federal government power are the general welfare clause, the commerce clause, and the "necessary and proper" clause.[1] Generations of hapless American high school students have been taught fantasy versions of these clauses, such that they graduate with the conviction that the federal government is duly authorized to do pretty much whatever it wants to do.

Let's consider the "general welfare" clause first. We read in Article I, Section 8 of the Constitution that Congress "shall have Power To lay and collect Taxes, Duties, Imposts and Excises, to pay the Debts and provide for the common Defence and general Welfare of the United States."[2] Does this mean the federal government has the power to implement *any* measure it thinks will redound to the general welfare? When Anti-Federalist opponents of the Constitution pointed to this clause with alarm, warning that the new government could thereby exercise whatever power it wanted on the grounds that it somehow promoted the general welfare, the Constitution's supporters assured them that such fears were unfounded. The federal government, they said, had only those powers expressly delegated to it.

James Madison was particularly adamant. The very structure of Article I, Section 8 of the Constitution, he said, ruled out such an interpretation. If the general welfare clause granted the federal government a *general power* to do anything that might advance the general welfare, why did this section of the Constitution then bother to list *specific powers* the government could exercise? Wouldn't these specifics have been superfluous and absurd, on the heels of a general grant of power that obviously included the powers that followed and made their enumeration unnecessary? There is no point, in other words, in *specifically* declaring (for example) that the federal government shall have the power to erect "needful Buildings" immediately after saying it may do *anything at all* it thinks will advance the general welfare. Thus Madison wrote in Federalist #41, "For what purpose could the enumeration of particulars be inserted, if these and all others were meant to be included in the preceding general power?" In 1792, he said:

> If Congress can employ money indefinitely to the general welfare, and are the sole and supreme judges of the general welfare, they may take the care of religion into their own hands; they may appoint teachers in every state, county, and parish, and pay them out of the public treasury; they may take into their own hands the education of children, establishing in like manner schools throughout the Union; they may assume the provision for the poor; they may undertake the regulation of all roads other than post-roads; in short, everything, from the highest object of state legislation down to the most minute object of police, would be thrown under the power of Congress.[3]

In other words, activities of the federal government that we have been taught to consider perfectly unobjectionable were, to Madison, clear and obvious violations of the Constitution that derived from a dishonest reading of the general welfare clause.

This remained Madison's view throughout his life. "In its fair and consistent meaning," he wrote in 1800, "[the general welfare clause] cannot enlarge the enumerated powers vested in Congress."[4] Madison was saying the same thing in the 1830s, noting that "it exceeds the possibility of belief" that supporters of limited government "should have silently permitted the introduction of words or phrases in a sense rendering fruitless the restrictions & definitions elaborated by them."[5]

Madison also noted that, of all the amendments the states proposed to limit the power of the new government shortly after they ratified the Constitution, not one sought to circumscribe the power of Congress under the general welfare clause—even though, if the expansive reading of the clause were correct, it was "evidently more alarming in its range, than all the powers objected to put together." Had the general welfare clause been understood to grant an unspecified reservoir of powers to the federal government, in other words, early Americans suspicious of government power would obviously have objected to it. People understood that the general welfare clause—which had also appeared in the Articles of Confederation—did no such thing. "It was taken for granted," said Madison, "that the terms were harmless; because explained & limited, as in the 'Articles of Confederation,' by the enumerated powers which followed them."[6]

This was Jefferson's view as well. To interpret the words "general welfare" as granting the federal government "a distinct and independent power to do any act they please, which might be for the good of the Union, would render all the preceding and subsequent enumerations of power completely useless." Such a reading, furthermore, "would reduce the whole instrument to a single phrase, that of instituting a Congress with power to do whatever would be for the good of the United States; and, as they would be the sole judges of the good or evil, it would be also a power to do whatever evil they please."[7]

Every tyrant claims to be advancing the general welfare. Having just fought against a government that claimed an undefined reservoir of powers, Americans would not have granted such a reservoir to their own government. If anything, the general welfare clause was a restriction on the power of the federal government: it had to exercise the powers delegated to it with an eye to the welfare of the country as a whole, not to the particular advantage of one state or section.[8]

It might be objected that Alexander Hamilton, the country's first secretary of the Treasury, took a different, more expansive view of the clause. Of that there is no doubt. But we may question how much weight Hamilton's position should carry. For one thing, prior to New York's ratification of the Constitution, Hamilton noted in Federalist #17 and #34 that the clause did not mean that an area like agriculture would come under the purview of the federal government.[9] But having given the people that assurance, Hamilton then declared, several years after the Constitution was ratified, that the clause *did* mean agriculture could be directed by the federal government.[10] Which of these opinions is more weighty: the one intended to explain the Constitution's intent to the people as they were deciding whether or not to ratify, or the opposite opinion given suddenly and after the people's decision had safely been made?

If we wish to cite Hamilton as a source, we might, while we are at it, quote from his remarks to the Constitutional Convention to the effect that the United States ought to have a president for life; a Senate whose members, appointed by the president, would serve for life; and state governors appointed by the president. We might likewise cite his view that the British government, which he hoped his own might come to resemble, was the best in the world. Finally, we could cite Hamilton's own admission that he was very much out of step with the rest of the Constitution's drafters. Then we might fully assess the relevance of Hamilton's views of the general welfare clause.

The Constitution's commerce clause declares that Congress will have power to "regulate Commerce with foreign Nations, and among the several States, and with the Indian tribes." It is the part about regulating commerce "among the several States" that has caused the mischief. As with the general welfare clause, the original understanding of the commerce clause—the understanding that informed the decisions of the ratifying conventions, and thus the interpretation to which they believed they were committing the American people—is not so hard to uncover. "Commerce" meant only trade or exchange—not, as its more ambitious interpreters have tried to claim, all gainful activity.[11] No reference to commerce at the Constitutional Convention, in the *Federalist*, or at the state ratifying conventions encompasses anything else. "Among the several States" meant exactly that: commerce between one state and another, not commerce that might happen to have an effect on another state.[12] For that matter, "regulate" in the eighteenth century meant to "make regular"—that is, to cause to function in a regular and orderly manner—as opposed to the word's modern meaning that suggests micromanagement and control. (This is the sense in which the Second Amendment's "well-regulated Militia" is to be understood, for example.) Thus, the purpose of the commerce clause was to establish a free-trade zone throughout the United States (thereby making commerce regular), and prevent states from disrupting the free movement of commerce.

That was certainly how James Madison understood and explained it: "'*Among* the several states' ... grew out of the abuses of the power by the importing states in taxing the non-importing, and was intended as a negative and preventive provision against injustice among the States themselves, rather than as a power to be used for the positive purposes of the General Government."[13]

By the nineteenth century, the Supreme Court was already pretending the commerce clause extended federal authority over commerce that merely *affected* other states. It thereby opened up a potentially limitless field of power to the federal government, since practically anything can be said to "affect" anything else in some way. By the twentieth century this had become a "*substantial* effects" rule, but in practice it still allowed the federal government to control whatever it wanted. Thus the federal government claimed the power to regulate the wages of a janitor in a building whose occupants happened to be engaged in interstate commerce. In *Wickard* v. *Filburn* (1942), the Court ruled that the federal government could regulate the amount of wheat grown on an individual's farm even though the wheat never left the state, and the farmer and his livestock consumed it themselves. Had they not grown and consumed that wheat, the argument went, they might have purchased it from another state, and hence their abstention from this purchase indirectly affected interstate commerce.

Following the upheavals of the New Deal Court in the late 1930s, the Supreme Court did not challenge the federal government's "commerce clause" claims by declaring even a single federal law unconstitutional on those grounds—until the anomalous 1995 case of *U.S.* v. *Lopez*. That case involved the federal Gun Free School Zones Act of 1990, which made it a federal crime to carry a firearm into a school zone. Some forty states already had similar legislation restricting guns in school zones on the books at the time this federal law was passed. Alfonso Lopez, Jr., who was convicted of violating the Act, objected that the federal government had had no constitutional authority to enact the law in the first place. The federal government argued that the potential presence of guns in schools would make students nervous, that nervous students would learn less and thus acquire an inferior education, that people with inferior educations would contribute less to the U.S. economy, that contributing less to the U.S. economy would have a substantial effect on interstate commerce, and that therefore the question of guns in schools could be regulated by the U.S. government. This line of reasoning, although not significantly more absurd than the federal government's commerce-clause justifications for many other laws, was too much even for the normally indulgent Supreme Court. But even here, with the exception of Justice Clarence Thomas, no one on the Court challenged the "substantial effects" rule itself; the Justices merely claimed that the federal government had not shown substantial effects on interstate commerce in this particular case. And although supporters of centralized government feared (and opponents hoped) that *Lopez* would serve as a precedent for the future, pushing the federal government back toward an honest interpretation of the commerce clause, no such thing occurred.

Meanwhile, the federal government has been extending its authority over countless areas of American life on the grounds (when indeed it bothers justifying itself at all) of flimsy to nonexistent connections to interstate commerce.

Finally, we come to the "necessary and proper" clause, which social studies teachers around the country cite to this day as an "elastic clause" that permits the federal government to exercise a broad array of powers not mentioned in the Constitution. The clause declares that Congress shall have the power to "make all Laws which shall be necessary and proper for carrying into Execution the foregoing Powers, and all other Powers vested by the Constitution in the Government of the United States, or in any Department or Officer thereof." Given the Framers' assurances about the limited nature of the government they were creating and their repeatedly expressed fears of unlimited government, we must look with skepticism at the claim that this or any constitutional clause was designed to be an "elastic clause." Such a thing would have defeated the purpose the Framers had in mind in drafting a written constitution.

A review of the statements of the Framers and ratifiers regarding this clause confirms our initial skepticism. Of course, it was not designed as an "elastic clause," an invitation to tyranny that would have horrified just about everyone. It was intended as a note of clarification only. It meant not that the federal government was thereby granted an array of unspecified powers, but that the government could perform simple tasks that were *clearly incidental* to carrying out its enumerated powers. Thus the power to erect "needful Buildings" would, by direct (rather than fanciful) implication, involve a power to purchase lumber for this purpose.

It is not difficult to uncover evidence of this broad consensus. The state ratifying conventions are full of assurances about the innocuous nature of the clause. Thus, in Virginia, George

Nicholas said "it was no augmentation of power," and Madison said the clause "gives no supplementary powers." Archibald Maclaine said in North Carolina that "the clause gives no new power." In Pennsylvania, Chief Justice Thomas McKean explained that it "gives to Congress no further powers than those enumerated." James Iredell said the same thing in North Carolina.[14]

This is the clause that our textbooks expect to carry the burden of explaining how our government could have grown to such proportions without violating the Constitution. What history shows, on the contrary, is that eminent Americans, even those who favored a powerful central government, agreed that the Constitution would have been *exactly the same* had this alleged elastic clause never been written. Even Alexander Hamilton noted that the Constitution would have been in no way different had this clause not been included at all. "It may be affirmed with perfect confidence," wrote Hamilton in Federalist #33, "that the constitutional operation of the intended government would be precisely the same" if the "necessary and proper" clause were "entirely obliterated."

"In sum," writes Harvard's Raoul Berger, "the records make plain that the necessary and proper clause was merely designed to specifically authorize the employment of *means* to effectuate, to carry into execution, granted powers, not to augment them; and they strongly read against the doctrine of implied *powers*."[15]

This interpretation of the "necessary and proper" clause continued to be insisted upon in the years following ratification of the Constitution. Jefferson defended this view in 1791, pointing out that necessary meant *necessary*, not merely "convenient";

governments will always find their oppressions convenient.[16] St. George Tucker, the great judge and law professor who wrote the highly regarded *View of the Constitution of the United States* (1803), echoed these sentiments.[17] So did political thinker and U.S. senator John Taylor, Judge Spencer Roane, and a great many others.[18] James Madison wrote in 1800 that this interpretation of the clause is "precisely the construction which prevailed during the discussions and ratifications of the Constitution." It "cannot too often be repeated," he continued, that this limited interpretation is "absolutely necessary" in order for the clause to be compatible with the character of the federal government, which is "possessed of particular and defined powers only" rather than "general and indefinite powers."[19]

Thus the three clauses most frequently abused on behalf of a central government of unlimited powers not only fail to support any such thing, but mean pretty much the opposite of what politicians and judges have tried to tell us they mean. The Tenth Amendment to the Constitution—"The powers not delegated to the United States by the Constitution, nor prohibited by it to the States, are reserved to the States respectively, or to the people"—in turn makes clear that broad constructions of these phrases, by which the federal government arrogates to itself an array of additional, unspecified powers, are inadmissible. Here, in this crucial amendment, was explicit recognition of what the Federalists themselves had insisted was already implicit in the Constitution as drafted. The Tenth Amendment was the written guarantee of the central principle that state ratifying conventions had been assured of as they were being urged to approve the Constitution: the proposed federal government will have only those powers granted to it and no others.

The various attempts to evade the Tenth Amendment's clear meaning over the years, and particularly since the 1940s, must be counted to the great intellectual discredit of those advancing them. In *U.S.* v. *Darby* (1942), the Supreme Court tried to describe the Amendment as a mere "truism," no more interesting than the tautological statement that all bachelors are unmarried. Left unexplained was why so many of the original states would have vigorously demanded the inclusion of a mere tautology, why the country's legal history would be replete with references to a tautology, or why Jefferson would have described a tautology as the cornerstone of the Constitution.

Another claim is that the Tenth Amendment was, in fact, meant to allow the federal government greater flexibility than so-called strict constructionists of the Constitution will admit. After all, the argument goes, while the Amendment says the federal government will have those powers "delegated" to it, it does not say "*expressly* delegated." This failure to include the word "expressly" has been cited as evidence that Congress was intended to possess a broad array of additional powers beyond just the ones specifically enumerated in Article I, Section 8. After all, the Articles of Confederation had used the word "expressly," so its absence in the Tenth Amendment had to be a deliberate omission.

This argument is exploded at once when we examine the state ratifying conventions, which each state held individually and to which it elected delegates who were given the task of deciding whether to adopt the Constitution. Time and again, the Constitution was portrayed by its supporters as granting only those powers that the states "expressly delegated" to it. That means the states themselves entered the Union with the express assurance that this was how the Constitution would be understood. It is this that matters to constitutional interpretation: *what were the people themselves told about the document they were to ratify?*

At the New York Convention, even Alexander Hamilton—as we have seen, one of the strongest advocates of a powerful central government and among the least committed to the cause of states' rights—declared that, in all federations, the proposed American one not excepted, "whatever is not expressly given to the Federal Head, is reserved to the members." The people, moreover, had "already delegated their sovereignty and their powers to their several [state] governments; and these cannot be recalled, and given to another, without an *express* act."[20] When New York ratified the Constitution, it accompanied its ratification with a brief rendition of the nature of the Union it understood itself to be joining: "Every power, jurisdiction, and right which is not by the said Constitution clearly delegated to the United States of America, or the departments of the government thereof remains to the people of the several States, or to their respective State governments."[21]

The people of half a dozen states were specifically assured that the proposed federal government would indeed possess only those powers expressly delegated to it. We may cite a few more of them here. Thus at the Pennsylvania Convention, James Wilson said that "everything not *expressly* mentioned will be presumed to be purposely omitted."[22] At the North Carolina Convention Governor Samuel Johnston explained that "Congress cannot assume any other powers than those *expressly* given them, without a palpable violation of the Constitution," adding that the "powers of Congress are all circumscribed, defined and clearly laid down. So far they may go, but no farther."[23] Charles Pinckney told the convention in South Carolina that the federal government could not execute or assume any powers except those that "were *expressly* delegated."[24] James Madison emphasized the same point repeatedly both in *The Federalist* and at his state's ratifying convention. In Federalist #40 he noted that "the general powers are limited; and that the States, in all unenumerated cases, are left in enjoyment of their sovereign and independent jurisdiction." In #45 he observed: "The powers delegated by the proposed Constitution to the federal government, are few and defined. Those which are to remain in the State governments are numerous and indefinite." At the Virginia Convention he noted that the federal government would have "defined and limited objects beyond which it cannot extend its jurisdiction."[25] In 1789, the *Salem Mercury* of Massachusetts published Roger Sherman's *Observations on the New Federal Constitution, and the Alterations That Have Been Proposed as Amendments*; Sherman was a Connecticut lawyer who signed the Constitution, and a future U.S. representative and senator. Sherman concurred with the above: "The powers vested in the federal government are particularly defined, so that each State still retains its sovereignty in what concerns its own internal government, and a right to exercise every power of a sovereign State, not *expressly* delegated to the government of the United States."[26]

Well into the early republic, the same assurances were regularly repeated, sometimes by the Federalists themselves—that is, the party in the early republic known for its support for a strong central government.[27] Thus Samuel Chase, as partisan a Federalist as ever lived, declared in *Calder* v. *Bull* (1798) that "the several State Legislatures *retain* all powers of *legislation*, delegated to them by the State Constitutions; which are not expressly taken away by the Constitution of the United States."[28]

When we survey the states' demands for constitutional amendments at the time of ratification, we consistently find reference to the "expressly delegated" principle. In Massachusetts, John Hancock proposed that the Constitution be amended so that "it be *explicitly* declared, that all powers not *expressly* delegated by the aforesaid Constitution are reserved to the several states, to be by them exercised."[29] John Adams, in turn, believed such an amendment would serve to diminish or remove people's apprehensions about the Constitution. The matter was then referred to a committee, whose subsequent report read, in part:

> And it is the opinion of this Convention, that [since] certain amendments and alterations in the said Constitution, would remove the fears and quiet the apprehensions of many of the good people of this Commonwealth, and more effectually guard against an undue administration of the Federal Government, the Convention do [*sic*] therefore recommend that the following alterations and provisions be introduced into the said Constitution. First, that it be *explicitly declared* that all powers not expressly delegated by the aforesaid Constitution, are reserved to the several States, to be by them exercised. [Seven other proposed amendments followed.]

New Hampshire proposed the same thing. So did Maryland and Pennsylvania. By means of such an amendment, these states sought explicit recognition of the principle that the Federalists themselves assured them was already there: that the federal government possessed only those powers "expressly delegated" to it.[30]

The absence of the word "expressly" in the Tenth Amendment to the Constitution was not a subterfuge by means of which the federal government could someday exercise a wide array of additional powers. In fact, the addition of the words "or to the people" (as in, all powers not delegated to the federal government are reserved to the states *or to the people, from whom they originated*) in tandem with the Ninth Amendment,[31] had essentially the same effect as the words "expressly delegated." Emmerich de Vattel, one of the great international lawyers of the eighteenth century, taught in his 1758 work *The Law of Nations* that *sovereigns possess all power they have not expressly delegated*, and therefore that any delegation of power by a sovereign must be construed strictly. In the American system, the sovereigns are the peoples of the various states.[32] Therefore, their delegations of power to the federal government, according to accepted norms of international law, are to be construed strictly, and their agent is to hold only those powers expressly delegated to it.[33]

Congressman John Page, who served in the Congress that drafted the Bill of Rights, agreed that the combination of the Ninth and Tenth Amendments had the effect of restoring the word "expressly." That was also the view of James Madison. Madison publicly noted, shortly after the ratification of the Constitution, that the state conventions had ratified on the understanding that the federal government would possess only "expressly delegated power." And indeed, Madison believed the Ninth and Tenth Amendments taken together had accomplished exactly that.[34] In fact, Thomas Tucker, the congressman who sought without success to add the word "expressly" to the amendment, was also the one who added "or to the people," a phrase he considered more important even than "expressly." He envisioned both of these additions as accomplishing the same end. Explicit reference to the principle of popular sovereignty in the Constitution would, by the American understanding of the existing "law of nations" (as "international law" was then known), confine the federal government to only those powers expressly delegated by the peoples of the states.[35]

The omission of "expressly" had a far less ambitious aim than is popularly understood today. It was intended to leave room for the federal government to exercise *clearly incidental* means to carrying out its assigned tasks. In the Virginia Ratifying Convention, for instance, Edmund Randolph noted the inability of the Articles of Confederation government to issue passports, even though such a power, while not "expressly delegated" to the Congress, was surely incidental to the diplomatic tasks entrusted to it. By omitting this *specific word*—"expressly"—which had yielded inconveniences in the past, the framers of the Amendment addressed this earlier difficulty. But by inserting the idea of popular sovereignty, they restored the *principle* that the federal government possessed only expressly delegated powers, and that any powers it might further exercise would have to be clearly incidental to the exercise of the delegated powers. Thus, whatever we may think of the decision to omit the word "expressly," the omission in no way justifies the view that the federal government possesses an endless source of additional, unspecified powers.

The historical record is much too clear and consistent for any other interpretation of the issues we have discussed in this chapter to have much chance of success. That is why critics typically give up trying to argue the matter. They change the subject, proposing instead that none of this matters anyway, since what the Framers may have written over 200 years ago is of no import to modern-day Americans. Even if this argument were true, it is silent on the question that really matters: how exactly are we to know what the original Constitution should be replaced with, in accordance with people's supposedly different outlook today? Who decides? The implicit answer is that we let federal judges decide on the evolving meaning of the Constitution. But this would merely give a small group of politically well-connected lawyers a monopoly on determining how Americans will be governed.[36] Such an arrangement sounds much less desirable when stated that way, which is why it never is stated that way.

Furthermore, since the Framers of the Constitution made clear that the clauses we examined above—general welfare, commerce, and necessary and proper—were very far from open-ended grants of power to the federal government, how can the mere passage of time transform these clauses into the broad grants of power that our critics want them to be? Even Alexander Hamilton insisted, in Federalist #78, that unless the people had solemnly and formally ratified a change in the meaning of the Constitution, the courts could not proceed on any other basis. "Until the people have, by some solemn and authoritative act, annulled or changed the established form, it is binding upon themselves collectively, as well as individually; and no presumption, or even knowledge, of their sentiments, can warrant their representatives in a departure from it, prior to such an act." Likewise, James Iredell, a leading North Carolina Federalist and the youngest of the original Supreme Court appointees, explained that the people had chosen "to be governed under such and such principles. They have not chosen to be governed or promised to submit upon any other."[37] Thomas Cooley, the distinguished Chief Justice of the Michigan Supreme Court, declared in 1868 that a court

> which should allow a change in public sentiment to influence it in giving construction to a written constitution not warranted by the intention of its founders, would be justly charged with reckless disregard of official oath and public duty.... A Constitution is not to be made to mean one thing at one time, and another at some subsequent time when the circumstances may have changed as perhaps to make a different rule in the case seem desirable.[38]

We're sometimes told that ours is a "living" Constitution that changes with the times. Again, this merely begs the question. *Who decides what these changes should be*? Judges? The Constitution does allow for amendment, which would secure the people's consent to any major changes, but this is not what advocates of the "living" Constitution have in mind. They mean the federal government will have a monopoly on deciding how the Constitution should be interpreted now and in the future. Suspicions that it might abuse this power, that it might suddenly discover a whole host of new powers for itself as it re-examines day by day what the Constitution really ought to mean, are a sign that we are being paranoid and unreasonable. We should instead adopt the tranquil outlook of Britney Spears, who told us: "I think we should just trust our president in every decision he makes and should just support that, you know, and be faithful in what happens."[39]

Thomas Jefferson took the opposite view. Should there be a desire to grant the federal government additional powers, it is better to do so the right way, with popular consent through the amendment process, than for the government itself simply to go ahead and exercise the powers, stretching the meaning of the

Constitution to do so. As he told a correspondent, "When an instrument admits two constructions [interpretations], the one safe, the other dangerous, the one precise, the other indefinite, I prefer that which is safe & precise. *I had rather ask an enlargement of power from the nation*, where it is found necessary, *than to assume it by a construction which would make our powers boundless*."[40]

A "living" constitution is precisely what the American colonists fought against in the American Revolution. The unwritten, "living" British constitution, they found, provided scant protection of their liberties. The colonists held fast to an older view of British constitutionalism, according to which a proposed measure was constitutional only if it conformed to customary practice.[41] This approach had given way to the principle that the criterion of constitutionality was not custom and tradition but simply the will of Parliament. This is why Americans insisted on a written constitution for their new country—they knew all too well what it was like to live under a "living" constitution whose meaning could not be definitively pinned down. If we'd like to spit in the faces of our ancestors who fought for American independence from the British, we should by all means advocate a "living Constitution."

In short, it was with good reason that Jefferson wrote, "In questions of power, then, let no more be heard of confidence in man, but bind him down from mischief by the chains of the Constitution."[42] That constitution had to be construed strictly if it were not to defeat the purpose of its drafting. "Our peculiar security is in possession of a written constitution," Jefferson wrote. "Let us not make it a blank paper by construction."[43] In other words, let us not interpret the Constitution so liberally that we destroy its deliberately crafted restraints on government power. One can only imagine what he would have thought of the Supreme Court of our day—which, in the face of all the evidence set forth above, can declare with a straight face, as it has numerous times, that "the power of Congress to authorize expenditure of public moneys for public purposes *is not limited by the direct grants of legislative power found in the Constitution*."[44]

Having established the limited nature of the federal government under the Constitution, we now consider the Jeffersonian answer to the urgent question: what is to be done if that government violates the Constitution? What options are available to the people?

To answer that question, we proceed to the presidential term of John Adams, who was elected in 1796. Events leading to the Quasi War with France were already in progress by the time Adams took office. Diplomatic relations between the United States and France had been cool for years by then. Alienated by (among other things) the American government's increasingly warm relations with Britain, as well as its refusal to repay its Revolutionary War debt to France (on the grounds that that debt had been contracted with the previous French regime rather than the revolutionary one), the French government, at war with the British, instituted a policy of seizing American ships trading with the British. The resulting Quasi War amounted to a series of relatively minor naval clashes between the two countries.

A war hysteria subsequently broke out, far out of proportion to the danger the country faced, which Adams himself privately acknowledged was minimal to nonexistent.[45] Noah Webster's newspaper warned that in the event of a French invasion, an American Executive Directory headed by Jefferson, Madison,

James Monroe, and Aaron Burr would take control of the country. *Porcupine's Gazette* condemned Jefferson as "the head of the democratic frenchified faction in this country." Jefferson had favored the French Revolution, it is true; his enthusiasm had even bordered on the grotesque at a time when France was convulsed by the Reign of Terror. But he was obviously not aiding the French or planning a Jacobin-style revolution, and in fact he later spoke of "the horrors of the French revolution" and "the murderous Jacobins of France."[46] Not surprisingly, correspondence between Jefferson and Madison during this period reflects their growing alarm at the fanaticism they saw enveloping their country. "Perhaps it is a universal truth that the loss of liberty at home is to be charged to provisions against danger, real or pretended, from abroad," wrote Madison.[47]

During the Quasi War, the federal government enacted four pieces of legislation that became known as the Alien and Sedition Acts of 1798. The Naturalization Act, the least controversial among them, extended the period required for foreigners to become American citizens, and was repealed four years later. The Alien Friends Act authorized the president to deport resident aliens considered "dangerous to the peace and safety of the United States," and expired in two years. The Alien Enemies Act, still on the books today, authorized the president to deport aliens whose home countries were at war with the United States.

Although Republicans objected to the Alien Acts on a variety of constitutional grounds, they were essentially not enforced, so we turn our attention to the Sedition Act, by far the Republicans' greatest source of concern.[48] That Act established fines and jail time

> if any person shall write, print, utter, or publish, or shall cause or procure to be written, printed, uttered, or published, or shall knowingly and willingly assist or aid in writing, printing, uttering, or publishing any false, scandalous and malicious writing or writings against the government of the United States, or either House of the Congress of the United States, or the President of the United States, with intent to defame the said government, or either House of the said Congress, or the said President, or to bring them, or either of them, into contempt or disrepute; or to excite against them, or either or any of them, the hatred of the good people of the United States, or to stir up sedition within the United States.

Congressional supporters of the Sedition Act, defended the legislation by citing the "general welfare" and "necessary and proper" clauses of the Constitution.[49]

In addition to the constitutional problems with the Sedition Act, its partisan nature seemed obvious. The president was a Federalist, and the Congress was dominated by Federalists. Under the Sedition Act, they could not be criticized. The vice president was the Republican Thomas Jefferson.* The Sedition Act imposed no penalties for criticizing him. That was fine by Jefferson, who believed calumny went with the territory when one entered politics, for it is "an injury to which duty requires every one to submit whom the public think

---

* Recall that in the 1790s, the Twelfth Amendment had not yet been added to the Constitution, so the candidate who received the greatest number of electoral votes became president, while the second-highest vote-getter became vice president. This was how John Adams, who belonged to the Federalist party, could have as his vice president Thomas Jefferson, the Republican.

proper to call to its councils." He would not "suffer calumny to disturb my tranquility."[50]

The convictions began quickly enough. Although Matthew Lyon, a U.S. congressman from Vermont, had fought in the American Revolution, that wasn't enough to save him from sedition charges for the crime of writing one letter and publishing another. The letter he wrote spoke of President Adams's "continual grasp for power" and his "thirst for a ridiculous pomp, foolish adulation, and selfish avarice." The letter he published was from an American in France who wondered why Adams had not been committed to "a mad house." Lyon was sentenced to four months in prison and a fine of $1,000. Stevens T. Mason, a U.S. senator from Virginia, joined by ordinary citizens from Vermont, collected the money to pay Lyon's fine. Popular opinion was very much in sympathy with Lyon following his arrest, so much so that he won re-election to the House while still incarcerated.[51]

Other convictions were equally egregious. Political writer James Callender was given a biased, kangaroo proceeding by Justice Samuel Chase, whose later impeachment by the House was motivated in part by outrage at his conduct in this case. Writer and lawyer Thomas Cooper, reflecting on his own trial, cautioned that Americans "may learn some useful lessons from this trial; and principally, that if they mean to consult their own peace and quiet, they will hold their tongues, and restrain their pens, on the subject of politics."[52]

What was to be done? Jefferson saw that some form of resistance was surely necessary, but what form should it take? In the face of unconstitutional federal laws, Jefferson—constitutionalist first; vice president second—believed a stronger response than mere petitions and protests was called for, but he also wanted the states to avoid the other extreme of secession. Although he believed in a state's right to withdraw from the Union (this being merely a logical extension of the principle of self-government, which was central to Jefferson's political philosophy), he thought that right should be exercised only as a last resort. What he sought was a mode of resistance that would allow a state to remain in the Union, but at the same time recognize its right to defend itself against federal usurpation. Nullification, in this view, was not an extreme remedy at all. It was the moderate middle ground. It was a central feature of Jeffersonian thought that "the true barriers of our liberty... are our State governments," and it was via nullification that Jefferson suggested those barriers be employed.[53]

The judiciary was, for Jefferson, certainly *not* the answer to such problems. For one thing, the Supreme Court in his day was packed with Federalists who would surely have upheld the constitutionality of the Alien and Sedition Acts. For another, the Supreme Court was itself a branch of the federal government, and thus not an impartial arbiter. And finally, the judiciary was composed of human beings no different from the rest of mankind. "To consider the Judges of the Superior Court as the ultimate Arbiters of Constitutional questions," he argued, "would be a dangerous doctrine which would place us under the despotism of an oligarchy. They have with others, the same passion for party, for power, and for the privileges of their corps—and their power is the more dangerous as they are in office for life, and not responsible, as the other functionaries are, to the Elective control. The Constitution has elected no single Tribunal. I know no safe depositary of the ultimate powers of society but the people themselves."[54]

It makes instructive reading to examine the correspondence between Thomas Jefferson and James Madison during 1798 and 1799, and to observe their heightened concern for the future of constitutional government in light of the misplaced war fever and especially the Alien and Sedition Acts. Unfortunately, the letters they might have written to each other regarding the details of what became the Virginia and Kentucky Resolutions in particular do not exist. Jefferson feared that Federalist postmasters were opening and reading their mail. He was ashamed that he could not speak his mind in his own country: "I know not which mortifies me most, that I should fear to write what I think or that my country bear such a state of things."[55] Jefferson later called the Sedition Act "a nullity as absolute and as palpable as if Congress had ordered us to fall down and worship a golden image."[56]

Jefferson drafted a series of resolutions that (1) described the nature of the federal Union, (2) condemned the Alien and Sedition Acts as gross violations of the Constitution, and (3) considered the proper response by the states. He gave these resolutions to Wilson Cary Nicholas, his neighbor and a member of the Virginia Senate. When Nicholas gave them to John Breckinridge (a member of the Kentucky legislature who had also been Jefferson's neighbor at one time), who happened to be passing through Virginia, both Jefferson and Nicholas trusted his assurances that the Kentucky legislature would pass them.[57]

According to Professor Marco Bassani, author of a recent study of Jefferson's political thought, these resolutions, which in modified form became the Kentucky Resolutions of 1798, contain "the whole of his theory of the federal union."[58] They begin with this pithy defense of the Jeffersonian view of the nature of the United States:

> 1. *Resolved,* That the several States composing the United States of America, are not united on the principle of unlimited submission to their general [federal] government; but that, by a compact under the style and title of a Constitution for the United States, and of amendments thereto, they constituted a general government for special purposes—delegated to that government certain definite powers, reserving, each State to itself, the residuary mass of right to their own self-government; and that *whensoever the general government assumes undelegated powers, its acts are unauthoritative, void, and of no force*: that to this compact each State acceded as a State, and is an integral part, its co-States forming, as to itself, the other party: that the government created by this compact was not made the exclusive or final judge of the extent of the powers delegated to itself; since that would have made its discretion, and not the Constitution, the measure of its powers; but that, as in all other cases of compact among powers having no common judge, *each party has an equal right to judge for itself, as well of infractions as of the mode and measure of redress*. [Emphasis added.]

Here, in brief, is the essential statement of the principles behind nullification. The states had not agreed to a system in which they would submit without protest to whatever the federal government should do. To the contrary, the states established a federal government with limited powers, and reserved for themselves all powers they did not delegate to that government.

Any measures the federal government should take beyond the powers delegated to it are absolutely void. The federal government, which the states themselves created, cannot hold a monopoly on constitutional interpretation and cannot decide for itself what the extent of its own powers are. That would mean the people were governed by the mere discretion of their rulers rather than by the Constitution. Since the federal government, either as a whole or in its branches, is not and cannot be an impartial arbiter of disputes between itself and the states of which it is composed, it is up to each state's own judgment to decide when the Constitution has been violated and how that violation is to be addressed. (As we shall see in chapter 4, although Jefferson deserves much credit for his exposition of these ideas, they in fact long preceded his Kentucky Resolutions.)

Much of the remainder of the Kentucky Resolutions involved an attack on the constitutionality of the Alien and Sedition Acts. The argument, in brief, was twofold: (1) restrictions on political speech violated the First Amendment; and (2) the states never delegated to the federal government the powers to be exercised under the Acts, and thus the exercise of those powers violated the Tenth Amendment. The federal government's appeal to the "general welfare" and "necessary and proper" clauses in defense of the legislation was, according to the Resolutions, an absurd violation of the original understanding of those phrases and tended toward the "destruction of all the limits prescribed to [the federal government's] power by the Constitution: that words meant by that instrument to be subsidiary only to the execution of the limited powers, ought not to be so construed as themselves to give unlimited powers, nor a part so to be taken, as to destroy the whole residue of the instrument."

The conclusion then returned to general principles. "This Commonwealth," read the text, "is determined, as it doubts not its Co-states are, tamely to submit to undelegated and consequently unlimited powers in no man or body of men on earth." It expressed confidence that the other states would see things the same way—namely, that the acts in question were clear violations of the Constitution, and indeed "altogether void and of no force."

John Breckinridge, who sponsored the Resolutions in the Kentucky House, argued that when the federal government enacted merely "impolitic" laws, the people should strive to repeal them. But when the federal government passed laws that extended *beyond its constitutional powers*, the people at the state level ought "to make a legislative declaration that, being unconstitutional, they are therefore void and of no effect." With regard to the Alien and Sedition Acts in particular, while Breckinridge hoped Congress might repeal them, or that decent judges might refuse to act upon them, he declared that the states could nullify them: "I hesitate not to declare it as my opinion that it is then the right and duty of the several States to nullify those acts, and to protect their citizens from their operation."[59] And to those who replied that federal judges had found the Acts to be constitutionally unobjectionable and so the matter was closed, Breckinridge replied: "Who are the judiciary? Who are they, but a part of the servants of the people created by the Federal compact? And if the servants of the people have a right, is it good reasoning to say that the people by whom and for whose benefit both they and the government were created, are destitute of that right?"[60]

In section eight of his draft of the Kentucky Resolutions, Jefferson had included the word "nullification," describing it as the "rightful remedy" in such situations, but a skittish legislature removed it. The use of that word had to await the Kentucky Resolutions of 1799, which read in relevant part:

> If those who administer the general government be permitted to transgress the limits fixed by that compact, by a total disregard to the special delegations of power therein contained, annihilation of the state governments, and the erection upon their ruins, of a general consolidated government, will be the inevitable consequence: That the principle and construction contended for by sundry of the state legislatures [here the reference is to states that had responded unfavorably to the Kentucky Resolutions of 1798], that the general government is the exclusive judge of the extent of the powers delegated to it, stop nothing short of despotism; since the discretion of those who administer the government, and not the constitution, would be the measure of their powers: That the several states who formed that instrument, being sovereign and independent, have the unquestionable right to judge of its infraction; and that *a nullification, by those sovereignties, of all unauthorized acts done under colour of that instrument, is the rightful remedy*: That this commonwealth does upon the most deliberate reconsideration declare, that the said alien and sedition laws, are in their opinion, palpable violations of the said constitution; and however cheerfully it may be disposed to surrender its opinion to a majority of its sister states in matters of ordinary or doubtful policy; yet, in momentous regulations like the present, which so vitally wound the best rights of the citizen, it would consider a silent acquiescence as highly criminal.[61]

There it is, as clear as anyone could ask for: "nullification . . . is the rightful remedy" against infractions of the Constitution.

The Virginia Resolutions of 1798 likewise protested the Alien and Sedition Acts and urged the states to take action against them.[62] Up until the very recent renewal of interest in these ideas, it was scarcely possible to imagine one of the feckless and docile American states confronting the federal government in such language as Virginia did in 1798:

> This Assembly doth explicitly and peremptorily declare, that it views the powers of the federal government, as resulting from the compact, to which the states are parties; as limited by the plain sense and intention of the instrument constituting the compact; as no further valid than they are authorized by the grants enumerated in that compact; and that in case of a deliberate, palpable, and dangerous exercise of other powers, not granted by the said compact, the states who are parties thereto, have the right, and are in duty bound, to interpose for arresting the progress of the evil, and for maintaining within their respective limits, the authorities, rights and liberties appertaining to them.

In Document IX of this book, Judge Abel P. Upshur considers various means of "interposing for arresting the progress of the evil" of usurpation, and concludes that the only avenue of redress by which a state may effectively interpose its authority is indeed nullification.

The Resolutions continue:

> The General Assembly doth also express its deep regret, that a spirit has in sundry instances, been manifested by the

> federal government, to enlarge its powers by forced constructions of the constitutional charter which defines them; and that implications have appeared of a design to expound certain general phrases (which having been copied from the very limited grant of power, in the former articles of confederation were the less liable to be misconstrued) so as to destroy the meaning and effect, of the particular enumeration which necessarily explains and limits the general phrases; and so as to consolidate the states by degrees, into one sovereignty.

This is a formal protest against broad interpretation of the Constitution, whereby the "general phrases" we examined earlier in this chapter are interpreted so loosely as to pretend the subsequent list of the federal government's powers did not exist. (In Madison's famous Report of 1800, he confirmed that the general welfare clause was what the Virginia legislature had had particularly in mind.)

The Virginia Resolutions close with an appeal to the other states to join with that state in declaring the Alien and Sedition Acts unconstitutional, and to take such measures as are necessary to protect the rights of the states and the people.

The initial draft of the Resolutions, as John Taylor introduced them into the Virginia legislature, referred to the Alien and Sedition Acts as "unconstitutional, and not law, but utterly null, void, and of no force or effect." The words following "unconstitutional" were later struck out with Taylor's consent. Taylor considered them superfluous, since it went without saying that an unconstitutional law was not law but rather void and of no effect.[63] That was a widely held position. Congressman James Barbour, who later served as governor of Virginia and

U.S. Secretary of War, concurred: "If the alien and sedition laws are unconstitutional, they are not law, and of course of no force." Another Republican agreed that "if they were unconstitutional, they, of course, were null and void."[64]

The principles of the Virginia Resolutions, Taylor contended, were essential to the maintenance of a federal republic. Should the states sit idly by as their reserved powers are invaded, vainly waiting years for elections to put things right, then "all powers whatsoever would gradually be absorbed by, and consolidated in, the general government." The states do not "hold their constitutional rights by the courtesy of Congress. . . . Congress is the creature of the States and of the people; but neither the States nor the people are the creatures of Congress. It would be evidently absurd, that the creature [Congress] should exclusively construe the instrument of its own existence [the Constitution]."[65]

For his part, Congressman Edward Livingston of New York declared in the U.S. House of Representatives that the states and the people must resist the unconstitutional acts in question:

> If regardless of our duty as citizens, and our solemn obligations as representatives; regardless of the rights of our constituents; regardless of every sanction, human and divine, we are ready to violate the Constitution we have sworn to defend—will the people submit to our unauthorized Acts? Will the states sanction our usurped power? Sir, they ought not to submit—they would deserve the chains which these measures are forging for them, if they did not resist.[66]

The Virginia and Kentucky Resolutions were not warmly received by the other states, which either ignored or denounced them. Delaware curtly dismissed the Resolutions as "a very unjustifiable interference with the general government and constituted authorities of the United States, and of dangerous tendency, and therefore not a fit subject for the further consideration of the General Assembly."[67] Rhode Island declared that in the private opinion of its legislators, the Alien and Sedition Acts were perfectly constitutional, indeed well "within the powers delegated to Congress, and promotive of the welfare of the United States."[68] The state legislature "cannot contemplate, without extreme concern and regret, the many evil and fatal consequences which may flow from the very unwarrantable resolutions aforesaid of the legislature of Virginia." (Thus the Alien and Sedition Acts themselves were perfectly constitutional, but Virginia's call to resistance was to be deplored.) The Massachusetts state senate "explicitly declare[d], that they consider the acts of Congress, commonly called 'the alien and sedition acts,' not only constitutional, but expedient and necessary." The Sedition Act, it said, was "wise and necessary," since "an audacious and unprincipled spirit of falsehood and abuse had been too long unremittingly exerted for the purpose of perverting public opinion, and threatened to undermine and destroy the whole fabric of the government." Not surprisingly, it denied the power of "any of the state governments to decide upon the constitutionality of the acts of the Federal Government."[69]

As we can see, much of the reason for these indignant replies was that many of the states issuing them supported the Alien and Sedition Acts whose constitutionality the Resolutions so robustly denied. In fact, as we'll see in chapter 3, some of the very states that professed to be so appalled at the Principles of '98—as the ideas contained in the Virginia and Kentucky Resolutions came to be known—themselves made use of them not ten years later. So we may take their shock and horror in 1798 with a grain of salt. (Remember, too, that these state legislatures were dominated by Federalists, the party that supported the Alien and Sedition Acts and in whose interests those laws had been drafted.)

Also significant is that it was not Jefferson's compact theory of the Union, discussed in greater detail in chapter 4, to which these states objected. Of the states issuing critical replies to the Resolutions, only Vermont actually called into question the idea that the Union had been formed as a compact among sovereign states. Thus the Jefferson/Madison conception of the Union was not itself a source of particular controversy.[70]

In light of the disappointing response by the other states, Virginia decided to draft a special report, to be written by James Madison, which would respond to the arguments advanced against the position Virginia had taken and consider whether any retreat from the Resolutions of '98 was warranted. The resulting Report of 1800 declared that having examined the matter with great care, Virginia saw no reason to withdraw or amend its Resolutions. To those states that had pointed to the Supreme Court as the arbiter of disputes over power between the federal government and the states, Madison argued in the Report that the judiciary, too, could commit transgressions against the Constitution and likewise had to be guarded against:

> The resolution supposed that dangerous powers, not delegated, may not only be usurped and executed by the other departments, but that the judicial department also may exercise or sanction dangerous powers beyond the grant of the Constitution; and, consequently, that the ultimate right of

> the parties to the Constitution, to judge whether the compact has been dangerously violated, must extend to violations by one delegated authority, as well as by another; by the judiciary, as well as by the executive, or the legislature.
>
> However true, therefore, it may be, that the judicial department is, in all questions submitted to it by the forms of the Constitution, to decide in the last resort, this resort must necessarily be deemed the last in relation to the authorities of the other departments of the government; not in relation to the rights of the parties to the constitutional compact, from which the judicial as well as the other departments hold their delegated trusts. On any other hypothesis, the delegation of judicial power would annul the authority delegating it; and the concurrence of this department with the others in usurped powers, might subvert forever, and beyond the possible reach of any rightful remedy, the very Constitution which all were instituted to preserve.[71]

In short, the Virginia and Kentucky Resolutions of 1798, along with the follow-up Report of 1800 and Kentucky Resolutions of 1799, held that (1) the federal government had been created when sovereign states granted it a few enumerated powers; (2) any powers not so delegated remained reserved to the states or the people, a point expressly stated in the Tenth Amendment; and (3) should the federal government exercise a power it had not been delegated, the states ought to interpose—that is, they ought to stand between their own people on the one side and the federal government's unconstitutional law on the other.

The Principles of '98 are essentially ignored and unknown today. No bicentennial commemoration was held in their honor in 1998. Even professional scholars have chosen ("mostly for ideological reasons," according to Professor Bassani) to downplay the Kentucky Resolutions in studies of Jefferson's thought, despite their centrality to his understanding of the Union. Dumas Malone spends six pages on the subject out of six entire volumes on Jefferson; Merrill Peterson's biography of over one thousand pages covers the Resolutions in four or five pages. R. B. Bernstein's study, often referred to as the best short biography of Jefferson, grants them a quarter of a page. Bernard Weisberger's study of the political battles culminating in the election of 1800 covers the Kentucky Resolutions in *one sentence*.[72]

This deliberate neglect has resulted in a distorted and biased rendering of American history. With the Virginia and Kentucky Resolutions and their doctrines downplayed and their subsequent history completely ignored, political decentralization and the defense of the powers of the states have come to be viewed as the political goals only of those who wish to preserve slavery and oppression. Much of the rest of this book (and much of what we have already said) is dedicated to disproving this unsupportable claim.

Historian Eugene Genovese made a good start toward this end when he considered the five Virginians who made the greatest intellectual contributions to the strict constructionist, states' rights interpretation of the Constitution: George Mason, Thomas Jefferson, John Randolph of Roanoke, St. George Tucker, and John Taylor of Caroline. "If strict construction and state rights were merely or essentially a façade for the defense of slavery," he said,

> we need to account for a disturbing and incontrovertible fact. Of the five, only Taylor was proslavery, and even he regarded it as an inherited misfortune to be tolerated, rather

> than celebrated. Mason and Randolph spoke out against slavery. Tucker wrote the first important plan for emancipation to come out of Virginia. And when the legislature ignored it, he appealed to the American people by including it as an appendix to his edition of Blackstone, which was widely read by those who aspired to the bar and, indeed, by a great many of those who, in the manner of the day, aspired to be proper gentlemen. In the minds of these five men, and to a considerable extent in their political practice, strict construction and state rights had little to do with slavery.[73]

The Principles of '98 had exactly nothing to do with slavery. And they did not perish when the eighteenth century drew to a close. To the contrary, in the years to come, these essential constitutional ideas would become commonplace even in the very states that had once denounced them. The next chapter discusses this forgotten part of American history, which not one American in one hundred learned about in school. For Americans who are frustrated by the ongoing and evidently unstoppable expansion of government power, the example of states that dared to oppose the federal government's violations of the Constitution might get them thinking. Which is probably why we never learn this material in the first place.

CHAPTER 3

American History and the Spirit of '98

BEFORE THEY TUMBLED DOWN THE ORWELLIAN MEMORY HOLE, the Principles of '98 enjoyed a long and distinguished life in American history. Media spokesmen today, who as usual know none of the pertinent history, have tried to associate nullification with disreputable causes. Our public servants in Washington are only too glad to see this false version of our history peddled to American audiences, since it casts in a perverse light anyone who might wish to employ these great Jeffersonian principles today—if they were thought up and used by slaveholders for wicked purposes, what kind of extremist would want to bring them back? This chapter seeks to recover some of our lost history, both for its own sake and to detoxify the idea of nullification, an unjustly maligned Jeffersonian remedy.

We saw in chapter 2 that the Principles of '98 had nothing to do with slavery, and that the key proponents of the states' rights, strict-constructionist view of the Constitution were not known for sympathy to slavery. The evidence in this chapter amplifies that argument many times over. References to the Principles of '98 over the six ensuing decades can be found all over the United States. "During conflicts between state and national authority," writes a historian of the Virginia and Kentucky Resolutions, "reports and resolutions adopted by state legislatures, messages from state chief executives, opinions of state appellate courts, and speeches of leading citizens all ring with the words of the Kentucky and Virginia Resolutions."[1] In Virginia in particular, the Resolutions were especially influential, forming the basis of legal education at the University of Virginia and the College of William and Mary until well after the Civil War.[2] And as we shall see, it was the northern states, and not the southern, that had more frequent recourse to these Jeffersonian principles.

It was New England, for example, that cited the Principles of '98 most insistently in the decades that followed the Virginia and Kentucky Resolutions. As the Napoleonic Wars raged in Europe in the early years of the nineteenth century, the rights of neutrals like the United States on the seas were increasingly disregarded, as both the British and French searched American ships for goods intended for the other side and seized any such cargoes. The British, furthermore, claimed the right to impress back into service any former members of the British navy they might find on board American merchant ships. In some cases, American citizens were seized. Jefferson, who sought to vindicate American rights, was sure that military action would be foolish, even suicidal. He chose economic warfare instead: in December 1807 he instituted an embargo that prevented American merchant ships from traveling to any foreign port anywhere in the world. The policy wound up having no effect on the behavior of Britain and France, but created great hardship and intense political opposition at home.

Jefferson's embargo devastated New England's maritime economy. New Englanders could take out insurance against seizure of their cargoes by Britain or France, but the complete cessation of international trade at the hands of Jefferson transformed their situation from challenging to impossible. The enforcement of the embargo was also a source of complaint: sweeping search powers, along with the authority to seize ships or even goods wherever they were to be found throughout the country on mere suspicion of intent to export, struck New Englanders as obnoxious and unconstitutional. Although protests were initially muted because the northern ports were frozen and commercial traffic was at a natural standstill, within months Jefferson faced the most intense opposition he had encountered in his two terms as president. We get a flavor of that opposition from the letters the third president received. The nicer ones condemned him as incompetent or a scoundrel. The nastier ones threatened him with assassination. One merchant urged him to "take off the embargo[,] return to Carter's Mountain and be ashamed of yourself, and never show your head in publick Company again."[3] Another correspondent said the President had set "aside and trampled on our most dearest rights bought by the blood of our ancesters [*sic*]. . . . You can not be considered any thing but a curse to this Nation and the whole wrath and indignation of an injured people is pointed at you!"[4] One especially desperate fellow wrote:

> PRESIDENT JEFFERSON
>
> I have agreed to pay four of my friends $400 to shoat you if you dont take off the embargo by the 10th of Oct 1808 which I shall pay them, if I have to work on my hands & nees for it. Here I am in Boston in a starving Condition. I

> have by working at jurney wurk got me a small house but what shall I git to eat? I cant eat my house & it is the same with all the Coopers. I cant git no work by working about on the warves for you have destroy'd all our Commerce & all the ships lie rotting in our harbours & if you dont take off the embargo before the 10 of Oct. you will be shott before the 1st of Jany 1809. You are one of the greatest tyrants in the whole world. You are wurs than Bonaparte a grate deel. I wish you could feal as bad as I feal with 6 Children round you crying for vittles & be half starved yours[elf &] then you would no how good it felt.[5]

Given the American colonists' history of evading British taxation and regulation of their trade, we can hardly be surprised that a new wave of American smuggling greeted Jefferson's policy. Goods were often transported to Canada and shipped from there instead. But it wasn't just private individuals who resisted; it was also state governments. When a federal collector at Oswego requested help in enforcing the embargo, for instance, New York's governor refused. For their part, the state courts of Rhode Island took action to prevent the detention of vessels.[6]

State opposition to the embargo on the grounds of its lack of constitutional sanction was also declared by means of formal protests. In January 1809, the Massachusetts legislature condemned the embargo as "in many respects, unjust, oppressive and unconstitutional, and not legally binding on the citizens of this state." It promised to protect the people against it: "It would be derogatory to the honour of the commonwealth to presume that it is unable to protect its subjects against all violations of their rights, by peaceable and legal remedies. While this state maintains its sovereignty and independence, all the citizens can find protection against outrage and injustice in the strong arm of the state government." It urged its people only to "abstain from forcible resistance" until all peaceful remedies "shall have been exhausted in vain."[7]

The following month, Governor Jonathan Trumbull of Connecticut spoke openly of state interposition: "Whenever our national legislature is led to overleap the prescribed bounds of their constitutional powers, on the State Legislatures, in great emergencies, devolves the arduous task—it is their right—it becomes their duty, to interpose their protecting shield between the right and liberty of the people, and the assumed power of the General Government."[8] The response of the Connecticut legislature, which supported the governor with vigor, deserves to be quoted at length:

> *Resolved*, That to preserve the Union, and support the constitution of the United States, it becomes the duty of the Legislatures of the States, in such a crisis of affairs, vigilantly to watch over, and vigorously to maintain, the powers not delegated to the United States, but reserved to the States respectively, or to the people; and that a due regard to this duty, will not permit this Assembly to assist, or concur in giving effect to the aforesaid unconstitutional act, passed, to enforce the Embargo.
>
> *Resolved*, That this Assembly highly approve of the conduct of his Excellency the Governor, in declining to designate persons to carry into effect, by the aid of *military power*, the act of the United States, enforcing the Embargo, and that his

> letter addressed to the Secretary for the Department of War, containing his refusal to make such designation, be recorded in the public records of this State, as an example to persons, who may hold places of distinguished trust, in this free and independent republic.
>
> *Resolved*, That the persons holding executive offices under this State, are restrained by the duties which they owe this State, from affording any official aid or co-operation in the execution of the act aforesaid.[9]

The following month the legislature of Rhode Island followed suit. It began by noting that “the dissolution of the Union may be more surely, and as speedily affected by the systematick oppression of the government, as by the inconsiderate disobedience of the people.” It then stated, as a matter of common sense, that “the people of this State” were “one of the parties to the Federal compact.” It was, therefore, “the duty of this General Assembly as the organ of their sentiments and the depository of their authority, to *interpose* for the purpose of protecting them from the ruinous inflictions of usurped and unconstitutional power.” Rhode Island’s resolutions read, in part:

> *Resolved*, That the several acts of the Congress of the United States laying an embargo, by the permanent interdiction of foreign commerce, and by the numerous and vexatious restrictions upon the coasting trade, do, in the opinion of this General Assembly, infringe upon the undeniable rights and privileges of the good people of this State.

> *Resolved*, That the act of Congress of the 9th of January last, enforcing the several embargo acts, is in many of its provisions unjust, oppressive, tyrannical and unconstitutional.
> *Resolved*, That to preserve the Union and to support the constitution of the United States, it becomes the duty of this General Assembly, while it is cautious not to infringe upon the constitution and delegated powers and rights of the General Government, to be vigilant in guarding from usurpation and violation, those powers and rights which the good people of this State have expressly reserved to themselves, and have ever refused to delegate.[10]

At the same time that they set forth such a confrontational position, these states by and large insisted on their fidelity to the Union, a fidelity that required them to resist unconstitutional federal acts rather than acquiesce in them. They likewise urged their representatives and senators to work against the embargo and its oppressive and unconstitutional enforcement, and perhaps even to amend the Constitution to make the matter as clear as possible. But as they urged these peaceful remedies, they also insisted that the law in question was unconstitutional and void, and not legally binding.

Conflict between New England and the federal government persisted into the War of 1812. The New England states objected that the president could call upon the militias of the several states only for the constitutional purposes of "execut[ing] the laws of the Union, suppress[ing] insurrections and repel[ling] invasions." To leave entirely within the hands of the president the determination of whether one of these exigencies actually held would, according to New England's argument, efface the just rights of the governors over their own militias. Called upon to decide the question, several Massachusetts judges concluded that such a power of determination was indeed reserved to the states. No power was given to the president or Congress to decide whether "the said exigencies do in fact exist. As this power is not delegated to the United States by the Federal Constitution, nor prohibited by it to the states, it is reserved to the states, respectively; and from the nature of the power, it must be exercised by those with whom the states have respectively entrusted the chief command of the militia [i.e., the state governors]."[11]

The Massachusetts legislature was not alone. The Connecticut legislature declared that "the conduct of his excellency the governor in refusing to order the militia of this State into the service of the United States on the requisition of the Secretary of War meets with the entire approbation of this Assembly."[12] U.S. Senator Timothy Pickering of Massachusetts expressly employed the language of the Principles of '98: "How are the powers reserved to the States respectively, or to the people, to be maintained, but by the respective States judging for themselves, and putting their negative on the usurpations of the general government?"[13]

As the war proceeded and a still more stringent embargo than that of Jefferson was imposed, the embargo controversy reemerged. State dissent once again adopted the language and concepts of the Principles of '98. The Massachusetts legislature condemned the embargo as unconstitutional and reaffirmed that state's right to protect its people against unconstitutional federal laws:

> A power to regulate Commerce is abused, when employed to destroy it; and a manifest and voluntary abuse of power sanctions the right of resistance, as much as a direct and palpable usurpation. The sovereignty reserved to the States, was reserved to protect the Citizens from acts of violence by the United States, as well as for purposes of domestic regulation. We spurn the idea that the free, sovereign and independent State of Massachusetts is reduced to a mere municipal corporation, without power *to protect its people, and to defend them from oppression, from whatever quarter it comes*. Whenever the national compact is violated, and the citizens of this state are oppressed by cruel and unauthorized laws, this legislature is bound to interpose its power, and wrest from the oppressor his victim.[14]

As if the appeal to the Principles of '98 were not clear enough in the passage just quoted, the Massachusetts legislature went on to make express reference to Madison, who was now the President: "This is the spirit of our Union, and thus has it been explained by the very man, who now sets at defiance all the principles of his early political life." It then listed its grievances, noting that the laws that oppressed them were "unconstitutional and void":

> *Resolved*, That "the act laying an embargo on all Ships and vessels in the Ports and harbors of the United States," passed by the Congress of the United States on the 16th day of December, 1813, contains provisions not warranted by the Constitution of the United States, and violating the rights of the People of this Commonwealth.

> *Resolved,* That the Inhabitants of the State of Massachusetts, have enjoyed, from its earliest settlement, the right of navigating from Port to Port within its limits and of fishing on its coasts; that the free exercise and enjoyment of these Rights are essential to the comfort and subsistence of a numerous class of its citizens; that the power of prohibiting to its Citizens the exercise of these rights was never delegated to the general government, and that all Laws passed by that Government, intended to have such an effect, are therefore unconstitutional and void.
>
> *Resolved,* That the people of this commonwealth, "have a right to be secure from all unreasonable searches and seizures of their Persons, Houses, Papers, and all their Possessions;" that all Laws rendering liable to seizure the property of a Citizen at the discretion of an Individual, without warrant from a Magistrate, issued on a complaint, supported on oath or affirmation, under the pretence that such property is "apparently on its way towards the territory of a foreign nation or the vicinity thereof," are arbitrary in their nature, tyrannical in their exercise, and subversive of the first principles of civil liberty.[15]

From a political point of view, the War of 1812 wound up essentially a draw, and the Treaty of Ghent signed in December 1814 reestablished the *status quo ante bellum.* From a military point of view, it was a British rout. As a result, Congress seriously entertained the prospect of military conscription. The constitutional objections, in turn, were not long in coming.[16] The legislature of Connecticut, for instance, described the ensuing bill as "not only intolerably burdensome and oppressive, but utterly subversive of the rights and liberties of the people of this State, and the freedom, sovereignty, and independence of the same, and inconsistent with the principles of the constitution of the United States." Were the bill passed, said the legislature, "it will become the imperious duty of the Legislature of this State to exert themselves to ward off a blow so fatal to the liberties of a free people."[17] The bill never did pass, but the very possibility that it could pass prompted the legislature to issue the following resolution: "That in case the plan and bill aforesaid, or any other bill on that subject, containing the principles aforesaid, shall be adopted, and assume the form of an act of Congress, the Governor of this state is hereby requested forthwith to convoke the General Assembly; and, to avoid delay, he is hereby authorized and requested to issue his proclamation, requiring the attendance of the members thereof at such time and place as he may appoint, to the end that opportunity may be given to consider what measures may be adopted to secure and preserve the rights and liberties of the people of this state, and the freedom, sovereignty and independence of the same."[18]

Daniel Webster likewise opposed the measure, and urged a similar remedy. Webster, who would later represent Massachusetts in both the House of Representatives and the Senate, and who was then serving as a U.S. congressman from New Hampshire, delivered in December 1814 one of the most effective speeches of a political career known for elegant oratory. Military conscription, he thundered, was incompatible with both the Constitution and the principles of a free society. It was, as twentieth-century conservatives like Russell Kirk would later argue, a case of government run completely amok, treating the citizens as if their very lives could be disposed of by politicians. "Where is it written in the Constitution," he demanded to know, "in what article or section is it contained, that you may take children from their parents, and parents from their children, and compel them to fight the battles of any war in which the folly or the wickedness of government may engage it?"[19]

Now if there is one thing Daniel Webster is remembered for in his speaking career, it is his devotion to and defense of a strong and indivisible American Union. His famous exchanges in the U.S. Senate with Robert Hayne and John C. Calhoun, in which he defended a nationalist theory of the Union that consigned the states to a distinctly subordinate position, are among his best-known speeches. (Contrary to popular legend, Webster was in fact the clear loser in the famed Webster-Hayne debate, whether from the point of view of public opinion, the press, or the Senate.)[20] Yet what did Webster think should be done if the conscription bill should pass? In that case, he said, it would be

> the solemn duty of the State Governments to protect their own authority over their own militia, and to *interpose* between their citizens and arbitrary power. These are among the objects for which the State governments exist; and their highest obligations bind them to the preservation of their own rights and the liberties of their people. I express these sentiments here... because I shall express them to my constituents. Both they and myself live under a constitution which teaches us that "the doctrine of nonresistance against arbitrary power and oppression is absurd, slavish, and destructive of the good and happiness of mankind" (New Hampshire Bill of Rights). With the same earnestness with which I now exhort you to forbear from these measures, I

> shall exhort them to exercise their unquestionable right of providing for the security of their own liberties.[21]

Thus even Daniel Webster, the great nationalist, called for interposition, the central theme of the Resolutions of '98.

Although the conscription bill did not pass, the federal government did enact a bill for the enlistment of minors. The legislature of Connecticut promptly passed An Act to Secure the Rights of Parents, Masters, and Guardians, which described the federal government's measure as "repugnant to the spirit of the constitution of the United States, and an unauthorized interference with the laws and rights of this State." The bill required judges to release on habeas corpus any minors enlisted without the consent of their parents. Anyone trying to remove a minor from the state for this purpose was subject to fine and imprisonment. Massachusetts followed suit.[22]

We encounter favorable references to the Principles of '98 in still other northern states. Thus in 1820, in the midst of a confrontation with the Second Bank of the United States, the Ohio legislature declared: "*Resolved by the General Assembly of the State of Ohio,* That in respect to the powers of the governments of the several states which compose the American Union, and the powers of the Federal Government, this General Assembly do recognize and approve the doctrines asserted by the Legislatures of Virginia and Kentucky, in their resolutions of November and December, 1798, and January 1800—and do consider that their principles have been recognized and adopted by a majority of the American people." Immediately preceding the Ohio legislature's resolutions was appended a report that described the election of Thomas Jefferson in 1800 as a referendum on the

Federalists, who had imposed the Alien and Sedition Acts on the country, and an indication of popular support for the Principles of '98:

> The States and the People recognized and affirmed the Doctrines of Kentucky and Virginia, by effecting a total change in the administration of the Federal Government [i.e., by replacing the Federalists with the Republicans]. In the pardon of Calender [*sic*], convicted under the Sedition Law, and in the remittance of his fine, the new Administration unequivocally recognized the decision and the authority of the States and of the people. Thus has the question whether the Federal Courts are the sole expositors of the Constitution of the United States, in the last resort or whether the States, "as in all other cases of compact among parties having no common judge," have an EQUAL RIGHT to interpret that Constitution FOR THEMSELVES, where their sovereign rights are involved, been decided against the PRETENSION OF THE FEDERAL JUDGES, by the people themselves, the true source of legitimate power.[23]

Nine years earlier, the legislature of Pennsylvania had approved a resolution whose indebtedness to the Principles of '98 should be obvious:

> The people of the United States by the adoption of the federal constitution established a general government for special purposes, reserving to themselves respectively, the rights and authorities not delegated in that instrument. To the compact thereby created, each state acceded in its character

> as a state, and is a party. The act of union thus entered into being to all intents and purposes a treaty between sovereign states, the general government by this treaty was not constituted the exclusive or final judge of the powers it was to exercise; for if it were so to judge then its judgment and not the constitution would be the measure of its authority.[24]

In 1826, the legislature of Virginia expressly renewed its support for the Virginia Resolutions of 1798 and Madison's Report of 1800, in light of the federal government's commitment to federally funded internal improvements without a constitutional amendment authorizing them. It also imposed a series of tariffs for the protection of domestic manufacturing that would benefit one section of the country at the expense of another. The principles asserted in those immortal documents, the legislature declared, "apply with full force against the powers assumed by Congress" in its own day.[25] The legislature renewed this protest the following year.

The confrontation between the federal government and South Carolina in 1832–1833 is typically the only time the standard version of American history makes reference to the Principles of '98 in the years following the Virginia and Kentucky Resolutions. We need not spend much time on historical background, since the story is a relatively familiar one compared to the other episodes we have covered thus far. The controversy stemmed from the federal government's protective tariff policy, culminating in the "Tariff of Abominations" of 1828. Many southerners believed the South suffered most of the losses from this policy, and the North reaped most of the gains. Southerners relied on sales in the world market for much of their produce, so protective tariffs in the United States could not help them. Meanwhile, the tariffs forced them to pay more for manufactured goods, and by discouraging Americans from buying foreign products, the tariffs deprived foreigners of the wherewithal with which to purchase southern exports and could lead to destructive economic retaliation.

Numerous southern legislatures condemned the protective tariff throughout the 1820s. As the legislature of North Carolina explained in its own solemn protest in 1828, "Manufactures, in the United States, are not an object of *general* interest but of *local* interest; and yet they have received from the Government, not only a moderate and just encouragement, under the operation of a tariff of duties on imports, for purposes of revenue, but a protection by an enormous duty upon importations; which palsies every effort of the agriculturist, withers the product of his industry, and greatly impairs foreign commerce."[26] South Carolina's Thomas Cooper described the tariff as "a system, whose effect will be to sacrifice the south to the north, by converting us into colonies and tributaries—to tax us for their own emolument—to claim the right of disposing of our honest earnings—to forbid us to buy from our most valuable customers—to irritate into retaliation our foreign purchasers, and thus confine our raw material to the home market—in short to impoverish the planter, and to stretch the purse of the manufacturer."[27]

The South's constitutional argument against the protective tariff was twofold. First, the Constitution envisioned the levying of tariffs for the purpose of raising revenue to meet government expenses, not for the purpose of granting protected status to domestic industry at the expense of consumers. Second, the Constitution called for government activity to be carried out with an eye to the general welfare, not the particular welfare of one section. The protective tariff, it seemed clear, involved the enrichment of northern industry at the expense of southern agriculture, and thus violated the general welfare clause. The South, said sometime senator and Jackson Administration vice president John C. Calhoun, was perfectly content to allow the North the incidental protection that even a revenue tariff would afford, but anything beyond this imposed a heavy and unfair burden on the South.

Perhaps in order to deflect attention from the merits of Calhoun's arguments on nullification, proponents of centralized government have sought to demonize the man himself, noting with gleeful satisfaction his support for the institution of slavery. We are to understand that a supporter of slavery cannot have anything of value to say, and that anything he does say is probably tainted by a desire to protect and expand slavery. But while Calhoun indeed did support slavery, so did Andrew Jackson, the slaveholding southern president who opposed both nullification and Calhoun himself.[28] Such critics are apparently unaware that northern abolitionists were known to refer to Calhoun's principles themselves, even citing him by name, in support of their own struggles against the fugitive slave laws.[29] Someone evidently forgot to tell them that they were not allowed to read or cite the wicked Calhoun, or that these ideas were all about protecting slavery. In this book, we leave aside the bigoted and childish nonsense that views everything southern as disreputable and dishonest, and adopt instead the forbidden course of following the abolitionists and treating the ideas on their merits.[30]

In 1828 Calhoun drafted the South Carolina Exposition and Protest. The Exposition was a lengthy constitutional and economic criticism of the federal government's tariff policy as well as a vigorous defense of nullification as a legitimate state response. The Protest, a brief and separate document condemning the federal government's tariff policy as unconstitutional, was approved by the South Carolina legislature. If relief was not forthcoming, these documents suggested, the state could well resort to nullification.

Calhoun's relationship with Andrew Jackson had been deteriorating throughout the President's first term, and indeed Calhoun had resigned as vice president by the end of 1832. He returned to South Carolina, where he filled an open U.S. Senate seat and opposed President Jackson in the open. The Tariff of 1832 had brought no real relief from the protective tariff policy that numerous southern legislatures considered constitutionally dubious. South Carolina elected delegates to a special convention that voted to nullify the tariffs of 1828 and 1832, declaring that the state's noncompliance would go into effect on February 1, 1833. Jackson responded with his famous Proclamation of December 10, 1832, that condemned nullification and warned South Carolina to desist from its course.

South Carolina did no such thing. To the contrary, its legislature protested what it considered the intimidating words and actions of President Jackson: "*Resolved*, That the principles, doctrines and purposes, contained in the said proclamation are inconsistent with any just idea of a limited government, and subversive of the rights of the states and liberties of the people." To the President's implicit threat to use force against his own people, South Carolina replied that "while this legislature has witnessed with sorrow such a relaxation of the spirit of our institutions, that a President of the United States dare venture upon this high handed measure, it regards with indignation the menaces which are directed against it, and the concentration of a standing army on our borders—that the state will repel force by force, and relying upon the blessings of God, will maintain its liberty at all hazards."[31]

In early 1833, as the fateful date approached, Jackson secured passage by Congress of the Force Bill, which authorized the use of force against South Carolina should it not collect the tariff in compliance with federal law. An ultimate collision was averted when a compromise was reached whereby the tariff would be gradually lowered over the next ten years. For good measure, South Carolina nullified the Force Bill.

The usual moral of the story is that no one state can successfully stand up to the federal government. I draw a different moral. South Carolina stared down the federal government and won for the South a program of tariff relief it might otherwise not have received. The compromise reached between the federal government and South Carolina demonstrates the value of nullification, not its fruitlessness.

The merits of South Carolina's constitutional argument are not our concern here. It could have been submitted to the arbitrament of the states as a whole, and the controversy decided there. There was no reason for a U.S. president to threaten the use of military force against his own people—the kind of thing Americans are taught to condemn when carried out by foreign regimes but to excuse and even celebrate as if it were something categorically different when done by their own.

So far we have seen nullification and the Principles of '98 employed on behalf of numerous causes, among them freedom of speech, free trade, state control of the militia, and opposition to conscription. We have also seen that the major architects of the idea were not supporters of slavery. The average American knows little to none of this. Should he hear the idea of nullification, he would likely suspect—borrowing from the comic-book version of American history he was doubtless forced to endure in junior high school—that it must have been nothing but a sinister means of defending slavery. Isn't that, after all, the only reason someone might support political decentralization?

This is one reason it is important to remember how the northern states employed the Principles of '98 in opposition to the return of runaway slaves. Now it is true that the Constitution (Article IV, Section 2) contains a fugitive-slave clause (made irrelevant when the Thirteenth Amendment was adopted): "No Person held to Service or Labour in one State, under the Laws thereof, escaping into another, shall, in Consequence of any Law or Regulation therein, be discharged from such Service or Labour, but shall be delivered up on Claim of the Party to whom such Service or Labour may be due." Thus it was argued that the northern states were misusing the Principles of '98, since the fugitive slave laws to which they objected were in fact authorized by the Constitution. On the other hand, the clause does not mean that absolutely any measures designed for the purpose of capturing runaway slaves would be constitutionally acceptable, and the Fugitive Slave Act of 1850 was in fact open to constitutional objection.[32] The lack of a proper jury trial for accused fugitives seemed to some states to conflict with their obligation to protect their citizens against kidnapping. Bystanders could be forced to assist in the capture of a fugitive, and stiff penalties were imposed for anyone who harbored or tried to obstruct the capture of a fugitive. On a more technical note, the Constitution requires judicial officers to be paid by fixed salaries, but the fugitive-slave commissioners were paid by fees. And not just any fees: such commissioners received ten dollars if they returned an accused fugitive to slavery, and only five if they set him free!

In northern states, nullification took the form of doing everything officials could to make enforcement of the act difficult if not impossible. State officials who lent their support to a fugitive-slave claimant were penalized and even impeached. Federal officials were not allowed to use local jails to house accused fugitives. Slaveholders coming to claim their slaves were required to go before federal fugitive-slave tribunals rather than simply snatching their slaves and absconding with them.

In a speech delivered in 1909, historian Robert Wild challenged his audience at the Wisconsin Bar Association to consider that those states (including Wisconsin itself) that chose to interfere with or resist the enforcement of the Fugitive Slave Act had in fact been *nullifiers*:

> There are gentlemen still in our own midst, some within the sound of my voice, who lived through and even participated in that great humanitarian movement, and I stand in their presence with reverence upon my lips and affection in my heart. But, I ask, speaking calmly from the standpoint of my unemotional text, did their acts differ in principle from those of the South Carolinians, save only in degree? Were they not also, purely and simply, nullifiers, acting, to be sure, in the spirit of a broad and sweet humanity, yet nullifiers none the less?[33]

One of the most vivid examples of a state's determination not to enforce a measure it considered constitutionally dubious involved Wisconsin, and a man named Joshua Glover. The story began in March 1854. Glover had been taken into custody by a federal marshal seeking to enforce the Fugitive Slave Act of 1850, on the grounds that Glover was himself a runaway slave. Sherman Booth, a local anti-slavery newspaper editor, frantically distributed handbills urging people to convene in the courthouse square to ensure the accused fugitive was not removed without a jury trial. With time running short, Booth ultimately abandoned the handbills and simply rode his horse throughout Milwaukee's business district, stopping at street corners to shout, "A man's liberty is at stake!"[34]

Several speakers addressed the mob that gathered before the jail in which Glover was being held. It was Booth in particular who roused the crowd into action. After he spoke, they forced their way into the jail and released Joshua Glover.

Not unexpectedly, Booth was arrested and brought before a federal district court. When he applied for a writ of habeas corpus, a judge of the Wisconsin State Supreme Court ordered him released. The state supreme court declared the Fugitive Slave Act to be unconstitutional and therefore void.

Before long Booth was arrested again, by the same federal marshal. This time he was found guilty of violating the Fugitive Slave Act, and imprisoned and fined. But once again he was released on order of the state supreme court.

Because the state supreme court was completely uncooperative in submitting a proper record of the case to the U.S. Supreme Court, no further action was taken until March 1857, when the U.S. Attorney was at last able to get a copy of that record. Finally, in December 1858, the U.S. Supreme Court ordered Booth turned over to federal custody. The state supreme court refused to comply.

In 1859, the Wisconsin legislature, heartily approving of its state supreme court's conduct, adopted a resolution in support of the Principles of '98. The U.S. Supreme Court's action, the legislature declared, was "without authority, void, and of no force." Its full statement, as anyone can see, was deeply indebted to the Kentucky Resolutions of 1798:

> *Resolved*, That the government formed by the Constitution of the United States was not the exclusive or final judge of the extent of the powers delegated to itself; but that, as in all other cases of compact among parties having no common judge, each party has an equal right to judge for itself, as well of infractions as of the mode and measure of redress.
> *Resolved*, that the principle and construction contended for by the party which now rules in the councils of the nation, that the general government is the exclusive judge of the extent of the powers delegated to it, stop nothing short of despotism, since the *discretion* of those who administer the government, and not the *Constitution*, would be the measure of their powers; that the several States which formed that instrument, being sovereign and independent, have the unquestionable right to judge of its infractions; and that a *positive defiance* of those sovereignties, of all unauthorized acts done or attempted to be done under color of that instrument, is the rightful remedy.[35]

The Virginia and Kentucky Resolutions and the Principles of '98 had in fact been appealed to all along in the Glover/Booth controversy, and not just in the Wisconsin legislature's 1859 statement. Several weeks after the capture of Glover, a handbill announced the establishment of the "Anti-Slave-Catchers' Mass Convention," which appealed to the defense of state sovereignty against federal usurpations:

> All the People of this State, who are opposed to being made SLAVES or SLAVE-CATCHERS, and to having the Free Soil of Wisconsin made the hunting-ground for Human Kidnappers, and all who are willing to unite in a STATE LEAGUE, to defend our State Sovereignty, our State Courts, and our State and National Constitutions, against the flagrant usurpations of U.S. Judges, Commissioners, and Marshals, and their Attorneys; and to maintain inviolate those great Constitutional Safeguards of Freedom—the WRIT OF HABEAS CORPUS and the RIGHT OF TRIAL BY JURY—as old and sacred as Constitutional Liberty itself; and all who are willing to sustain the cause of those who are prosecuted, and to be prosecuted in Wisconsin, by the agents and executors of the Kidnapping Act of 1850, for the alleged crime of rescuing a human being from the hands of kidnappers, and restoring him to himself and to Freedom, are invited to meet at YOUNGS' HALL, IN THIS CITY, THURSDAY, APRIL 13TH, at 11 o'clock A.M., to counsel together, and take such action as the exigencies of the times, and the cause of imperiled Liberty demand.[36]

Byron Paine, a knowledgeable abolitionist respected for his oratory by friend and foe alike, argued before the Wisconsin

Supreme Court that "the great point of the controversy upon this subject is whether the Federal Government is the exclusive judge of its own powers, or whether the States have not also the right to judge upon that matter." He declared that the federal government, having been created by the states to perform certain limited functions, could not reach beyond its expressly delegated powers; this principle, he said, was "not denied in theory by any one." He referred again and again to the Virginia and Kentucky Resolutions and to Madison's Report of 1800. Abram Smith and Edward Whiton, two justices of the Wisconsin Supreme Court, cited Jefferson, Madison, and the right of state interposition. Justice Smith contended that "the real danger to the union" came not from nullification, but "in acquiescence in measures which violate the Constitution."[37]

This history may be all very impressive, but everything changed after 1865, right? Weren't the states forced into a subordinate position? Of course not. The nature of sovereignty will not permit such a thing. In 1869, a year after the Fourteenth Amendment was adopted, even the Supreme Court reaffirmed the "expressly delegated" principle in the case of *Lane County v. Oregon*:

> Both the states and the United States existed before the Constitution. The people, through that instrument, established a more perfect union by substituting a national government, acting, with ample power, directly upon the citizens, instead of the Confederate government [i.e., the government under the Articles of Confederation], which acted with powers, greatly restricted, only upon the states. But in many articles of the Constitution the necessary existence of the States, and,

> within their proper spheres, the independent authority of the States, is distinctly recognized. To them nearly the whole charge of interior regulation is committed or left; to them and to the people all powers not expressly delegated to the national government are reserved. The general condition was well stated by Mr. Madison in the *Federalist*, thus: "The Federal and State governments are in fact different agents and trustees of the people, constituted with different powers and designated for different purposes."[38]

Still, it is very common in current discussions of nullification to hear critics say the Civil War "settled" the issue. Now for one thing, the Civil War had nothing to do with nullification, though the southern secession was indeed based upon the (correct) compact theory of the Union, to be discussed in the next chapter. In fact, many supporters of nullification, including the now-reviled Calhoun, supported nullification precisely in order to preserve the Union against secessionists who would sever it. But even if nullification *had* been at stake, what moral significance can we attach to the statement that war "settled" the issue? If I say the sky is blue and you say it is brown and green, and then you throw a brick at my head, does that make the sky brown and green? Would a parent tell his bloodied son that his unfortunate fate at the hands of the school bully proved the poor kid must have been wrong? Would we not consider it unspeakably grotesque and morally outrageous to declare that the U.S. Army "settled" the issue of the Plains Indians?[39]

The merits of the constitutional arguments advanced by the states we have studied in this chapter, although interesting in themselves, are not what concern us. What is important is the history itself, the brute fact that the states once did resist the federal government when they believed it had gone beyond its legitimate powers. This is not a newfangled idea that emerged in the twenty-first century out of opposition to George W. Bush or Barack Obama. It is a regular feature of American history, employed for honorable purposes from the earliest days of the republic.

CHAPTER 4

What Is (or Are) the United States, Anyway?

WHAT WAS THE UNITED STATES SUPPOSED TO BE, ANYWAY? That may sound like an odd question. It is, in fact, the most important question of all. The history of state resistance we reviewed in chapter three, as well as the idea of nullification itself, are based on a particular understanding of the nature of the Union that the Constitution brought into existence. Was the United States created by a group of independent political societies that established a federal government as their agent, reserving all undelegated powers to themselves? Or was the United States the creation of a single, undifferentiated American people? That may sound like a distinction without a difference to those new to the subject, but it amounts to perhaps the most significant controversy in early American history—and perhaps in all of American history. Was the United States intended to be just another run-of-the-mill centralized polity, of the kind that would appear with a vengeance in the nineteenth century, or did the

Framers of the Constitution have something less formulaic in mind?

What most American children learn when they study American history in school is what might be called the nationalist theory of the Union, which was expounded by the likes of Daniel Webster and jurist Joseph Story, the latter of whom composed the influential *Commentaries on the Constitution of the United States* (1833). There was no systematic nationalist theory until Story's *Commentaries*.[1] This version of American history and constitutionalism conceives of the United States as deriving from a single sovereign people rather than from an agreement among states and the various peoples thereof. In this view, the United States is just another modern unitary state, in which a monopolistic central authority is the source of all power, and any lesser bodies (in this case, the states) derive their own powers and privileges from this central authority.

What we hear much less about, and what our law students do not learn about at all, is the alternative and far more historically plausible compact theory of the Union, set forth by the likes of Thomas Jefferson, John Taylor, St. George Tucker, Spencer Roane, Abel Upshur, John C. Calhoun, Littleton Waller Tazewell, and others. Hardly anyone reads Judge Abel P. Upshur's book, *A Brief Enquiry into the True Nature and Character of Our Federal Government* (1840), a point-by-point refutation of Justice Story's *Commentaries* that is at least as serious a work as the one it opposes. The compact theory, which Upshur sought to uphold against the nationalist version put forth by Story, held that the United States had been formed when the peoples of each of the thirteen states, each acting in its sovereign capacity, ratified the Constitution in the months and years following its drafting in 1787. (The very fact that the states voted separately to ratify the Constitution, and that the Constitution was not ratified by a single, consolidated vote of all individuals in the original thirteen states, is an important piece of evidence to compact theorists that the states, rather than some single American people, created the federal Union.) They delegated to that government a small number of enumerated powers, reserving the remainder to themselves. As we have seen, Thomas Jefferson and others further proposed that the states may refuse to enforce a federal law that exceeded the powers they had delegated to the central government. According to the compact theory, therefore, the United States consists not of a single, aggregated people, but of particular peoples, organized into distinct states.

For compact theorists, therefore, nullification amounts to the legitimate exercise of sovereignty by sovereign bodies in defense of their liberties against a federal government that was supposed to be the agent, not the master, of the states.[2] The nationalist view, by contrast, would condemn nullification as illegal and possibly treasonous. We leave to the student as an exercise to determine where the true spirit of treason was to be found: in the states that upheld the Constitution by resisting unconstitutional encroachments, or in politicians who imposed unconstitutional measures on the people.

The nationalist view denies that the states established the federal government or that the United States is a league or compact among states. The ratification of the Constitution by state holds no significance for the nature of the Union, according to this view. Ratification was an act not of the states but of the whole people, who alone are sovereign even if they happen to have expressed that sovereignty through the intermediary of state conventions. State resistance to federal power, according to this reading of the American tradition, can be conceived of only as insubordination. The states are essentially helpless to defend themselves against the federal government, and must instead depend for the maintenance of their liberties on such notoriously unreliable mechanisms as national elections—as if elections alone could prevent unjust or wicked federal legislation—or the Supreme Court.

Proponents of the nationalist view attempt to undermine the political and historical integrity of the states by suggesting that the peoples of the American colonies (the precursors of the states) had already become amalgamated into a single people before the Declaration of Independence was signed, and thus well before the Constitution was ratified. According to the nationalist view, as early as the colonial period we see a single people being forged out of the various British North American settlements. From this alleged "single people" the nationalists derive the idea that the American Union itself was the creation of a "single people" instead of what it obviously was: the creation of the various peoples of the several states.

Joseph Story set forth the nationalist reading of American history, in which "one people" began to coalesce during colonial times, as follows:

> Although the colonies were independent of each other in respect to their domestic concerns, they were not wholly alien to each other. On the contrary, they were fellow-subjects, and for many purposes one people. Every colonist had a right to inhabit, if he pleased, in any other colony; and as a British subject, he was capable of inheriting lands by descent in

> every other colony. The commercial intercourse of the colonies, too, was regulated by the general laws of the British Empire, and could not be restrained or obstructed by colonial legislation.[3]

Likewise, John Jay, the first Chief Justice of the United States, argued that "all the people of this country were then subjects of the King of Great Britain, and owed allegiance to him, and all the civil authority then existing or exercised here flowed from the head of the British Empire. They were in [a] strict sense fellow subjects, and in a variety of respects one people."[4]

But do these facts really prove what their advocates tell us they do? For instance, if the people of the various American colonies were "one people" because they had all been subject to the same sovereign during their history within the British Empire, that would have made them "one people" with Jamaica and Canada as well. The facts cited by Story and Jay, according to Upshur, do indeed "prove a unity between all the colonies and *the mother country*, and show that these, taken together, are, in the strictest sense of the terms, 'one people'; but I [Upshur] am at a loss to perceive how they prove that two or more parts or subdivisions of the same empire necessarily constitute 'one people.'"[5] Upshur concluded: "If a common allegiance to a common sovereign, and a common subordination to his jurisdiction, are sufficient to make the people of different countries 'one people,' it is not perceived (with all deference to Mr. Chief Justice Jay) why the people of Gaul, Britain and Spain might not have been 'one people' while Roman provinces."[6]

Each of the colonies did owe allegiance to the British king, it is true, but this was not a common allegiance of a single people to a common head. It was an individual allegiance held separately by each colonial government.[7] The colonies were not amalgamated simply because each of them separately owed allegiance to the same sovereign.

When Andrew Jackson composed his proclamation during his 1832–1833 confrontation with South Carolina over nullification, he too advanced the weak "one people" argument with reference to the American colonies. "In our colonial state," he wrote, "although dependent on another power, we very early considered ourselves connected by common interest with each other."[8] Littleton Waller Tazewell, in turn, whose career included service in the U.S. House, the U.S. Senate, and as governor of Virginia, composed a series of articles that amounted to a point-by-point refutation of Jackson's proclamation. He said of Jackson's "one people" argument:

> A more flimsy pretext, from which to infer the existence of a single community, could not easily have been selected.... Mark, no social connection of any sort, is affirmed to have actually existed; it is merely said, that we very early considered ourselves as connected. And by what was this imaginary connection constituted? Were we inhabitants of a common territory, the vacant and unoccupied parts of which were admitted to belong to all? No. Did we profess the same religious faith? No. Did there exist any one institution, which having been created or preserved by all, was therefore common to all? No. By what tie then did this People consider themselves to be connected, in their colonial state? Why, by the single tie of a supposed common interest. No man before President Jackson, ever thought of inferring the existence of a community from such a fact, which if believed to

> be sufficient to produce the effect, would consolidate, probably, one-half of the People of the whole world into one community, and by so doing, would dissolve more than the half of all the societies now existing, whose members do not even consider themselves connected by any such tie.[9]

The colonists' common experiences as British subjects cannot render them one people, particularly when we recall, with Upshur:

> The people of one colony owed no allegiance to the government of any other colony, and were not bound by its laws. The colonies had no common legislature, no common treasury, no common military power, no common judicatory. The people of one colony were not liable to pay taxes to any other colony, nor to bear arms in its defence; they had no right to vote in its elections; no influence nor control in its municipal government, no interest in its municipal institutions. There was no prescribed form by which the colonies could act together, for any purpose whatever.[10]

There was likewise no official capacity in which the colonies could act politically as one people. When intercolonial confederations *were* proposed during the colonial period, the colonists either resisted them entirely (as when they fought off the royally imposed Dominion of New England in the 1680s or refused to accede to Benjamin Franklin's Albany Plan of Union in 1754), or consented only after insisting on maintaining a veto power on what the confederation might do (as when Massachusetts insisted on a veto less than a decade after the defensive Confederation of New England was established in 1643).[11]

Furthermore, Upshur wonders, if the thirteen states really had constituted "one people," what would have been the status of states that chose not to ratify the Constitution? Could the others have coerced them into the Union, or treated them as if they were already part of it—as the nationalist, "one people" theory seems to demand? As it turned out, Rhode Island did not ratify until 1790—two years after the document had gone into effect over other states. During that time it never occurred to anyone that the U.S. government, by virtue of all the states having become "one people," had any political power over that recalcitrant state. In Federalist #43, in fact, James Madison had noted that if some states refused to ratify, then "no political relations can subsist between the assenting and dissenting states."

Alexis de Tocqueville, the best-known foreign observer of the United States in the nineteenth century, in concluding that the compact theory was the correct one, dismissed the claim that the people of the states ever constituted "one people" in any politically relevant sense. The Union, he wrote in *Democracy in America*, was "formed by the voluntary agreement of the states; and these, in uniting together, have not forfeited their nationality, nor have they been reduced to the condition of one and the same people."[12] The great British libertarian (or "classical liberal") Richard Cobden, in turn, adopted Tocqueville's view, citing him as "our highest European authority."[13]

The people of the colonies were, therefore, separate and distinct. As Upshur put it, they were "separate and distinct in their creation; separate and distinct in the forms of their governments; separate and distinct in the changes and modifications of their governments, which were made from time to time; separate and distinct in political functions, political rights, and in political duties."[14]

In September 1774, the First Continental Congress convened, months after the British imposed the hated Coercive Acts on the colonies. Did this alleged government in fact represent the maturation of a single American people? Joseph Story thought so: the existence and operation of the Continental Congress, he contended, demonstrated that "the united colonies must be considered as being a nation *de facto*."[15] The Continental Congress, to Story, represented a general, national government that was organized with the consent of the sovereign people taken in the aggregate. Yet the acts of the Continental Congress appeared in the form of resolutions rather than as laws or commands. The Congress had no more powers than those for which it could win the various colonies' consent. It could offer counsel, but it could require nothing. It did not reflect a governing structure that derived from authority bestowed by "one people," or could be conceived of as a general or national government. The colonies remained just as distinct as before.[16]

The Second Continental Congress convened in May 1775 in the wake of the Battles of Lexington and Concord, and then remained in session throughout what became the War for Independence. This, too, was organized as an institution to coordinate the joint action of sovereigns, not as a national government representing a consolidated American people. No matter how great its population or how many delegates it sent, each colony had one vote in this congress. A national government, which absorbed the people of the states into a single people, would not have been organized that way. There was nothing in the powers exercised by this congress from 1775 through 1781 that was inconsistent with the retention by the states of their sovereignty and independence. Even if for certain limited purposes they may have wished to collaborate, they did so not at the command of a single, unified sovereign, but as dictated by their own good judgment as individual political entities.

Even the power to wage war, which is universally regarded as one of the chief attributes of sovereignty, was not held exclusively by the Continental Congress. Before the Declaration of Independence, Massachusetts, Connecticut, and South Carolina fitted out vessels to cruise against the British, the troops of Connecticut took Ticonderoga, and New Hampshire authorized its executive to issue letters of marque and reprisal.[17] When, in June 1776, the Congress took up the task of drafting laws pertaining to treason, it was declared that the crime would be considered as directed against the colonies individually rather than as confederated together—not something they would have done had they imagined themselves to be operating under a national government that a single sovereign people had endowed with authority.[18]

The Declaration of Independence itself made clear how the original thirteen colonies, which became states when they declared independence from Britain, thought of themselves. Today, common usage has led most Americans to think of the word "state" as referring to a subordinate political entity within a larger union, as in the centralized United States of the present time. But when the states used the word "state" in the Declaration, they meant it in the same way that Spain and Italy are states—sovereign, independent political units. In the Declaration, the states referred to themselves in the plural, and not as constituting a single entity. Thus: "The history of the present King of Great Britain is a history of repeated injuries and usurpations, all having in direct object the establishment of an absolute Tyranny over *these States*" (emphasis added). When the term "united States of America" was used, the word "united" was not capitalized, as if they were bestowing a name upon a united federation of states. To the contrary, these were the states of America, united in their determination to break their respective political bonds with Britain but not united in the sense of having somehow dissolved their various sovereignties into one.

The Declaration declares the independence of thirteen sovereign states, each of which may exercise all those powers traditionally associated with sovereignty (as my particular emphasis below indicates):

> We, therefore, the Representatives of the united States of America, in General Congress, Assembled, appealing to the Supreme Judge of the world for the rectitude of our intentions, do, in the Name, and by Authority of the good People of these Colonies, solemnly publish and declare, That these united Colonies are, and of Right ought to be Free and Independent States, that they are Absolved from all Allegiance to the British Crown, and that all political connection between them and the State of Great Britain, is and ought to be totally dissolved; and *that as Free and Independent States, they have full Power to levy War, conclude Peace, contract Alliances, establish Commerce, and to do all other Acts and Things which Independent States may of right do.*

Likewise, the treaty of alliance between the United States and France on February 6, 1778, acknowledges an agreement between "the most Christian King and the United States of North America, to wit, New Hampshire, Massachusetts Bay, Rhode Island, Connecticut, New York, New Jersey, Pennsylvania, Delaware, Maryland, Virginia, North Carolina, South Carolina, and Georgia." The same formula is used in a treaty of amity and commerce with the Netherlands in October 1782, reached "between their High Mightinesses, the States General of the United Netherlands, and the United-States of America, to wit, New Hampshire, Massachusetts, Rhode-Island and Providence Plantations, Connecticut, New-York, New-Jersey, Pennsylvania, Delaware, Maryland, Virginia, North-Carolina, South-Carolina and Georgia." A similar treaty with Sweden the following year was ratified between "the King of Sweden, of the Goths and Vandals, &c. &c. &c. and the Thirteen United States of North America, to wit, New Hampshire, Massachusetts Bay, Rhode Island, Connecticut, New York, New Jersey, Pennsylvania, the counties of Newcastle, Kent and Sussex on Delaware, Maryland, Virginia, North Carolina, South Carolina, and Georgia."

When in formal diplomatic statements of this kind the term "united States of America" (with the "u" either capitalized or not, depending on the document) is used, it is understood as an interchangeable way of referring to all thirteen states separately, as in the above treaty with Sweden. And of course, when the states won their independence from Britain, the resulting Treaty of Paris (1783) declared: "His Britannic Majesty acknowledges the said United States, viz., New Hampshire, Massachusetts Bay, Rhode Island and Providence Plantations, Connecticut, New York, New Jersey, Pennsylvania, Maryland, Virginia, North

Carolina, South Carolina and Georgia, to be free sovereign and independent states."

On top of that, the people of the states sure *believed* they were sovereign: the Articles of Confederation, which gave legal sanction to the then-existing Congress, proclaimed in 1781 that "each state retains its sovereignty, freedom, and independence, and every power, jurisdiction, and right, which is not by this Confederation expressly delegated to the United States, in Congress assembled." There it is, as clear as anyone could ask for: *each state retains its sovereignty, freedom, and independence*. The states would have had to be sovereign in the first place in order for them to *retain* that sovereignty in 1781. Thus their status as separate and distinct sovereign states is officially acknowledged in the 1780s, meaning that any collapsing of the distinct peoples of the states into "one people" could not have occurred prior to that date.

But no action so collapsing them occurred after that date, either. Nor could it, for sovereignty is neither partible nor alienable. The great international lawyer Emmerich de Vattel observed in *The Law of Nations* (1758) that "several sovereign and independent states may unite themselves together by a perpetual confederacy, without ceasing to be, each individually, a perfect state. They will together constitute a federal republic: their joint deliberations will not impair the sovereignty of each member, though they may, in certain respects, put some restraint on the exercise of it, in virtue of voluntary engagements."[19] This was the view that Virginia jurist St. George Tucker set forth in his influential 1803 edition of Blackstone, when he explained that the states retained the legal and constitutional right to resume those sovereign powers that they merely "suspended" during such time as they continued to "delegate" them to the United States under the Constitution.[20] Thomas Jefferson said in effect the same thing: "The Constitution of the United States is a compact of independent nations subject to the rules acknowledged in similar cases."[21]

Returning for a moment to the Articles of Confederation, one objection to our position might be that the full name of that document, the Articles of Confederation *and Perpetual Union*, indicates some type of permanent surrender of sovereignty (if such a thing were possible) into a permanent union. If the states belong to a perpetual union, the argument goes, they must no longer be sovereign, for a sovereign would necessarily retain the right to choose to withdraw from any federation it had joined. Unfortunately for the poor souls advancing this claim, their ignorance of what the word "perpetual" meant in the context of eighteenth-century diplomacy has led them down a dead end. For an agreement to be "perpetual" meant only that it had no built-in sunset provision.[22] Hence numerous long-forgotten eighteenth-century treaties claimed to be "perpetual"; if our critics were correct about the meaning of that word, these agreements would still be in effect today. We might also note that even if "perpetual" *had* meant permanent, which it did not, this alleged permanence evidently did not stop the people of the states from discarding it and establishing a new one when they abandoned the Articles and adopted the Constitution.

What of the fact that the Constitution itself begins with the words "We, the People" rather than "We, the States"? Does this not prove that the United States was founded by a single, aggregated American people rather than by the people as citizens of the various states? As it turns out, the original text of the Constitution indeed began "We, the States." The change to "We, the People," was made by the Committee on Style. The reason was that it was impossible to know in advance which states would choose to ratify the Constitution and which would not. Thus, anything in the form "We, the People of the States of..." or "We, the States of..." would have been purely conjectural, and perhaps even insulting to state populations that would have been suspicious enough of the new Constitution without its Preamble seeming to take their approval for granted.[23] The reader may judge for himself the likelihood that the Committee on *Style* would have been permitted to make a substantive change to the Constitution's text, or that a change dramatically altering the nature of the Union would have been accepted without debate, as this one was.

If the states are the fundamental building blocks of the United States, and they maintain their sovereignty and their rights of self-government, one can at least understand how the conclusion follows that the states have the right to protect themselves against abuse by means of nullification. A nullifying state is exercising its prerogative as the agent of its sovereign people to defend them against an unconstitutional law. For the nationalists, on the other hand, nullification is simple insubordination. They would not view it as the sovereign people of a state protecting itself from encroachment on the part of an overweening federal government. They cannot see in it anything other than an insurrection involving an arbitrary group of individuals.

I'll never forget a scholarly colloquium I attended in 2003 on the compact versus nationalist debate. Of the fifteen academics in attendance, only Professor Clyde Wilson and I consistently defended the Jefferson-Roane-Upshur version of American constitutionalism, while the rest defended the Webster-Story version.

One of their scholars finally admitted to us that although, strictly speaking, we were indeed correct from a historical point of view, Webster's nationalist view was more "poetic." Oh.

The history of Virginia, in particular, both exemplifies the compact theory of the union and points to the colonial origins of the idea of nullification. As the controversy between the American colonies and the British government intensified over the course of the 1760s, Virginians appealed to their side of the story against the mother country. Richard Bland, who served in the House of Burgesses, began his 1766 pamphlet *An Inquiry into the Rights of the British Colonies* by revisiting his colony's early history. In coming to these shores, he said, Virginia's settlers had availed themselves of the natural right to emigrate. They had come to a new land by their own effort and at their own expense, and were no longer subject to English law, having fallen under the "Law of Nature" instead.

That meant Virginians had not been in a subordinate position but had chosen of their own free will to enter a mutually binding relationship with the Crown. They expected future kings to abide by James I's promise that Virginia's form of government would never be altered. Virginia could be taxed only by its representatives, and possessed "such Freedoms and Privileges as belong to the Free People of England." The Crown had repeated this guarantee numerous times, said Bland, in its commissions to Virginia's royal governors. Thomas Jefferson amplified this narrative of Virginia's history in his *Summary View of the Rights of British America*. Of course, what followed from this version of Virginia history, in which Virginians had chosen to be governed by the king, was that if he went beyond his traditional authority and attempted to interfere with the internal governance of the colony, they could withdraw their commission to the king.

The colonists had brought with them all the liberties of native-born Britons, including the right to govern themselves in their internal affairs and to tax themselves. British kings had subsequently confirmed this understanding, with this interpretation of events being, in the words of the Virginia Resolves against the Stamp Act in 1765, "constantly recognized by the kings and people of Great Britain." When the Stamp Act was imposed on the colonies in 1765, therefore, and the British attempted to bypass Virginia's legislature and tax them for revenue, Virginians denounced it as a violation of this original understanding.

In early 1766, Richard Henry Lee went a step further and organized the citizens of his county into the Westmoreland Association, which became a locus of resistance to British encroachments on American liberty. Those who joined pledged their loyalty to George III, but only to the extent that such loyalty did not come at the expense of "our Constitutional Rights and Liberty." That is to say, Virginia's right of internal self-government had to be recognized. Because the Stamp Act violated this foundational principle, they indicated that anyone who enforced it would be punished.[24]

This insistence that laws made in violation of Virginia's traditional rights of self-government ought to be considered void did not go away. In 1774, in the wake of the hated Coercive Acts, Thomson Mason (brother of George Mason, who became the father of the Bill of Rights) published a series of letters in Virginia newspapers under the name "British American" that pushed these ideas further still. Since Americans had no representation in Parliament, the acts of that body could not bind them. Those acts were "absolutely void, and m[ight] be legally resisted."[25] In February 1775, Virginia's Richard Henry Lee wrote to Samuel Adams of Boston about certain pending British legislation. "Should such Acts pass," he urged, "will it not be proper for all America to declare them essentially vile and void?"[26]

The preamble to Virginia's republican constitution of 1776 spelled out Virginia's understanding of its legal status before the world, as it had been explicated by Bland and Jefferson. *Virginia had the exclusive authority to govern for Virginia.* The grievances listed in the preamble of that document revolve almost entirely around the issue of Virginia's traditional rights to self-government—economics barely appears; religion, not at all. The right to self-government was later reaffirmed in the Articles of Confederation, Article II of which described the states as having maintained their "sovereignty, freedom, and independence." Virginians were persuaded to adopt the federal Constitution in 1788 on the grounds that that sovereignty would hardly be affected by the proposed confederation. Virginia would still govern for Virginia, as she had in the past.[27] This is the consistent theme, from the colonial period through the early republic.

With all the emphasis that is normally placed on the Constitution's Framers, we are apt to neglect the importance of the *ratifiers*, for it is they whose interpretation of the Constitution—and in particular, the precise nature of what they believed they were getting into—is of ultimate importance. At Virginia's ratifying convention, Patrick Henry raised the concern that phrases like "general welfare" could be exploited by ambitious politicians who wanted to exercise powers beyond those outlined in Article I, Section 8 of the Constitution. Federalist Edmund Randolph, who had been Virginia's attorney general for the past decade, assured everyone that Henry's fears were unfounded, for all rights were declared in the Constitution to be "completely vested in the people, unless expressly given away. Can there be a more pointed or positive reservation?" In other words, this was a strictly limited and federal government. Henry Lee explained to the convention that when "a question arises with respect to the legality of any power," we need simply ask, "Is it enumerated in the Constitution? . . . It is otherwise arbitrary and unconstitutional."[28]

Randolph further explained:

> If in the ratification we put words to this purpose—that all authority not given, is retained by the people, and may be resumed when perverted to their oppression; and that no right can be cancelled, abridged, or restrained, by the Congress, or any officer of the United States; I say, if we do this, I conceive that, as this stile [*sic*] of ratification would manifest the principles on which Virginia adopted it, we should be at liberty to consider as a violation of the Constitution, every exercise of a power not expressly delegated therein—I see no objection to this. It is demonstrably clear to me, that rights not given are retained, and that liberty of religion, and other rights are secure.[29]

Historian Kevin Gutzman, an expert on colonial and early republican Virginia, explains that it was precisely on the understanding and assurances laid out by Randolph and other supporters of the Constitution that Virginians ratified that document. "In the event of the violation of any of [Virginia's] reserved rights, the Federalists said, Virginians would only need to point to the conditions on which they had ratified, and their claim to exemption from the disputed statute would be recognized."[30] George Nicholas, who would become Kentucky's first attorney general, explained it thus:

> If thirteen individuals are about to make a contract, and one agrees to it, but at the same time declares that he understands its meaning, signification and intent, to be, what the words of the contract plainly and obviously denote; that it is not to be construed so as to impose any supplementary condition upon him, and that he is to be exonerated from it, whensoever any such imposition shall be attempted—I ask whether in this case, these conditions on which he assented to it, would not be binding on the other twelve? In like manner these conditions will be binding on Congress. They can exercise no power that is not expressly granted them.[31]

Randolph and Nicholas were not merely influential Federalists at the convention, though that would have been quite enough for their assurances of the limited nature of the proposed federal government to mean something. More significantly still, they belonged to the five-man committee that was to draw up Virginia's ratification instrument. They were in a unique position to articulate the understanding that would govern Virginia's ratification. Their particular "stile of ratification" went on to have the most profound influence on Virginia politics and American history.[32] Virginia would be exonerated from any attempt to impose "any supplementary condition"—that is, any exercise of federal power apart from those she agreed to in the Constitution—upon her.

Virginians kept this limited view of the Constitution and the federal Union very much in mind into the 1790s. Disturbed by Alexander Hamilton's financial program, particularly the federal assumption of state debts, Patrick Henry drafted a resolution for the Virginia legislature in 1790 in which he borrowed from the language of the assurances of Randolph and Nicholas that the federal government would have only those powers expressly delegated to it. Therefore, the legislature protested that the proposed assumption of the state debts "goes to the exercise of a power not expressly granted to the General government." The House passed it that day, the Senate six weeks later.

By the end of the year, the Virginia General Assembly had passed a further resolution, or memorial, regarding the federal assumption policy. Note well what should, by now, bc familiar themes:

> During the whole discussion of the federal constitution, by the convention of Virginia, your memorialists were taught to believe, "that every power not granted, was retained"; under this impression, and upon this positive condition, [which was] declared in the instrument of ratification, the said Government was adopted by the people of this Commonwealth; but your memorialists can find no clause in the constitution, authorizing Congress to assume debts of the states! As the guardians, then, of the rights and interests of their constituents; as sentinels placed by them over the ministers of the Federal Government, to shield it from their encroachments, or at least to sound the alarm when it is threatened

> with invasion; they can never reconcile it to their consciences silently to acquiesce in a measure which violates that hallowed maxim—a maxim, on the truth and sacredness of which, the Federal Government depended for its adoption in this Commonwealth.[33]

Here, as clearly as we could ask for, we find repeated the relevant themes of Virginia's ratifying convention. Henry reminds Virginians that they had been assured all through that convention that all powers not delegated to the federal government were retained by the states. Noting the dubious constitutional basis for Alexander Hamilton's financial program, in particular the federal assumption of the state debts, Henry then observes that it must be Virginia's right to shield its people from the unconstitutional encroachments of the federal government. We are getting very close to the Principles of '98, from a committee that included Henry Lee and Patrick Henry.

As we have seen, it was not the skeptics of the Constitution who insisted in Virginia's ratifying convention that their state entered the Union on the strict condition that it be exonerated should the new government stray beyond its delegated powers. This was the assurance that *the Federalists themselves* gave to those who were skeptical of the Constitution. So we should not be surprised to discover, with historian William Wirt Henry, that the 1790 document from the Virginia legislature, quoted above, "was the work of the advocates, as well as of the opponents, of the Constitution."[34] Colonel Henry Lee, for example, had been a vigorous proponent of the Constitution during the ratifying convention, but after observing the behavior of Congress he went so far as to write to James Madison: "To disunite is dreadful to my mind; but dreadful as it is, I consider it a lesser evil than union on the present conditions."[35] (In August 1799, Jefferson told Madison the same thing: those who cherished liberty, he said, ought to "sever ourselves from that union we so much value, rather than give up the rights of self-government which we have reserved, and in which alone we see liberty, safety and happiness."[36])

What all this means, according to Professor Gutzman, is that Nicholas and Randolph's explanation of the Constitution* and by extension the significance of Virginia's ratification, had come to be seen as completely authoritative by the overwhelming majority of Virginia's political leadership. As in the Imperial Crisis and the Confederation period, Virginians conceived of their interstate union as precisely a *federal* union, a union among parties that were on an equal footing (thirteen contracting parties, as Nicholas had put it). Virginia, not America, remained the primary political unit, the United States government a convenience.

Virginians continued to draw out the implications of these views over the course of the 1790s. According to John Taylor of Caroline, the great Virginian political pamphleteer, "The confederation is not a compact of individuals; it is a compact of states." It was therefore the responsibility of the state legislatures to monitor the federal government and, if necessary, to prevent the enforcement of laws that violated the Constitution.

---

* Nicholas and Randolph, the reader will recall, were Federalists who served on the five-man committee to draft Virginia's ratification instrument. They spoke of a limited federal Union from whose unauthorized exercises of power Virginia would be exonerated.

Constitutions *are* violated, Taylor said, and it would be absurd to expect the federal government to enforce the Constitution against itself. If the very federal judges the Constitution was partly intended to restrain were the ones exclusively charged with enforcing it, then "America possesses only the effigy of a Constitution." The states, the very constituents of the Union, had to do the enforcing.[37]

So by the time of the Virginia and Kentucky Resolutions of 1798 and their doctrines of interposition and nullification, there was nothing new or unusual about such views. They were merely the logical implications of assurances *by Federalists* at the ratifying convention, assurances that had dominated Virginia's constitutional thought in the ensuing decade. Those resolutions, in other words, "floated like leaves on the stream of the Virginia constitutional tradition of Jefferson's *A Summary View of the Rights of British America*, Richard Bland's *An Inquiry into the Rights of the British Colonies*, John Taylor's pamphlets of the 1790s, and the Richmond Convention's instrument of ratification (as explicated by George Nicholas and Edmund Randolph)." In form and content they belonged to the tradition of Patrick Henry's Stamp Act Resolves of 1765 and his General Assembly Resolution of 1790.[38]

Historians have sometimes tried to claim that Jefferson, the anonymous author of the Kentucky Resolutions, hastily devised nullification as an ad hoc response to the Alien and Sedition Acts' assaults on civil liberties.[39] But as we have just seen, nullification was in fact the culmination of a decade's worth of Virginian political thought traceable to the ratifying convention, and even further back with the inspiration they derived from Bland's *Inquiry* and Jefferson's *Summary View* and what those documents said about the status of Virginia vis-à-vis Britain at the time of her creation and throughout the colonial period. There was nothing ad hoc about it.

The principle of local self-government and against interference from distant central authorities was central to Virginian political thought both before and after the War for Independence. This is a key point of continuity between late colonial Virginia and the Virginia and Kentucky Resolutions of 1798. Professor Gutzman observes, "As during the Imperial Crisis, so after the enactment of the federal Constitution, Virginians put their state first and the distant authority they had erected for their state's convenience—formerly in Great Britain, now in the federal capital—somewhere down the list."[40]

As late as 1825, the year before his death, Jefferson prepared for the Virginia legislature another series of resolutions reaffirming these principles. He called them "The Solemn Declaration and Protest of the Commonwealth of Virginia, on the Principles of the Constitution of the United States of America, and on the Violation of Them." He decided against pursuing them, since an amendment granting the federal government the disputed power (in this case, federally funded internal improvements) was before the Congress, and because he thought it better for a state other than Virginia to take the lead. It remains a useful document in what it reveals about the consistency of Jefferson's thought over time. Here, yet again, we see reflected the understanding of the nature of ratification that the Federalists themselves had described thirty-seven years earlier at the ratifying convention:

> The States in N. America which confederated to establish their independence of the government of Great Britain, of

> which Virginia was one, became, on that acquisition, free and independent states, and as such authorized to constitute governments, each for itself, in such form as it thought best.
>
> They entered into a compact (which is called the Constitution of the US. of America), by which they agreed to unite in a single Government as to their relations with each other, and with foreign nations, and as to certain other articles particularly specified. They retained at the same time, each to itself, the other rights of independent government, comprehending mainly their domestic interests....
>
> But the federal branch has assumed in some cases and claimed in others, a right of enlarging its own powers by constructions, inferences, and indefinite deductions, from those directly given, which this assembly does declare to be usurpations of the powers retained to the independent branches, mere interpolations into the compact, and direct infractions of it....

Jefferson then had Virginia protest her loyalty to the Union, while at the same time noting that there was but one thing worse than disunion:

> Whilst the General assembly thus declares the rights retained by the states, rights which they never have yielded, and which this state will never voluntarily yield, they do not mean to raise the banner of disaffection, or of separation from their sister-states, co-parties with themselves to this compact. They know and value too highly the blessings of their union as to foreign nations and questions arising among themselves, to consider every infraction to be met by

> actual resistance; they respect too affectionately the opinions of those possessing the same rights under the same instrument, to make every difference of construction a ground of immediate rupture. They would indeed consider such a rupture as among the greatest calamities which could befall them; but not the greatest. There is yet one greater, submission to a government of unlimited powers.[41]

To my mind, Jefferson's compact theory, and the long tradition of thinkers who supported and amplified it, are immediately persuasive to anyone approaching the subject without prejudice. And it is in light of their exegesis of the American experience that the tradition of nullification makes the most sense and can be most readily defended. As we noted at the beginning of this chapter, few Americans have ever been exposed to it. No law student learns about it. Almost no undergraduates encounter it at any length, since their professors tend to be unfamiliar with the relevant texts. But if we are to make sense of American history, the Constitution, and the options before us as we confront Jefferson's nightmare—namely, a government that acknowledges no fixed limits to its power—we have an obligation to understand it.

CHAPTER 5

Nullification Today

WHY DO WE UNTHINKINGLY ASSUME that political monopolies are a good thing, even though we are rightly suspicious of all other sorts of monopoly? Why are ideas like Jefferson's principle of nullification so difficult for many of us to accept? The answer, I am convinced, lies in the widespread and deeply held preconceptions we have absorbed from our earliest years in school. We have been taught to believe that the best—indeed the only—way to organize society is for an infallible and irresistible central authority to issue commands to lesser, subordinate bodies. These subordinate bodies, in turn, exist at the pleasure of the central authority. They enjoy no independent existences of their own. Any liberties they enjoy may be invaded or cancelled at any time.

As Western liberty was being born over the course of the second millennium, a different model of society was followed. After the Roman Empire disintegrated, no continent-wide empire took its place. "Instead of experiencing the hegemony of a universal empire," writes historian Ralph Raico, "Europe evolved into a mosaic of kingdoms, principalities, city-states, ecclesiastical domains, and other entities."[1] It was the decentralized nature of European political life, the lack of a single, supreme political authority, that contributed to the development of liberty.[2] Princes risked losing population (and their tax base) if they engaged in excessive taxation or interference in their peoples' economic lives. People could simply move to another, less oppressive jurisdiction, which was never too far away.

Should you ever be interested in a graduate course in political philosophy, minus the tuition costs, you should overlook the soporific title and read Robert Nisbet's classic *The Quest for Community*. In that book, a Columbia University sociologist argues that "the single most decisive influence upon Western social organization has been the rise and development of the centralized territorial state." He sets out to examine "the conflict between the central power of the political State and the whole set of functions and authorities contained in church, family, gild, and local community."[3] Instead of a variety of power centers offsetting and competing with each other, a single, irresistible central authority became the central organizing principle of Western political life. The traditional liberties and functions of these lesser associations were absorbed or cancelled by this central power. One of the book's chapters is titled, appropriately enough, "The State as Revolution."

In the early seventeenth century, Johannes Althusius theorized about the political order that preceded the rise of the modern centralized state in his book *Politica Methodice Digesta, Atque Exemplis Sacris et Profanis Illustrata*, or simply *Politica*. Althusius began not with individuals but with the family, which he took to be the fundamental political unit. Groups of families, he explained, may organize to form villages. Groups of villages and towns may organize to form provinces, which in turn may group together to form a kingdom or state. An empire is composed of these various states along with free cities (which are directly answerable to the emperor). To the extent that Althusius believed in or employed the concept of sovereignty, he seemed to imagine it residing in the symbiotic relation of all these lesser groups as they unite for a common purpose. The individual or group exercising political power at the highest level—whether a monarch or something else—merely reflects this concord.

Whatever the ultimate locus of sovereignty, Althusius was quite clear about where it did *not* reside: in the ruling individual or group who happens to occupy the seat of power in a central government. The society Althusius envisioned was far too rich and variegated for a single power center to dominate all others. Althusius, in short, was describing what we might call a *federative polity*. It is a society in which power is shared by various social authorities, not held monopolistically by a central government. These social authorities have rights and liberties of their own, which preceded the central authority and cannot be arbitrarily interfered with or cancelled by it.

Against the federative polity is the model with which most of us are more familiar—what we might call the *modern state*.[4] The modern state, about which Thomas Hobbes theorized in the seventeenth century, envisions society not as composed of a diverse array of social authorities but as consisting of nothing other than an undifferentiated aggregate of isolated individuals. These individuals, in turn, endow a central government with the power to rule over them. No other social authority precedes this central government, and thus no competing power centers in society have the power or political wherewithal to resist the great Leviathan.[5] It is the very opposite of a federative polity, for its starting point is a mere aggregate of individuals, and its ending point is a sovereign who is logically and temporally greater than all other groups in society.

No doubt there is a certain macabre logic to the organization of the modern state. It seems rational and efficient. That is because we have never been introduced to any other way of arranging society. As I have written elsewhere:

> In a federative polity, when another social authority blocked the authority of the central government—medieval towns, for example, won many of their liberties by confronting the king and making demands of him, particularly when he needed their aid during war—it was a normal event, even a virtue. But the modern state trains its citizens to think otherwise. When another institution attempts to resist the encroachments of the central government of a modern state, it is guilty of *treason*. What was once a virtue now becomes the gravest possible crime. The nation, citizens are taught to believe, is "one and indivisible." This new morality inclines the people to view the central government's suppression of lesser bodies as something natural and normal, and resistance by those bodies as reprehensible and unpatriotic. . . . No longer restrained by these smaller authorities and their potential for resistance, the central governments of modern states became capable of all manner of atrocities, of which the twentieth century afforded one gruesome example after another.[6]

Those who oppose the centralized structure of the modern state are typically accused of harboring sinister intentions—but in light of the modern state's track record, including the unprecedented barbarism of its wars, its totalitarian revolutions, and its genocides, the moral presumption should be the other way around.

Indeed, the predatory modern state against which Althusius theorized corrupts everything it touches. Its centralization of power was directly responsible for the atrocities, domestic and international, of the twentieth century. Federative polities had by no means been free of outrages and enormities, but the age of genocide had to await the rise of the modern state. The suppression of lesser social authorities meant that the central government faced fewer and fewer obstacles as it expanded its power. This process of centralization was excused by the Left on the grounds that only a strong central authority could liberate individuals from the oppressions, all too real, of lesser social authorities. It was welcomed by some on the Right who saw a convenient mechanism for overriding moral decisions it disapproved of on the part of local communities.

Both sides got more than they bargained for. This Frankenstein monster, it turns out, creates more oppressions than it liberates us from, and consistently distorts or undermines moral virtues, from filial piety and thrift to personal responsibility and hard work. In the American case, its extravagance and irresponsibility have brought the country to the brink of economic catastrophe.[7]

I am suggesting that we do what has so often become the first principle of sound thinking: turn the conventional wisdom on its head. We have been taught to believe in the modern state; in political centralization. Nearly all modern political philosophers defend some form of it. Instead, we should give the moral benefit of the doubt to movements for political decentralization in the United States and around the world, which challenge the absorption of all power by an irresistible central authority. There has been no more destructive force in the history of the world than the modern state. There is nothing sinister about thinking in different ways. To the contrary, it is probably the most intellectually and politically liberating thing we can do.

That this is a morally and philosophically serious position should be obvious. But try advancing it in modern America, where generations of students are never given the opportunity to consider it. They are instead imbued with the principles of the modern state, their great and glorious protector. Because they accept these premises so unthinkingly, and are usually not even aware of their own assumptions, it becomes impossible for them to respond to alternatives other than with a string of clichés in defense of the status quo. You would have better luck debating a zombie.

Unexamined premises and assumptions can lead us thoughtlessly down paths we would not choose if we studied important questions thoroughly and systematically. A lot of people were taken in by the American politician who promised that he and his party

> would totally eliminate states' rights altogether: Since for us the state as such is only a form, but the essential is its content, the nation, the people, it is clear that everything else must be subordinated to its sovereign interests. In particular we cannot grant to any individual state within the nation and

> the state representing it state sovereignty and sovereignty in point of political power.

Whoops—that wasn't an American politician. My mistake. That was Adolf Hitler in *Mein Kampf*. The future dictator went on in that book to promise that the "mischief of individual federated states . . . must cease and will some day cease. . . . National Socialism as a matter of principle must lay claim to the right to force its principles on the whole German nation without consideration of previous federated state boundaries."[8] No nullification for him.

Now the question remains: can the honorable if moribund tradition of state resistance to unconstitutional federal power be resuscitated, or are Americans too deeply in thrall to the myth that unlimited submission to federal authority is the only course available to them, and is what makes them good and loyal Americans?

At the time of this book's publication, the passage of a health-care reform bill despite deeply rooted popular opposition has ignited popular interest in the possibilities offered by nullification. The legislatures of several states were already voting to nullify that law even before it was passed. As we have seen, this was not the first time a state let the federal government know in advance that proposed legislation would be nullified; Connecticut did the same thing with the conscription bill in 1814. These state proposals take different forms—some would be simple acts of legislation, while others would be amendments to state constitutions. But the principle is the same: to protect the people of a state from federal penalties they might suffer if they do not purchase an insurance package that makes them compliant with a federal health-care law. In Missouri, thirty legislators joined the lieutenant governor at a rally in January 2010 endorsing an amendment to the state constitution that would nullify any attempt by the federal government to force residents of that state to purchase health insurance. In Virginia, the state House and Senate voted overwhelmingly for legislation, later signed by the governor, that declared, "No resident of this Commonwealth, regardless of whether he has or is eligible for health insurance coverage under any policy or program provided by or through his employer, or a plan sponsored by the Commonwealth or the federal government, shall be required to obtain or maintain a policy of individual insurance coverage."[9] By the time of this printing, health-care nullification had been enacted into law in three states, had passed at least one house of the legislature in six others, and was pending in seventeen more. With the Internal Revenue Service unclear about whether it will directly punish those who do not wish to purchase more health insurance than they think they need, the possibility of large-scale civil disobedience remains an open question.

Not surprisingly, we often discover in the language of these measures the themes of the Principles of '98. Thus, in February 2010, the Idaho House passed House Bill 391, which makes express reference to the state's reserved powers under the Tenth Amendment:

> The power to require or regulate a person's choice in the mode of securing health care services, or to impose a penalty related thereto, is not found in the Constitution of the United States of America, and is therefore a power reserved to the people pursuant to the Ninth Amendment, and to the

> several states pursuant to the Tenth Amendment. The state of Idaho hereby exercises its sovereign power to declare the public policy of the state of Idaho regarding the right of all persons residing in the state of Idaho in choosing the mode of securing health care services free from the imposition of penalties, or the threat thereof, by the federal government of the United States of America relating thereto.[10]

If these provisions are to be more than rhetoric, the states enacting them will have to stand ready to defend their people if and when the federal government tries to exact punishment on those peaceful individuals who choose not to comply with its coercive edict. This defense will need to take various forms. Houston attorney Jeff Matthews proposes several:

> (1) No court of this state shall relinquish jurisdiction over any citizen of this state on the subject matter of federal health care legislation to any federal court in this state.
> (2) No judge in this state shall issue orders to levy or execute on the property of any citizen of this state to collect any amounts assessed against the citizen for failure to comply with any provision of federal health care legislation. Any person who violates this provision shall be subject to any disciplinary sanction available by the state bar, including suspension and/or disbarment.
> (3) Any federal judge in this state shall be subject to *sua sponte* and citizen-initiated grievance procedures before the state bar for exercising jurisdiction over any citizen of this state in cases involving federal health care legislation. Any person who violates this provision may be subject to any

> disciplinary sanction available by the state bar, including suspension and/or disbarment.
> (4) No federal or state officer in this state shall levy or execute on the property of any citizen of this state to collect any amounts assessed against the citizen for failure to comply with any provision of federal health care legislation....
> (5) No bank, credit union, trustee, investment broker or other depository in this state shall be authorized to pay over to any federal authority any sums claimed due under any writ of garnishment, if such writ is for purposes of collecting any amounts assessed against a citizen of this state for failure to comply with any provision of federal health care legislation....[11]

Opponents of the new health insurance mandate are also pursuing a more traditional legal option, with thirteen state attorneys general filing suit in opposition to various aspects of the law. This is a form of state interposition as well, even if not as radical as open defiance.

As we noted in chapter 1, numerous other federal laws in addition to the health insurance mandate are being examined for constitutionality by states prepared to employ Jefferson's remedy. There are far more state nullification initiatives, pending or already passed, than we can discuss here. To keep abreast of them, consult the Legislative Tracking page at TenthAmendmentCenter.com, far and away the best and most thorough website for following the spread of nullification and other localist initiatives. I post regularly about this subject at my own site, TomWoods.com.

Would each episode of nullification have to be resolved in some way? In other words, would the states have to amend the

Constitution, either expressly granting the federal government the disputed power or expressly withholding it, every time a state nullified a federal law? Most of the time this seems unnecessary. The country is surviving just fine in the midst of ongoing state defiance on medical marijuana and other issues. If we wound up with a Union in which some states were in fact different from others, it would not be a catastrophe to be deplored. *That would be the United States as the Founders envisioned it.*

Now it will be objected that nullification can't work because the federal government has the states right where it wants them: if push comes to shove, no one will want to antagonize the politicians in Washington for fear of losing "federal funding." That is a serious obstacle, to be sure. Of course, the problem would be mitigated to some extent if the states were to nullify unfunded federal mandates, thereby saving money. The more states engage in nullification, moreover, the more difficult it will be for politicians in Washington to get away with penalizing them all.

This is the essential point: if the people of the states are determined not to obey a law they consider unconstitutional, that law simply will not be enforced. The federal government can rant and rave all it likes. It won't matter. Recall again the case of Joshua Glover. The people of Wisconsin refused to support the federal government's campaign against Glover and Sherman Booth. Historian H. Robert Baker, author of *The Rescue of Joshua Glover* (2006), describes the situation:

> The rescue of Joshua Glover had, by 1860, become a national event. Wisconsin's steadfast resistance had morphed from a fugitive slave rescue to *the interposition of the state with such intensity that all federal officers—from a*

> *deputy marshal to the chief justice of the U.S. Supreme Court—had been stung by the defiance.* Most off-putting to them was its success. Despite immense pressure, the stand against the Fugitive Slave Act survived again and again at the polls.[12]

Thus we see how difficult it is for the federal government to enforce a constitutionally dubious law when the people are determined to resist.

If the Constitution could be safely amended to incorporate something of the spirit of '98, that would make the states' task easier. For one thing, we would not need to engage in a lengthy historical and constitutional disquisition to persuade skeptics every time we wished to employ it. Amending the Constitution, which I myself would have dismissed out of hand only a few years ago, will be met with resistance. Why, there's nothing wrong with the Constitution as it is, some will say—we just need to enforce the document as written. For one thing, that just isn't working. And this objection misfires on two additional counts. First, it can indeed be useful simply to clarify what is already implicit. As we have seen, the Tenth Amendment itself, which Jefferson described as the cornerstone of the Constitution, was only codifying what the states had been assured was already implicit in the Constitution as drafted. Clarifying the reserved powers of the states, or the correct, pre-1937 interpretation of the commerce clause, would be a waste of time only if the Tenth Amendment was a waste of time.

Second, there *is* something wrong with the Constitution as it exists today: the Seventeenth Amendment, to name just one such problem. The direct election of U.S. senators, instituted by the Seventeenth Amendment, is routinely described as a glorious and progressive advance over the backward, stupid system of the Framers, whereby U.S. senators were to be chosen by the state legislatures. In fact, that amendment has played a central role in advancing the centralization of power in Washington, D.C. I do not recall, in my own high school social-studies class, being encouraged to consider *why* the Framers decided to elect senators this way, and why they deliberately chose not to elect them as we do today. Today, senators get elected by holding fundraisers in major U.S. cities and collecting donations from all over the country. This does not exactly make them beholden to their states. To the contrary, it makes them beholden to their donors. As the Framers envisioned it, the state legislatures' power to choose U.S. senators would limit the extent to which the latter could be bought off, and maximize the influence that the states would exercise over them. Thus Fisher Ames of Massachusetts referred to U.S. senators as "ambassadors of the states." It was taken for granted that the state legislatures would instruct their senators, and thereby keep them on relatively short leashes.[13]

As a result, writes Professor Todd Zywicki of George Mason University Law School, the Senate once "played an active role in preserving the sovereignty and independent sphere of action of state governments. . . . Rather than delegating lawmaking authority to Washington, state legislators insisted on keeping authority close to home. . . . As a result, the long-term size of the federal government remained fairly stable and relatively small during the pre-Seventeenth-Amendment era."[14]

The chances that we might have a rational debate over the Seventeenth Amendment are essentially zero. Any discussion that did take place would occur at a strictly third-grade level, with supporters of the present system breathlessly posing as champions of "democracy" in the face of heretics and Neanderthals. But with the destruction of the Senate as the representative forum of the states, we do need the reintroduction of *some* form of state negative on the federal government. If nullification itself, which (like the Tenth Amendment) Jefferson took to be unavoidably implicit in the very nature of the Constitution, cannot be expressly enshrined in the Constitution, we might consider a second-best alternative whereby, say, a vote of two-thirds of the states could overturn a federal law. We need an institutional structure in which another force within the United States may say no after the federal government has said yes. Anyone who doesn't think the federal government has been saying yes to itself a teensy bit too much might consider, just for starters, the $100 trillion in unfunded liabilities for which our wise leaders, who continue to hand out "free" benefits as if nothing is wrong, have made absolutely no provision.[15]

The Constitution includes two mechanisms for the ratification of amendments: either Congress introduces the amendment and three-fourths of the states ratify it, or the states themselves convene in a convention for the purpose of amending the Constitution, with three-fourths of them having to vote to ratify any amendments proposed there. The far preferable way to introduce the kind of amendment I propose, because potentially less circus-like, is the former, in which Congress introduces the amendment and sends it out to the states for ratification.[16] Now since Congress is itself the problem, it is unlikely to be the solution. Unless, that is, it gets spooked at the prospect of the states acting on their own, and thus preemptively introduccs the amendment in question in order to head off such a possibility.

In the meantime, if the states really want to be serious, and their people are educated enough in their real history to back them up, they might consider establishing federal tax escrow accounts. Proposed so far in Oklahoma, Georgia, and Washington state, legislation establishing such accounts seeks to neutralize the federal government's ability to threaten and intimidate the states. All federal taxes would first go to the state's department of revenue. From there, legislators would consider the constitutionality of various aspects of the federal government's budget and then contribute from the escrow account an appropriate amount. Any leftover monies would either be returned to the people or spent on projects currently funded by federal grants. Yes, this would be a very different way of doing things. That's precisely the point. The current way of doing things has made a joke of the Constitution, to say nothing of pushing the country toward bankruptcy.

Another way nullification might be pursued is by means of jury nullification, which holds that juries must judge not just the facts of a case but also the law itself. Although few people realize it, the consensus among the Founding Fathers was that jury nullification was an essential defense mechanism for a free people.[17] This, then, becomes an additional means by which the people's determination not to enforce an unconstitutional law may be effected. Theophilus Parsons, who supported the Constitution in Massachusetts' ratification convention in 1788, and who turned down John Adams' offer to serve as U.S. attorney general in order to become Chief Justice of Massachusetts, took precisely this position. He wrote: "An Act of usurpation is *not obligatory—it is not law*. Any man may be justified in his resistance to it. Let him be considered as a criminal by the General

Government—yet his own *fellow citizens alone* can convict him. They are *his jury*—and if they pronounce him innocent, *not all the powers of congress can hurt him*—and innocent they certainly will pronounce him, if the *supposed* law which he resisted was an act of usurpation."[18]

Nothing is more certain than the demonization of this worthy cause and those who support it. Even though they are following in the footsteps of eminent Americans, they will be portrayed as cranks with sinister motives. Note that our wise public servants are not portrayed as having sinister motives. From time to time they may make "mistakes," but their intentions are good and they seek only to serve us. Those who resist them, on the other hand, are wicked and perverse. They must be crushed. They must be smeared and made into objects of hatred. Government is supposed to grow, our wise public servants and their favored constituencies are supposed to enrich themselves, and the rest of us are supposed to sit back and take it. The natural right of Ivy Leaguers to try out their theories on the American public shall not be infringed.

Demonization of those who favor nullification has already begun to occur at the state level. When, in late 2009, State Representative Susan Lynn introduced a nullification resolution into the Tennessee legislature in anticipation of the federal government's health care legislation, she was met by the usual hysteria with which the political establishment greets deviations from the narrow range of allowable opinion. According to the *Nashville City Paper*, "Rep. Mike Turner, chairman of the House Democrats' political caucus, said Tuesday Rep. Susan Lynn's comments harkened back to Civil War-era arguments." Representative Turner himself went on to unbosom his own thoughts: "Susan Lynn is yearning for times gone by. Maybe we could put the poor people back to sharecropping and slavery and let the people up at the big house have all the nice things. We've already had that fight about states' rights."[19]

That's one seriously convoluted remark, but the best I can make out, Turner is saying something like this: since Susan Lynn questions the federal government's constitutional authority on health care, she is an enemy of the people who is living in the past. If we listen to her, we may as well bring back slavery!

Listen again to Turner's *non sequitur*: "We've already had that fight about states' rights." In other words, we've already established that the experts who rule us in Washington know what's best. We've already decided that it's better for the federal government to exercise whatever powers it wants, and for the states to content themselves as administrative units dictated to by an imperial capital. You think the states might instead need to protect themselves from Washington, that perhaps the federal government just might overstep its constitutional bounds? What are you, a supporter of slavery?

Now even if, as I suspect is the case, Turner didn't know anything about the use of nullification on behalf of human freedom time and again in American history, and even if he'd never heard the name of Joshua Glover, what could justify such a vicious and absurd attack on the inoffensive Susan Lynn? What kind of numbskull would think she or her supporters favored *slavery*?

Turner does not actually believe what he is saying. He knows it, we know it, and he knows we know it. He is engaged in the familiar ritual of smearing the good name of anyone who dares to deviate from that glorious continuum from Hillary Clinton to Mitch McConnell that we laughingly call the "mainstream." He hopes that by associating someone with slavery, he can make that person odious in the minds of those who don't bother to investigate the matter for themselves.

That doesn't work anymore. In early 2010, Keith Olbermann said that when white men call Barack Obama "flippant" or "arrogant," they are using racist code words. No normal person believes that. Most people have figured out what these crazy accusations are really all about: suppressing opinions of which the Establishment disapproves, by trying to terrify opponents of the regime into silence. But sledgehammer tactics like this don't actually suppress anything. They just make people sympathetic to the targets of the character assassination, since they know the charges are phony, as usual.

Nullification is a principle that defends the freedom of all Americans, who are equally threatened by a government that acts without limits. And it is not Birmingham 1963 any longer. Demographic trends of the past several decades show blacks moving in large numbers *to* the South, the only section of the country where a majority of blacks polled say they are treated fairly. Times have changed. *Federal* policies, especially but not exclusively related to the "war on drugs," have helped turn black communities into war zones. Under the present system of federal supremacy, states are forbidden to adopt humane alternatives. Are we so pleased with the outcome that such alternatives are really unthinkable?

As we join together against a common foe, it is long past time that we started treating each other as human beings, rather than as categories. We ought to recall Murray Rothbard's refusal to accept that "our enemy today is the poor, who are robbing the rich; the blacks, who are robbing the whites; or the masses, who are robbing heroes and businessmen." To the contrary, he said, it is the government that is "robbing all classes, rich and poor, black and white, worker and businessman alike" and "ripping us all off."

> We must strip the mystical veil of sanctity from *our* rulers just as Tom Paine stripped the sanctity from King George III. And in this task we libertarians are not the spokesmen for any ethnic or economic class; we are the spokesmen for all classes, for all of the public; we strive to see all of these groups united, hand in hand, in opposition to the plundering and privileged minority that constitutes the rulers of the state.[20]

When the issue of nullification arose in the 2010 Texas gubernatorial race, with both Texas governor Rick Perry and challenger Debra Medina making reference to the compact theory of the Union, the Establishment went berserk. MSNBC's Chris Matthews, who knows nothing of the history in this book, exploded that these were the principles of Jim Crow (Jim Crow, of course, having been validated by the U.S. Supreme Court!), and demanded to know if Medina thought she was John Calhoun, whatever that was supposed to mean. This is the media's standard procedure. Never actually deign to tell us where our arguments are wrong; just point and shout, "Eek! An unapproved opinion!" Matthews then told the two other middle-aged white men on his program that the Tea Party demonstrations weren't "diverse."

The problem with this strategy, if we overlook for the sake of argument how creepy and Orwellian it is, is that it relies on the expectation that Americans are waiting by their televisions to be told what ideas they may support. Now that Keith Olbermann says that people who drive pickup trucks are likely to have sinister intentions, I rather doubt this number is as great as it may once have been. An increasing number of Americans seem to pride themselves on *defying* the monitors of approved opinion.

It was just as amusing and predictable during the Texas gubernatorial race to observe historian and constitutional law professor Sanford Levinson rushing to assure Texans and the American public that there was nothing to see here, that of course they could not resist their wise overlords no matter what Thomas Jefferson had tried to tell them. In fact, Levinson evidently figured he'd make it easier for Americans to make up their minds on the issue by obscuring Jefferson's connection to the idea; we wouldn't want to confuse the stupid rubes who might be inclined to listen respectfully to an idea traceable to Jefferson. Jefferson, said Levinson, "appeared to suggest" that Kentucky could declare the Sedition Act unconstitutional and void.[21] That's like saying the Declaration of Independence "appeared to suggest" that the states ought to separate from Britain. As we've seen, Jefferson didn't "appear" to "suggest" such a remedy—he came out and said exactly this, and insisted that *this power was essential if the federal government was to be kept limited*. There was nothing equivocal about it at all. Jefferson's whole view of the Union is contained in the very document Levinson wants to dismiss in a contemptuous sentence.

Especially misleading is Levinson's by-the-book argument that Virginia and Kentucky found no support for their arguments in 1798:

> They received the support of no other states (even those that opposed the Sedition Act), and several states went out of their way to denounce the notion. The Rhode Island Legislature forthrightly resolved that the Constitution places "in the federal courts, exclusively, and in the Supreme Court of the United States, ultimately, the authority of deciding on the constitutionality of any act or law of the Congress of the United States."[22]

For one thing, the *vast bulk* of the states that protested the Virginia and Kentucky Resolutions expressly affirmed, in their very replies to Virginia and Kentucky, their own support of the Alien and Sedition Acts, which they considered perfectly constitutional. The official communications of Massachusetts, Pennsylvania, Connecticut, New Hampshire, Vermont (specifically in its reply to Kentucky), Rhode Island, and New York (the latter of which simply declared that no unconstitutional acts had been committed, without mentioning the disputed legislation by name) all took this position. Delaware simply said it wouldn't deign to argue the matter; it is unclear why we should even bother with such a flippant response. None of the states south of Virginia drafted any replies to the Virginia and Kentucky Resolutions' invitation to similar action at all, and the existing evidence makes it difficult to uncover why they failed to do so. The most thorough study of the matter, by F. M. Anderson, found it likely that "the South Carolina legislature failed to act upon the resolutions of Virginia and Kentucky because it sympathized with the protest against the Alien and Sedition Laws but scarcely knew its own mind upon the matter of the remedy." Anderson concluded as follows: "South of the Potomac, where the Republican strength was rapidly rising, it had not yet been sufficiently consolidated to secure expressions of approval for even a portion of the resolutions; but it was strong enough to prevent any formal disapproval of them, as in the North."[23] In brief, the *only* state that replied to Virginia and/or Kentucky that did not make approving reference to the Alien and Sedition Acts was Delaware, whose response was so curt as to be worthless. This is not good news for Sanford Levinson, who either does not know this history or chooses to distort it. It means he is trying to win the argument by noting (1) how many states disagreed with Virginia and Kentucky at the time, but without adding (2) that *virtually all* of these states thought it was perfectly constitutional and right to throw people in jail for criticizing the president or Congress. Well, no wonder those states disagreed with Virginia and Kentucky, which were objecting to that very thing! If anything, this *strengthens* the case for nullification, for what other recourse was available at a time when most of the judges and most of the states had completely lost their minds?

Levinson also fails to make note of the widespread recourse to and respect for the Principles of '98 that we observe over the ensuing decades. That, too, might give people ideas, and we can't have that. He quotes the Rhode Island legislature in 1799 and its criticism of the Principles of '98, without mentioning what the Rhode Island legislature was saying only ten years later. Let us rectify that omission right now: "The people of this State," declared the Rhode Island legislature in 1809, "as one of the parties to the Federal compact, have a right to express their sense of any violation of its provisions and it is the duty of this General Assembly as the organ of their sentiments and the depository of their authority, to *interpose* for the purpose of protecting them from the ruinous inflictions of usurped and unconstitutional power."[24]

No, Rhode Island didn't support Virginia and Kentucky in 1799, when it drafted its response to those states. Levinson is right about that. But isn't it a teensy-weensy bit worth mentioning that only a decade later that very same state was *embracing* the very principles it had once spurned? Isn't Rhode Island's open challenge to the federal government in 1809, *employing the language and principles of the Virginia and Kentucky Resolutions*, a little bit more important than a letter its legislature wrote in 1799? Don't actions, after all, speak louder than words?

It wasn't just Rhode Island, of course; as we saw in chapter 3, within ten to fifteen years many of the states that had once been critical of Virginia and Kentucky were themselves speaking of the right of state interposition, and in the ensuing decades so were other states that in 1798 had not even been admitted to statehood yet. Recall the Ohio legislature's 1820 resolution in support of the Virginia and Kentucky Resolutions that declared the Principles to have been "recognized and adopted by a majority of the American people."[25] So revered were these documents, in fact, that Andrew Jackson himself, in the course of opposing South Carolina's act of nullification, was at pains to square his own position with that of the Virginia Resolutions.[26]

Not a word about any of this from Sanford Levinson. Nullification was merely something Jefferson once "appeared to suggest," was later tried by South Carolina, and that was that. Nothing about the centrality of the Virginia and Kentucky Resolutions in Virginian legal education, nothing about New England's use of interposition, nothing about the appeal to the Kentucky Resolutions over sixty years later in Wisconsin's opposition to fugitive-slave laws, and certainly nothing about the origins of nullification in mainstream Virginian political thought stretching back to that state's ratification convention and beyond.

If you, dear reader, can come up with an innocent explanation for so systematic an omission, your imagination is better than mine.

Nullification is not a silver bullet, of course. It cannot solve all problems, and carrying it through effectively will be difficult. But is that so surprising? The economic and political interests that benefit from the current system, in which the federal government does as it wishes without effective check from any quarter, swarms of federal employees line their pockets in the name of serving the public good, and countless pressure groups win lucrative special privileges for themselves, are formidable. *Any* attempt to reverse the process is going to be an uphill battle. If we are waiting for a remedy that will work like magic, we will be waiting a long time.

The federal courts will never allow the states to get away with nullification, skeptics may say. Perhaps so, but is this any different from saying that the federal government as a whole will object to nullification? No one doubts that the federal courts will object. The question is whether this should matter. Not for nothing did Jefferson describe the federal judiciary as "working like gravity by night and by day, gaining a little today and a little tomorrow, and advancing its noiseless step like a thief over the field of jurisdiction, until all shall be usurped from the states, and the government of all be consolidated into one."[27] The federal courts have done nothing, at least since the 1930s, as the rest of the federal government has dismantled the restraints on its power that the Framers of the Constitution clearly and obviously instituted. It would be farcical even by the federal courts' standards for them to decide that the one thing they *will* condemn is the states' efforts to restore these constitutional limitations. Whether or not one particular branch of the federal government is unhappy with state resistance is beside the point; as we've seen in the case of medical marijuana and are about to see in other aspects of American life, when the people of a state have determined to stand up to the federal government, merely being handed a declaration by that same government ordering them to cut it out is unlikely to divert them. Any such pronouncement by a federal court should itself be nullified, if not simply ignored.

Nullification efforts can play an important educational role even when unsuccessful. The very idea that the federal government might do something unconstitutional hardly enters into political discussion today. The vast bulk of Americans proceed through twelve years of government-funded education that (by an interesting coincidence) teaches them all about the wonders of the federal government, how lost they'd be without it, and how foolish it would be to worry that the Constitution might not authorize most of what it does. The very attempt at nullification and the ensuing controversy and debate can give rise to a veritable seminar in American history and constitutionalism, thereby filling the gaps that remain in most Americans' formal education.

Jon Roland, whose Constitution Society website has garnered over 100 million page views, proposes a state "Federal Action Review Commission," an institution that might first be established in one of the states where awareness of constitutional issues is relatively higher. The commission's rotating membership would be drawn from a pool of constitutional scholars compiled by some branch of the state government. It would meet with great frequency, perhaps even weekly, and be charged with the task of reviewing recent congressional legislation for constitutionality. Should a federal law be found unconstitutional, the commission would declare it so, and issue an edict ordering state officials not to cooperate in its execution. Citizens of the state would be urged not to cooperate. A state fund would be established to provide legal support to those who refused their cooperation with an unconstitutional federal law.[28]

A radical step? No doubt. But since nothing else has worked, and pursuing the same failed strategy again and again holds little promise, what alternative exists? Plenty of people make nice salaries writing think-tank reports, some of them quite good, about the benefits of freedom in this or that area. Isn't it time to supplement all the report-writing with vigorous, constitutional action in the tradition of Jefferson? It can scarcely be doubted where the Sage of Monticello's sympathies would lie if he had the misfortune of seeing what had become of his country.

We cannot know in advance how Roland's proposal would work out in practice. On the one hand, the historians and legal scholars who would be chosen for the commission would by and large be drawn from professions dominated by people who think things are just fine, and that the federal government's present size and activities are perfectly in line with the Constitution. But there are some mitigating factors. This lame result would not occur in all states. In places like Texas, as well as in the West and Pacific Northwest, enough sensible and knowledgeable people could well be appointed to make things interesting. And these days, enough uneasiness exists about certain federal actions that even conventional legal thinkers might be willing to consider taking a stand against them—especially if an informed and angry population urged them to do so.

Roland suspects the following outcome. In a state like Texas, where a critical mass of the population may, in fact, understand the constitutional issues at stake, the commission would nevertheless start out timidly, declaring unconstitutional only the most egregious but still relatively minor federal activities. The very fact of declaring any federal action to be unconstitutional, though, would provoke debate and discussion among the general public. Faced with the possibility that something real might actually be done about federal lawlessness for a change, the public may well demand still more such findings, thereby emboldening the commission further. This momentum would undoubtedly spread to other states, where candidates for office may even find it in their interest to champion the constitutional cause.

Roland suggests that immediately using the commission for the purpose of large-scale constitutional challenges could backfire, in that it could lead to the suppression of the commission itself. It should proceed more gradually, he says, in tandem with popular support and education. How rapidly or cautiously such a commission should proceed ultimately depends on the status of public opinion in each particular state, and the degree to which the people of that state are willing to make a stand against violations of the Constitution. Either way, it is a worthwhile step forward to keep the idea of constitutional limitations on government before the general public on a regular basis. The very existence of such a commission would strike at the superstitious reverence Americans are taught to have for the federal government, portrayed in all our textbooks as a benevolent force innocently pursuing the common good. It would suggest that the federal government is, as Jefferson taught, something to be on guard against, not the glorious source of costless benefits granted by selfless crusaders for justice. There comes a time to put away foolish things. Now is that time.

I have long been skeptical that any government, constitutional or otherwise, can remain limited over time. If we grant one sector of society both a monopoly on the initiation of violence and the related power to tax, and then hand it a piece of paper and ask it to stay limited, we should know in advance what is certainly going to happen. Lysander Spooner, abolitionist and anarchist, once said that the Constitution has either authorized the government we have now or has been helpless to prevent it. "In either case," he starkly concluded, the Constitution "is unfit to exist."

At the same time, institutional restraints that pit power against power might postpone or hobble a regime's growth. That is what Jefferson's remedy seeks to do. Jefferson knew that the natural tendency was for power to advance and liberty to give ground. So he sought to slow down that process however he could—including by recourse to nullification.

In earlier times, advocates tried to make nullification more palatable to skeptics by assuring them that it would be used only infrequently and as an absolutely last resort. Today this assurance hardly seems necessary. The regime in Washington has grown so destructive and parasitic, its activities so inimical to the welfare, liberties, and prosperity of the people and so remote from any conception of constitutionally limited government, that supporters of nullification need not apologize for disrupting its plans. That, in fact, is the point. They should be congratulated for doing what they can to slow it down. Again, *nothing else has worked.*

Recall the words of the Kentucky Resolutions of 1799: "If those who administer the general government be permitted to transgress the limits fixed by that compact, by a total disregard to the special delegations of power therein contained, annihilation of the state governments, and the erection upon their ruins, of a general consolidated government, will be the inevitable consequence." Can an honest observer doubt that this unheeded warning has come to pass? Has the time not come to follow the advice of the man who consistently predicted this outcome?

We have been helpless spectators long enough. Even if some opponents of government growth might have blanched at nullification a few decades ago, they can hardly reject it out of hand now. How much longer do we have to fail before we admit that maybe something different, something we might have scorned years ago, but that has been used to good effect and for honorable purposes in the past, might now be necessary? If anything is going to change, we must employ every mechanism of defense that Thomas Jefferson bequeathed to us, not just the ones that won't offend Katie Couric or the *New York Times*.

Nullification is about learning to exercise our rights, whether the courts or the politicians want us to or not. Instead of waiting for our liberties to be handed back to us, we in our states can follow Jefferson's noble example and take the lead in saying no to the ambitions of a government that would have horrified the founding generation. For, as Lord Byron said, "Who would be free, themselves must strike the blow."

Part II

Eleven Essential Documents

I.

James Madison and the "Duty" to Interpose

The Virginia Resolutions of 1798

The Virginia Resolutions of 1798, introduced in chapter 2 and referred to throughout this book, were drafted by James Madison and agreed to by the legislature of Virginia in December 1798.

Resolved, That the General Assembly of Virginia doth unequivocally express a firm resolution to maintain and defend the Constitution of the United States, and the Constitution of this state, against every aggression, either foreign or domestic; and that they will support the government of the United States in all measures warranted by the former.

That this Assembly most solemnly declares a warm attachment to the union of the states, to maintain which it pledges its powers; and that, for this end, it is their duty to watch over and oppose every infraction of those principles which constitute the only basis of that union, because a faithful observance of them can alone secure its existence and the public happiness.

That this Assembly doth explicitly and peremptorily declare, that it views the powers of the federal government as resulting from the compact to which the states are parties, as limited by the plain sense and intention of the instrument constituting that compact, as no further valid than they are authorized by the grants enumerated in that compact; and that, in case of a deliberate, palpable, and dangerous exercise of other powers, not granted by the said compact, the states, who are parties thereto, have the right, and are in duty bound, to interpose, for arresting the progress of the evil, and for maintaining, within their respective limits, the authorities, rights, and liberties, appertaining to them.

That the General Assembly doth also express its deep regret, that a spirit has, in sundry instances, been manifested by the federal government to enlarge its powers by forced constructions of the constitutional charter which defines them; and that indications have appeared of a design to expound certain general phrases (which, having been copied from the very limited grant of powers in the former Articles of Confederation, were the less liable to be misconstrued) so as to destroy the meaning and effect of the particular enumeration which necessarily explains and limits the general phrases, and so as to consolidate the states, by degrees, into one sovereignty, the obvious tendency and inevitable result of which would be, to transform the present republican system of the United States into an absolute, or, at best, a mixed monarchy.

That the General Assembly doth particularly PROTEST against the palpable and alarming infractions of the Constitution, in the two late cases of the "Alien and Sedition Acts," passed at the last session of Congress; the first of which exercises a power nowhere delegated to the federal government, and which, by uniting legislative and judicial powers to those of executive, subverts the general principles of free government, as well as the particular organization and positive provisions of the Federal Constitution; and the other of which acts exercises, in like manner, a power not delegated by the Constitution, but, on the contrary, expressly and positively forbidden by one of the amendments thereto,—a power which, more than any other, ought to produce universal alarm, because it is levelled against the right of freely examining public characters and measures, and of free communication among the people thereon, which has ever been justly deemed the only effectual guardian of every other right.

That this state having, by its Convention, which ratified the Federal Constitution, expressly declared that, among other essential rights, "the liberty of conscience and the press cannot be cancelled, abridged, restrained, or modified, by any authority of the United States," and from its extreme anxiety to guard these rights from every possible attack of sophistry and ambition, having, with other states, recommended an amendment for that purpose, which amendment was, in due time, annexed to the Constitution,—it would mark a reproachful inconsistency, and criminal degeneracy, if an indifference were now shown to the most palpable violation of one of the rights thus declared and secured, and to the establishment of a precedent which may be fatal to the other.

That the good people of this commonwealth, having ever felt, and continuing to feel, the most sincere affection for their brethren of the other states; the truest anxiety for establishing and perpetuating the union of all; and the most scrupulous fidelity to that Constitution, which is the pledge of mutual friendship, and the instrument of mutual happiness,—the General Assembly doth solemnly appeal to the like dispositions in the other states, in confidence that they will concur with this commonwealth in declaring, as it does hereby declare, that the acts aforesaid are unconstitutional; and that the necessary and proper measures will be taken *by each* for cooperating with this state, in maintaining unimpaired the authorities, rights, and liberties, reserved to the states respectively, or to the people.

That the governor be desired to transmit a copy of the foregoing resolutions to the executive authority of each of the other states, with a request that the same may be communicated to the legislature thereof, and that a copy be furnished to each of the senators and representatives representing this state in the Congress of the United States.

II.

Virginia Informs the People

Address of the General Assembly to the People of the Commonwealth of Virginia January 23, 1799

The Virginia Legislature explained the Resolutions of 1798 to the people of Virginia in an accompanying document, which is extracted below.

Fellow-citizens: Unwilling to shrink from our representative responsibilities, conscious of the purity of our motives, but acknowledging your right to supervise our conduct, we invite your serious attention to the emergency which dictated the subjoined resolutions. Whilst we disdain to alarm you by ill-founded jealousies, we recommend an investigation guided by the coolness of wisdom, and a decision bottomed on firmness, but tempered with moderation.

It would be perfidious in those intrusted with the GUARDIANSHIP OF THE STATE SOVEREIGNTY, and acting under the solemn obligation of the following oath,—"I do swear that I will support the Constitution of the United States,"—not to warn you of encroachments, which, though clothed with the pretext of necessity, or disguised by arguments of expediency, may yet establish precedents which may ultimately devote a generous and unsuspicious people to all the consequences of usurped power.

Encroachments springing from a government WHOSE ORGANIZATION CANNOT BE MAINTAINED WITHOUT THE CO-OPERATION OF THE STATES, furnish the strongest excitements upon the state legislatures to watchfulness, and impose upon them the strongest obligation TO PRESERVE UNIMPAIRED THE LINE OF PARTITION.

The acquiescence of the states, under infractions of the federal compact, would either beget a speedy consolidation, by precipitating the state governments into impotency and contempt, or prepare the way for a revolution, by a repetition of these infractions until the people are aroused to appear in the majesty of their strength. It is to avoid these calamities that we exhibit to the people the momentous question, whether the Constitution of the United States shall yield to a construction which defies every restraint, and overwhelms the best hopes of republicanism.

Exhortations to disregard domestic usurpation, until foreign danger shall have passed, is an artifice which may be forever used; because the possessors of power, who are the advocates for its extension, can ever create national embarrassments, to be successively employed to soothe the people into sleep, whilst that power is swelling, silently, secretly, and fatally. Of the same character are insinuations of a foreign influence, which seize upon a laudable enthusiasm against danger from abroad, and distort it by an unnatural application, so as to blind your eyes against danger at home.

The Sedition Act presents a scene which was never expected by the early friends of the Constitution. It was then admitted that the state sovereignties were only diminished by powers specifically enumerated, or necessary to carry the specified powers into effect. Now, federal authority is deduced from implication; and from the existence of state law, it is inferred that Congress possess a similar power of legislation; whence Congress will be endowed with a power of legislation in all cases whatsoever, and the states will be stripped of every right reserved, by the concurrent claims of a paramount legislature.

The Sedition Act is the offspring of these tremendous pretensions, which inflict a death-wound on the sovereignty of the states.

For the honor of American understanding, we will not believe that the people have been allured into the adoption of the Constitution by an affectation of defining powers, whilst the *preamble* would admit a construction which would erect the will of Congress into a power paramount in all cases, and therefore limited in none. On the contrary, it is evident that the objects for which the Constitution was formed were deemed attainable only by a particular enumeration and specification of each power granted to the federal government; reserving all others to the people, or to the states. And yet it is in vain we search for any specified power embracing the right of legislation against the freedom of the press.

Had the states been despoiled of their sovereignty by the generality of the preamble, and had the federal government been endowed with whatever they should judge to be instrumental towards the union, justice, tranquillity, common defence, general welfare, and the preservation of liberty, nothing could have been more frivolous than an enumeration of powers.

All the preceding arguments, arising from a deficiency of constitutional power in Congress, apply to the Alien Act; and this act is liable to other objections peculiar to itself. If a suspicion that aliens are dangerous, constitutes the justification of that power exercised over them by Congress then a similar suspicion will justify the exercise of a similar power over natives; because there is nothing in the Constitution distinguishing between the power of a state to permit the residence of natives and aliens. It is, therefore, a right originally possessed, and never surrendered, by the respective states, and which is rendered dear and valuable to Virginia, because it is assailed through the bosom of the Constitution, and because her peculiar situation renders the easy admission of artisans and laborers an interest of vast importance.

But this bill contains other features, still more alarming and dangerous. It dispenses with the trial by jury; it violates the judicial system; it confounds legislative, executive, and judicial powers; it punishes without trial; and it bestows upon the President despotic power over a numerous class of men. Are such measures consistent with our constitutional principles? And will an accumulation of power so extensive in the hands of the executive, over aliens, secure to natives the blessings of republican liberty?

If measures can mould governments, and if an uncontrolled power of construction is surrendered to those who administer them, their progress may be easily foreseen, and their end easily foretold. A lover of monarchy, who opens the treasures of corruption by distributing emolument among devoted partisans, may at the same time be approaching his object and deluding the people with professions of republicanism. He may confound monarchy and republicanism, by the art of definition.

He may varnish over the dexterity which ambition never fails to display, with the pliancy of language, the seduction of expediency, or the prejudices of the times; and he may come at length to avow, that so extensive a territory as that of the United States can only be governed by the energies of monarchy; that it cannot be defended, except by standing armies; and that it cannot be united, except by consolidation.

Measures have already been adopted which may lead to these consequences. They consist:

In fiscal systems and arrangements, which keep a host of commercial and wealthy individuals embodied and obedient to the mandates of the treasury;—

In armies and navies, which will, on the one hand, enlist the tendency of man to pay homage to his fellow-creature who can feed or honor him; and on the other, employ the principle of fear, by punishing imaginary insurrections, under the pretext of preventive justice;—

In swarms of officers, civil and military, who can inculcate political tenets tending to consolidation and monarchy, both by indulgences and severities, and can act as spies over the free exercise of human reason;—

In restraining the freedom of the press, and investing the executive with legislative, executive, and judicial powers, over a numerous body of men.

And, that we may shorten the catalogue, in establishing, by successive precedents, such a mode of construing the Constitution as will rapidly remove every restraint upon federal power.

Let history be consulted; let the man of experience reflect; nay, let the artificers of monarchy be asked what further materials they can need for building up their favorite system.

These are solemn but painful truths; and yet we recommend it to you not to forget the possibility of danger from without, although danger threatens us from within. Usurpation is indeed dreadful; but against foreign invasion, if that should happen, let us rise with hearts and hands united, and repel the attack with the zeal of freemen who will strengthen their title to examine and correct domestic measures, by having defended their country against foreign aggression.

Pledged as we are, fellow-citizens, to these sacred engagements, we yet humbly, fervently implore the Almighty Disposer of events to avert from our land war and usurpation, the scourges of mankind; to permit our fields to be cultivated in peace; to instill into nations the love of friendly intercourse; to suffer our youth to be educated in virtue, and to preserve our morality from the pollution invariably incident to habits of war; to prevent the laborer and husbandman from being harassed by taxes and imposts; to remove from ambition the means of disturbing the commonwealth; to annihilate all pretexts for power afforded by war; to maintain the Constitution; and to bless our nation with tranquillity, under whose benign influence we may reach the summit of happiness and glory, to which we are destined by *nature* and *nature's God.*

III.

Unconstitutional Laws Are Void

The Kentucky Resolutions of 1798

The Kentucky Resolutions of 1798 were approved by the Kentucky House and Senate in November 1798.

1. Resolved, That the several states composing the United States of America are not united on the principle of unlimited submission to their general government; but that, by compact, under the style and title of a Constitution for the United States, and of amendments thereto, they constituted a general government for special purposes, delegated to that government certain definite powers, reserving, each state to itself, the residuary mass of right to their own self-government; and that whensoever the general government assumes undelegated powers, its acts are unauthoritative, void, and of no force; that to this compact each state acceded as a state, and is an integral party; that this government, created by this compact, was not made the exclusive or final judge of the extent of the powers delegated to itself,

since that would have made its discretion, and not the Constitution, the measure of its powers; but that, as in all other cases of compact among powers having no common judge, each party has an equal right to judge for itself, as well of infractions as of the mode and measure of redress.

2. *Resolved,* That the Constitution of the United States having delegated to Congress a power to punish treason, counterfeiting the securities and current coin of the United States, piracies and felonies committed on the high seas, and offences against the laws of nations, and no other crimes, whatsoever; and it being true, as a general principle, and one of the amendments to the Constitution having also declared, that "the powers not delegated to the United States by the Constitution, nor prohibited by it to the states, are reserved to the states respectively, or to the people,"—therefore, also, the same act of Congress, passed on the 14th day of July, 1798, and entitled "An Act in Addition to the Act entitled 'An Act for the Punishment of certain Crimes against the United States;'" as also the act passed by them on the 27th day of June, 1798, entitled "An Act to punish Frauds committed on the Bank of the United States," (and all other their acts which assume to create, define, or punish crimes other than those so enumerated in the Constitution,) are altogether void, and of no force; and that the power to create, define, and punish, such other crimes is reserved, and of right appertains, solely and exclusively, to the respective states, each within its own territory.

3. *Resolved,* That it is true, as a general principle, and is also expressly declared by one of the amendments to the Constitution, that "the powers not delegated to the United States by the Constitution, nor prohibited by it to the states, are reserved to

the states respectively, or to the people;" and that, no power over the freedom of religion, freedom of speech, or freedom of the press, being delegated to the United States by the Constitution, nor prohibited by it to the States, all lawful powers respecting the same did of right remain, and were reserved to the states, or the people; that thus was manifested their determination to retain to themselves the right of judging how far the licentiousness of speech, and of the press, may be abridged without lessening their useful freedom, and how far those abuses which cannot be separated from their use, should be tolerated rather than the use be destroyed; and thus also they guarded against all abridgment, by the United States, of the freedom of religious principles and exercises, and retained to themselves the right of protecting the same, as this, stated by a law passed on the general demand of its citizens, had already protected them from all human restraint or interference; and that, in addition to this general principle and express declaration, another and more special provision has been made by one of the amendments to the Constitution, which expressly declares, that "Congress shall make no law respecting an establishment of religion, or prohibiting the free exercise thereof, or abridging the freedom of speech, or of the press," thereby guarding, in the same sentence, and under the same words, the freedom of religion, of speech, and of the press, insomuch that whatever violated either throws down the sanctuary which covers the others,—and that libels, falsehood, and defamation, equally with heresy and false religion, are withheld from the cognizance of federal tribunals. That therefore the act of Congress of the United States, passed on the 14th of July, 1798, entitled "An Act in Addition to the Act entitled 'An Act for the Punishment of certain Crimes against the United States,'" which does abridge the freedom of the press, is not law, but is altogether void, and of no force.

4. *Resolved*, That alien friends are under the jurisdiction and protection of the laws of the state wherein they are; that no power over them has been delegated to the United States, nor prohibited to the individual states, distinct from their power over citizens; and it being true, as a general principle, and one of the amendments to the Constitution having also declared, that "the powers not delegated to the United States by the Constitution, nor prohibited by it to the states, are reserved to the states, respectively, or to the people," the act of the Congress of the United States, passed on the 22d day of July, 1798, entitled "An Act concerning Aliens," which assumes powers over alien friends not delegated by the Constitution, is not law, but is altogether void and of no force.

5. *Resolved*. That, in addition to the general principle, as well as the express declaration, that powers not delegated are reserved, another and more special provision inserted in the Constitution from abundant caution, has declared, "that the migration or importation of such persons as any of the states now existing shall think proper to admit, shall not be prohibited by the Congress prior to the year 1808." That this commonwealth does admit the migration of alien friends described as the subject of the said act concerning aliens; that a provision against prohibiting their migration is a provision against all acts equivalent thereto, or it would be nugatory; that to remove them, when migrated, is equivalent to a prohibition of their migration, and is, therefore, contrary to the said provision of the Constitution, and *void*.

6. *Resolved*, That the imprisonment of a person under the protection of the laws of this commonwealth, on his failure to

obey the simple order of the President to depart out of the United States, as is undertaken by the said act entitled, "An Act concerning Aliens," is contrary to the Constitution, one amendment in which has provided, that "no person shall be deprived of liberty without due process of law;" and that another having provided, "that, in all criminal prosecutions, the accused shall enjoy the right of a public trial by an impartial jury, to be informed as to the nature and cause of the accusation, to be confronted with the witnesses against him, to have compulsory process for obtaining witnesses in his favor, and to have assistance of counsel for his defence," the same act undertaking to authorize the President to remove a person out of the United States who is under the protection of the law, on his own suspicion, without jury, without public trial, without confrontation of the witnesses against him, without having witnesses in his favor, without defence, without counsel—contrary to these provisions also of the Constitution—is therefore not law, but utterly void, and of no force.

That transferring the power of judging any person who is under the protection of the laws, from the courts to the President of the United States, as is undertaken by the same act concerning aliens, is against the article of the Constitution which provides, that "the judicial power of the United States shall be vested in the courts, the judges of which shall hold their offices during good behavior," and that the said act is void for that reason also; and it is further to be noted that this transfer of judiciary power is to that magistrate of the general government who already possesses all the executive, and a qualified negative on all legislative powers.

7. *Resolved,* That the construction applied by the general government (as is evident by sundry of their proceedings) to

those parts of the Constitution of the United States which delegate to Congress power to lay and collect taxes, duties, imposts, excises; to pay the debts, and provide for the common defence and general welfare, of the United States, and to make all laws which shall be necessary and proper for carrying into execution the powers vested by the Constitution in the government of the United States, or any department thereof, goes to the destruction of all limits prescribed to their powers by the Constitution; that words meant by the instrument to be subsidiary only to the execution of the limited powers, ought not to be so construed as themselves to give unlimited powers, nor a part to be taken as to destroy the whole residue of the instrument; that the proceedings of the general government, under color of those articles, will be a fit and necessary subject for revisal and correction at a time of greater tranquillity, while those specified in the preceding resolutions call for immediate redress.

8. *Resolved*, That the preceding resolutions be transmitted to the senators and representatives in Congress from this commonwealth, who are enjoined to present the same to their respective houses, and to use their best endeavors to procure, at the next session of Congress, a repeal of the aforesaid unconstitutional and obnoxious acts.

9. *Resolved*, lastly, That the governor of this commonwealth be, and is, authorized and requested to communicate the preceding resolutions to the legislatures of the several states, to assure them that this commonwealth considers union for special national purposes, and particularly for those specified in their late federal compact, to be friendly to the peace, happiness, and prosperity, of all the states; that, faithful to that compact, according to the plain intent and meaning in which it was understood

and acceded to by the several parties, it is sincerely anxious for its preservation; that it does also believe, that, to take from the states all the powers of self-government and transfer them to a general and consolidated government, without regard to the special government, and reservations solemnly agreed to in that compact, is not for the peace, happiness, or prosperity of these states; and that, therefore, this commonwealth is determined, as it doubts not its co-states are, to submit to undelegated and consequently unlimited powers in no man, or body of men, on earth; that, if the acts before specified should stand, these conclusions would flow from them—that the general government may place any act they think proper on the list of crimes, and punish it themselves, whether enumerated or not enumerated by the Constitution as cognizable by them; that they may transfer its cognizance to the President, or any other person, who may himself be the accuser, counsel, judge, and jury, whose suspicions may be the evidence, his order the sentence, his officer the executioner, and his breast the sole record of the transaction; that a very numerous and valuable description of the inhabitants of these states, being, by this precedent, reduced, as outlaws, to absolute dominion of one man, and the barriers of the Constitution thus swept from us all, no rampart now remains against the passions and the power of a majority of Congress, to protect from a like exportation, or other grievous punishment, the minority of the same body, the legislatures, judges, governors, and counsellors of the states, nor their other peaceable inhabitants, who may venture to reclaim the constitutional rights and liberties of the states and people, or who for other causes, good or bad, may be obnoxious to the view, or marked by the suspicions, of the President, or be thought dangerous to his or their elections, or other interests, public or personal; that the friendless alien has been selected as the safest subject of a first experiment; but the citizen will soon follow, or rather has already followed; for already has a Sedition Act marked him as a prey: That these and successive acts of the same character, unless arrested on the threshold, may tend to drive these states into revolution and blood, and will furnish new calumnies against republican governments, and new pretexts for those who wish it to be believed that man cannot be governed but by a rod of iron; that it would be a dangerous delusion were a confidence in the men of our choice to silence our fears for the safety of our rights; that confidence is every where the parent of despotism; free government is founded in jealousy, and not in confidence; it is jealousy, and not confidence, which prescribes limited constitutions to bind down those whom we are obliged to trust with power; that our Constitution has accordingly fixed the limits to which, and no farther, our confidence may go; and let the honest advocate of confidence read the Alien and Sedition Acts, and say if the Constitution has not been wise in fixing limits to the government it created, and whether we should be wise in destroying those limits; let him say what the government is, if it be not a tyranny, which the men of our choice have conferred on the President, and the President of our choice has assented to and accepted, over the friendly strangers, to whom the mild spirit of our country and its laws had pledged hospitality and protection; that the men of our choice have more respected the bare suspicions of the President than the solid rights of innocence, the claims of justification, the sacred force of truth, and the forms and substance of law and justice.

In questions of power, then, let no more be said of confidence in man, but bind him down from mischief by the chains of the Constitution. That this commonwealth does therefore call on its co-states for an expression of their sentiments on the acts concerning aliens, and for the punishment of certain crimes herein before specified, plainly declaring whether these acts are or are not authorized by the federal compact. And it doubts not that their sense will be so announced as to prove their attachment to limited government, whether general or particular, and that the rights and liberties of their co-states will be exposed to no dangers by remaining embarked on a common bottom with their own; but they will concur with this commonwealth in considering the said acts as so palpably against the Constitution as to amount to an undisguised declaration that the compact is not meant to be the measure of the powers of the general government, but that it will proceed in the exercise over these states of all powers whatsoever. That they will view this as seizing the rights of the states, and consolidating them in the hands of the general government, with a power assumed to bind the states, not merely in cases made federal, but in all cases whatsoever, by laws made, not with their consent, but by others against their consent; that this would be to surrender the form of government we have chosen, and live under one deriving its powers from its own will, and not from our authority; and that the co-states, recurring to their natural rights not made federal, will concur in declaring these void and of no force, and will each unite with this commonwealth in requesting their repeal at the next session of Congress.

IV.

Nullification Is the "Rightful Remedy"

The Kentucky Resolutions of 1799

In November 1799 Kentucky approved these follow-up resolutions to its famous resolutions of the previous year, and took the opportunity to address those states that had received them unfavorably. Here for the first time the word "nullification" was employed in an official document to describe Jefferson's remedy. This document was largely overlooked in the country as a whole, owing to the death of George Washington several weeks later, around the time the newspapers in the various states might have received it.

The house, according to the standing order of the day, resolved itself into a committee of the whole house, on the state of the commonwealth, (Mr. Desha in the chair,) and, after some time spent therein, the speaker resumed the chair, and Mr. Desha reported, that the committee had taken under consideration sundry resolutions passed by several state legislatures, on the subject of the Alien and Sedition Laws, and had come to a resolution thereupon, which he delivered in at the clerk's table, where it was read and unanimously agreed to by the house, as follows:

The representatives of the good people of this commonwealth, in General Assembly convened, having maturely considered the answers of sundry states in the Union to their resolutions, passed the last session, respecting certain unconstitutional laws of Congress, commonly called the Alien and Sedition Laws, would be faithless, indeed, to themselves, and to those they represent, were they silently to acquiesce in principles and doctrines attempted to be maintained in all those answers, that of Virginia only excepted. To again enter the field of argument, and attempt more fully or forcibly to expose the unconstitutionality of those obnoxious laws, would, it is apprehended, be as unnecessary as unavailing. We cannot, however, but lament that, in the discussion of those interesting subjects by sundry of the legislatures of our sister states, unfounded suggestions, and uncandid insinuations, derogatory to the true character and principles of this commonwealth, have been substituted in place of fair reasoning and sound argument. Our opinions of those alarming measures of the general government, together with our reasons for those opinions, were detailed with decency and with temper, and submitted to the discussion and judgment of our fellow-citizens throughout the Union. Whether the like decency and temper have been observed in the answers of most of those states who have denied, or attempted to obviate, the great truths contained in those resolutions, we have now only to submit to a candid world. Faithful to the true principles of the federal union, unconscious of any designs to disturb the harmony of that Union, and anxious only to escape the fangs of despotism, the good people of this commonwealth are regardless of censure or calumniation. Lest, however, the silence of this commonwealth should be construed into an acquiescence in the doctrines and principles advanced, and attempted to be maintained, by the said answers; or lest those of our fellow-citizens, throughout the Union, who so widely differ from us on those important subjects, should be deluded by the expectation that we shall be deterred from what we conceive our duty, or shrink from the principles contained in those resolutions,—therefore,

Resolved, That this commonwealth considers the federal Union, upon the terms and for the purposes specified in the late compact, conducive to the liberty and happiness of the several states: That it does now unequivocally declare its attachment to the Union, and to that compact, agreeably to its obvious and real intention, and will be among the last to seek its dissolution: That, if those who administer the general government be permitted to transgress the limits fixed by that compact, by a total disregard to the special delegations of power therein contained, an annihilation of the state governments, and the creation, upon their ruins, of a general consolidated government, will be the inevitable consequence: That the principle and construction, contended for by sundry of the state legislatures, that the general government is the exclusive judge of the extent of the powers delegated to it, stop nothing short of *despotism*—since the discretion of those who administer the government, and not the *Constitution*, would be the measure of their powers: That the several states who formed that instrument, being sovereign and independent, have the unquestionable right to judge of its infraction; and, *That a nullification, by those sovereignties, of all unauthorized acts done under color of that instrument, is the rightful remedy*: That this commonwealth does, under the most deliberate reconsideration, declare, that the said Alien and Sedition Laws are, in their opinion, palpable violations of the said Constitution; and however cheerfully it may be disposed to surrender its opinion to a majority of its sister states, in matters of ordinary or doubtful policy, yet, in momentous regulations like the present, which so vitally wound the best rights of the citizen, it would consider a silent acquiescence as highly criminal: That although this commonwealth, as a party to the federal compact, will bow to the laws of the Union, yet it does, at the same time, declare, that it will not now, nor ever hereafter, cease to oppose, in a constitutional manner, every attempt, from what quarter soever offered, to violate that compact: And finally, in order that no pretexts or arguments may be drawn from a supposed acquiescence, on the part of this commonwealth, in the constitutionality of those laws, and be thereby used as precedents for similar future violations of the federal compact; this commonwealth does now enter against them, its solemn PROTEST.

V.

The Federal Government Will Not Police Itself

Virginia General Assembly Report of 1800

James Madison

In 1799, the government of Virginia decided to compose a reply to the arguments raised by the states that had objected to the principles laid out in the Virginia Resolutions of 1798, and in the process to explain the Virginia Resolutions further. The result is the Report of 1800 (sometimes called Madison's Report or the Virginia Report of 1800), adopted in January 1800. It is a very lengthy document, so I have omitted the detailed discussion of the unconstitutionality of the Alien and Sedition Acts themselves—which, while interesting, is not central to the purpose of this book.

Whatever room might be found in the proceedings of some of the states who have disapproved of the resolutions of the General Assembly of this commonwealth, passed on the 21st day of December, 1798, for painful remarks on the spirit and manner of those proceedings, it appears to the committee most consistent with the duty, as well as dignity of the General Assembly, to hasten an oblivion of every circumstance which might be construed into a diminution of mutual respect, confidence, and affection, among the members of the Union.

The committee have deemed it a more useful task, to revise, with a critical eye, the resolutions which have met with this disapprobation; to examine fully the several objections and arguments which have appeared against them; and to inquire whether there be any errors of fact, of principle, or of reasoning, which the candour of the General Assembly ought to acknowledge and correct.

The first of the resolutions is in the words following:

> *Resolved, That the General Assembly of Virginia doth unequivocally express a firm resolution to maintain and defend the Constitution of the United States, and the Constitution of this state, against every aggression, either foreign or domestic, and that they will support the government of the United States in all measures warranted by the former.*

No unfavourable comment can have been made on the sentiments here expressed. To maintain and defend the Constitution of the United States, and of their own state, against every aggression, both foreign and domestic, and to support the government of the United States in all measures warranted by their Constitution, are duties which the General Assembly ought always to feel, and to which, on such an occasion, it was evidently proper to express its sincere and firm adherence.

In their next resolution—*The General Assembly most solemnly declares a warm attachment to the union of the states, to maintain which it pledges all its powers; and that, for this end, it is its duty to watch over and oppose every infraction of those principles, which constitute the only basis of that union, because a faithful observance of them can alone secure its existence and the public happiness.*

The observation just made is equally applicable to this solemn declaration, of warm attachment to the union, and this solemn pledge to maintain it; nor can any question arise among enlightened friends of the union, as to the duty of watching over and opposing every infraction of those principles which constitute its basis, and a faithful observance of which can alone secure its existence, and the public happiness thereon depending.

The third resolution is in the words following:

> *That this Assembly doth explicitly and peremptorily declare, that it views the powers of the Federal Government, as resulting from the compact, to which the states are parties, as limited by the plain sense and intention of the instrument constituting that compact; as no farther valid than they are authorized by the grants enumerated in that compact; and that in case of a deliberate, palpable and dangerous exercise of other powers, not granted by the said compact, the states who are parties thereto have the right, and are in duty bound, to interpose for arresting the progress of the evil, and for maintaining within their respective limits, the authorities, rights, and liberties appertaining to them.*

On this resolution, the committee have bestowed all the attention which its importance merits; they have scanned it not merely with a strict, but with a severe eye; and they feel confidence in pronouncing, that, in its just and fair construction, it is unexceptionably true in its several positions, as well as constitutional and conclusive in its inferences.

The resolution declares, *first*, that "it views the powers of the Federal Government, as resulting from the compact to which the states are parties;" in other words, that the Federal powers are derived from the Constitution, and that the Constitution is a compact to which the states are parties.

Clear as the position must seem, that the federal powers are derived from the Constitution, and from that alone, the committee are not unapprised of a late doctrine, which opens another source of federal powers, not less extensive and important, than it is new and unexpected. The examination of this doctrine will be most conveniently connected with a review of a succeeding resolution. The committee satisfy themselves here with briefly remarking, that in all the contemporary discussions and comments which the Constitution underwent, it was constantly justified and recommended, on the ground, that the powers not given to the government, were withheld from it; and that, if any doubt could have existed on this subject, under the original text of the Constitution, it is removed, as far as words could remove it, by the [10th] amendment, now a part of the Constitution, which expressly declares, "that the powers not delegated to the United States, by the Constitution, nor prohibited by it to the states, are reserved to the states respectively, or to the people."

The other position involved in this branch of the resolution, namely, "that the states are parties to the Constitution or compact," is, in the judgment of the committee, equally free from objection. It is indeed true, that the term "states," is sometimes used in a vague sense, and sometimes in different senses, according to the subject to which it is applied. Thus, it sometimes means the separate sections of territory occupied by the political societies within each; sometimes the particular governments, established by those societies; sometimes those societies as organized into those particular governments; and, lastly, it means the people composing those political societies, in their highest sovereign capacity. Although it might be wished that the perfection of language admitted less diversity in the signification of the same words, yet little inconveniency is produced by it, where the true sense can be collected with certainty from the different applications. In the present instance, whatever different constructions of the term "states," in the resolution, may have been entertained, all will at least concur in that last mentioned; because, in that sense, the Constitution was submitted to the "states," in that sense the "states" ratified it; and, in that sense of the term "states," they are consequently parties to the compact, from which the powers of the federal government result.

The next position is, that the General Assembly views the powers of the federal government, "as limited by the plain sense and intention of the instrument constituting that compact," and "as no farther valid than they are authorized by the grants therein enumerated." It does not seem possible, that any just objection can lie against either of these clauses. The first amounts merely to a declaration, that the compact ought to have the interpretation plainly intended by the parties to it; the other to a declaration, that it ought to have the execution and effect intended by them. If the powers granted, be valid, it is solely because they are granted: and, if the granted powers are valid, because granted, all other powers not granted, must not be valid.

The resolution, having taken this view of the federal compact, proceeds to infer, "that, in case of a deliberate, palpable, and dangerous exercise of other powers, not granted by the said compact, the states, who are parties thereto, have the right and are in duty bound to interpose for arresting the progress of the evil, and for maintaining within their respective limits, the authorities, rights, and liberties appertaining to them."

It appears to your committee to be a plain principle, founded in common sense, illustrated by common practice, and essential to the nature of compacts, that, where resort can be had to no tribunal, superior to the authority of the parties, the parties themselves must be the rightful judges in the last resort, whether the bargain made has been pursued or violated. The Constitution of the United States was formed by the sanction of the states, given by each in its sovereign capacity. It adds to the stability and dignity, as well as to the authority of the Constitution, that it rests on this legitimate and solid foundation. The states, then, being the parties to the constitutional compact, and in their sovereign capacity, it follows of necessity, that there can be no tribunal above their authority, to decide in the last resort, whether the compact made by them be violated; and, consequently, that, as the parties to it, they must themselves decide, in the last resort, such questions as may be of sufficient magnitude to require their interposition.

It does not follow, however, that because the states, as sovereign parties to their constitutional compact, must ultimately decide whether it has been violated, that such a decision ought to be interposed, either in a hasty manner, or on doubtful and inferior occasions. Even in the case of ordinary conventions between different nations, where, by the strict rule of interpretation, a breach of a part may be deemed a breach of the whole, every part being deemed a condition of every other part and of the whole, it is always laid down that the breach must be both wilful and material to justify an application of the rule. But in the case of an intimate and constitutional union, like that of the United States, it is evident that the interposition of the parties, in their sovereign capacity, can be called for by occasions only, deeply and essentially affecting the vital principles of their political system.

The resolution has accordingly guarded against any misapprehension of its object, by expressly requiring for such an interposition, "the case of a *deliberate*, *palpable*, and *dangerous* breach of the Constitution, by the exercise of *powers not granted* by it." It must be a case, not of a light and transient nature, but of a nature *dangerous* to the great purposes for which the Constitution was established. It must be a case, moreover, not obscure or doubtful in its construction, but plain and *palpable*. Lastly, it must be a case not resulting from a partial consideration, or hasty determination; but a case stamped with a final consideration and *deliberate* adherence. It is not necessary, because the resolution does not require that the question should be discussed, how far the exercise of any particular power, ungranted by the Constitution, would justify the interposition of the parties to it. As cases might easily be stated, which none would contend ought to fall within that description; cases, on the other hand, might, with equal ease, be stated, so flagrant and so fatal, as to unite every opinion in placing them within that description.

But the resolution has done more than guard against misconstruction, by expressly referring to cases of a *deliberate, palpable,* and *dangerous* nature. It specifies the object of the interposition which it contemplates, to be solely that of arresting the progress of the *evil* of usurpation, and of maintaining the authorities, rights, and liberties appertaining to the states, as parties to the Constitution.

From this view of the resolution, it would seem inconceivable that it can incur any just disapprobation from those who, laying aside all momentary impressions, and recollecting the genuine source and object of the Federal Constitution, shall candidly and accurately interpret the meaning of the General Assembly. If the deliberate exercise of dangerous powers, palpably withheld by the Constitution, could not justify the parties to it, in interposing even so far as to arrest the progress of the evil, and thereby to preserve the Constitution itself, as well as to provide for the safety of the parties to it, there would be an end to all relief from usurped power, and a direct subversion of the rights specified or recognised under all the state constitutions, as well as a plain denial of the fundamental principle on which our independence itself was declared.

But it is objected that the judicial authority is to be regarded as the sole expositor of the Constitution, in the last resort; and it may be asked for what reason, the declaration by the General Assembly, supposing it to be theoretically true, could be required at the present day and in so solemn a manner.

On this objection it might be observed, *first*, that there may be instances of usurped power, which the forms of the Constitution would never draw within the control of the judicial department; *secondly*, that if the decision of the judiciary be raised above the authority of the sovereign parties to the Constitution, the decisions of the other departments, not carried by the forms of the Constitution before the judiciary, must be equally authoritative and final with the decisions of that department. But the proper answer to the objection is, that the resolution of the General Assembly relates to those great and extraordinary cases, in which all the forms of the Constitution may prove ineffectual against infractions dangerous to the essential rights of the parties to it. The resolution supposes that dangerous powers, not delegated, may not only be usurped and executed by the other departments, but that the judicial department also may exercise or sanction dangerous powers beyond the grant of the Constitution; and, consequently, that the ultimate right of the parties to the Constitution, to judge whether the compact has been dangerously violated, must extend to violations by one delegated authority, as well as by another; by the judiciary, as well as by the executive, or the legislature.

However true, therefore, it may be, that the judicial department, is, in all questions submitted to it by the forms of the Constitution, to decide in the last resort, this resort must necessarily be deemed the last in relation to the authorities of the other departments of the government; not in relation to the rights of the parties to the constitutional compact, from which the judicial as well as the other departments hold their delegated trusts. On any other hypothesis, the delegation of judicial power would annul the authority delegating it; and the concurrence of this department with the others in usurped powers, might subvert for ever, and beyond the possible reach of any rightful remedy, the very Constitution which all were instituted to preserve.

The truth declared in the resolution being established, the expediency of making the declaration at the present day, may safely be left to the temperate consideration and candid judgment of the American public. It will be remembered that a frequent recurrence to fundamental principles, is solemnly enjoined by most of the state constitutions, and particularly by our own, as a necessary safeguard against the danger of degeneracy to which republics are liable, as well as other governments, though in a less degree than others. And a fair comparison of the political doctrines not unfrequent at the present day, with those which characterized the epoch of our revolution, and which form the basis of our republican constitutions, will best determine whether the declaratory recurrence here made to those principles, ought to be viewed as unseasonable and improper, or as a vigilant discharge of an important duty. The authority of constitutions over governments, and of the sovereignty of the people over constitutions, are truths which are at all times necessary to be kept in mind; and at no time perhaps more necessary than at the present.

The fourth resolution stands as follows:

> *That the General Assembly doth also express its deep regret, that a spirit has in sundry instances, been manifested by the federal government, to enlarge its powers by forced constructions of the constitutional charter which defines them; and that indications have appeared of a design to expound certain general phrases, (which, having been copied from the very limited grant of powers in the former articles of confederation, were the less liable to be misconstrued,) so as to destroy the meaning and effect of the particular enumeration which nec-*

> *essarily explains, and limits the general phrases; and so as to consolidate the states, by degrees, into one sovereignty, the obvious tendency and inevitable result of which would be, to transform the present republican system of the United States into an absolute, or, at best, a mixed monarchy.*

The *first* question here to be considered is, whether a spirit has in sundry instances been manifested by the Federal Government to enlarge its powers by forced constructions of the constitutional charter.

The General Assembly having declared its opinion merely by regretting in general terms that forced constructions for enlarging the federal powers have taken place, it does not appear to the committee necessary to go into a specification of every instance to which the resolution may allude. The alien and sedition-acts being particularly named in a succeeding resolution, are of course to be understood as included in the allusion. Omitting others which have less occupied public attention, or been less extensively regarded as unconstitutional, the resolution may be presumed to refer particularly to the bank law, which from the circumstances of its passage, as well as the latitude of construction on which it is founded, strikes the attention with singular force; and the carriage tax, distinguished also by circumstances in its history having a similar tendency. Those instances, alone, if resulting from forced construction and calculated to enlarge the powers of the Federal Government, as the committee cannot but conceive to be the case, sufficiently warrant this part of the resolution. The committee have not thought it incumbent on them to extend their attention to laws which have been objected to, rather as varying the constitutional distribution of powers in the

Federal Government, than as an absolute enlargement of them; because instances of this sort, however important in their principles and tendencies, do not appear to fall strictly within the text under review.

The other questions presenting themselves, are—1. Whether indications have appeared of a design to expound certain general phrases copied from the "articles of confederation" so as to destroy the effect of the particular enumeration explaining and limiting their meaning. 2. Whether this exposition would by degrees consolidate the states into one sovereignty. 3. Whether the tendency and result of this consolidation would be to transform the republican system of the United States into a monarchy.

1. The general phrases here meant must be those "of providing for the common defence and general welfare."

In the "articles of confederation," the phrases are used as follows, in Art. VIII. "All charges of war, and all other expenses that shall be incurred *for the common defence and general welfare*, and allowed by the United States in Congress assembled, shall be defrayed out of a common treasury, which shall be supplied by the several states, in proportion to the value of all land within each state, granted to, or surveyed for any person, as such land and the buildings and improvements thereon shall be estimated, according to such mode as the United States in Congress assembled shall from time to time direct and appoint."

In the existing Constitution, they make the following part of Sec. 8, "The Congress shall have power to lay and collect taxes, duties, imposts, and excises, to pay the debts, and to provide for the common defence and general welfare of the United States."

This similarity in the use of these phrases in the two great federal charters, might well be considered, as rendering their meaning less liable to be misconstrued in the latter; because it will scarcely be said, that in the former they were ever understood to be either a general grant of power, or to authorize the requisition or application of money by the old Congress to the common defence and general welfare, except in the cases afterwards enumerated, which explained and limited their meaning; and if such was the limited meaning attached to these phrases in the very instrument revised and remodelled by the present Constitution, it can never be supposed that when copied into this Constitution, a different meaning ought to be attached to them.

That, notwithstanding this remarkable security against misconstruction, a design has been indicated to expound these phrases in the Constitution, so as to destroy the effect of the particular enumeration of powers by which it explains and limits them, must have fallen under the observation of those who have attended to the course of public transactions. Not to multiply proofs on this subject, it will suffice to refer to the debates of the federal legislature, in which arguments have on different occasions been drawn, with apparent effect, from these phrases, in their indefinite meaning.

To these indications might be added, without looking farther, the official report on manufactures, by the late Secretary of the Treasury, made on the 5th of December, 1791; and the report of a committee of Congress, in January, 1797, on the promotion of agriculture. In the first of these it is expressly contended to belong "to the discretion of the national legislature to pronounce upon the objects which concern the *general welfare*, and for which, under that description, an appropriation of money is requisite and proper. And there seems to be no room for a doubt, that whatever concerns the general interests of LEARNING, of AGRICULTURE, of MANUFACTURES, and of COMMERCE, are within the sphere of the national councils, *as far as regards the application of money*." The latter report assumes the same latitude of power in the national councils, and applies it to the encouragement of agriculture by means of a society to be established at the seat of government. Although neither of these reports may have received the sanction of a law carrying it into effect, yet, on the other hand, the extraordinary doctrine contained in both, has passed without the slightest positive mark of disapprobation from the authority to which it was addressed.

Now, whether the phrases in question be construed to authorize every measure relating to the common defence and general welfare, as contended by some; or every measure only in which there might be an application of money, as suggested by the caution of others; the effect must substantially be the same, in destroying the import and force of the particular enumeration of powers which follow these general phrases in the Constitution. For it is evident that there is not a single power whatever, which may not have some reference to the common defence, or the general welfare; nor a power of any magnitude, which, in its exercise, does not involve or admit an application of money. The government, therefore, which possesses power in either one or other of these extents, is a government without the limitations formed by a particular enumeration of powers; and consequently, the meaning and effect of this particular enumeration is destroyed by the exposition given to these general phrases.

This conclusion will not be affected by an attempt to qualify the power over the "general welfare," by referring it to cases where the *general welfare* is beyond the reach of *separate* provisions by the *individual states*; and leaving to these their jurisdictions, in cases to which their separate provisions may be competent. For, as the authority of the individual states must in all cases be incompetent to general regulations operating through the whole, the authority of the United States would be extended to every object relating to the general welfare, which might, by any possibility, be provided for by the general authority. This qualifying construction, therefore, would have little, if any tendency, to circumscribe the power claimed under the latitude of the terms "general welfare."

The true and fair construction of this expression, both in the original and existing federal compacts, appears to the committee too obvious to be mistaken. In both, the Congress is authorized to provide money for the common defence and *general welfare*. In both, is subjoined to this authority, an enumeration of the cases to which their powers shall extend. Money cannot be applied to the *general welfare* otherwise than by an application of it to *some particular* measures, conducive to the general welfare. Whenever, therefore, money has been raised by the general authority, and is to be applied to a particular measure, a question arises whether the particular measure be within the enumerated authorities vested in Congress. If it be, the money requisite for it may be applied to it; if it be not, no such application can be made. This fair and obvious interpretation coincides with, and is enforced by the clause in the Constitution, which declares, that "no money shall be drawn from the treasury, but in consequence of appropriations by law." An appropriation of money to the general welfare would be deemed rather a mockery than an observance of this constitutional injunction.

2. Whether the exposition of the general phrases here combated would not, by degrees, consolidate the states into one sovereignty, is a question concerning which the committee can perceive little room for difference of opinion. To consolidate the states into one sovereignty, nothing more can be wanted, than to supersede their respective sovereignties in the cases reserved to them, by extending the sovereignty of the United States, to all cases of the "general welfare," that is to say, to *all cases whatever.*

. . . These observations appear to form a satisfactory reply to every objection which is not founded on a misconception of the terms employed in the resolutions. There is one other, however, which may be of too much importance not to be added. It cannot be forgotten, that among the arguments addressed to those who apprehended danger to liberty from the establishment of the General Government over so great a country, the appeal was emphatically made to the intermediate existence of the state governments, between the people and that government, to the vigilance with which they would descry the first symptoms of usurpation, and to the promptitude with which they would sound the alarm to the public. This argument was probably not without its effect; and if it was a proper one then, to recommend the establishment of the Constitution, it must be a proper one now, to assist in its interpretation.

The only part of the two concluding resolutions that remains to be noticed, is the repetition in the first, of that warm affection to the union and its members, and of that scrupulous fidelity to the Constitution, which have been invariably felt by the people of this state. As the proceedings were introduced with these sentiments, they could not be more properly closed than in the same manner. Should there be any so far misled as to call in question the sincerity of these professions, whatever regret may be excited by the error, the General Assembly cannot descend into a discussion of it. Those, who have listened to the suggestion, can only be left to their own recollection of the part which this state has borne in the establishment of our national independence, in the establishment of our national Constitution, and in maintaining under it the authority and laws of the Union, without a single exception of internal resistance or commotion. By recurring to these facts, they will be able to convince themselves, that the representatives of the people of Virginia, must be above the necessity of opposing any other shield to attacks on their national patriotism, than their own consciousness, and the justice of an enlightened public; who will perceive in the resolutions themselves, the strongest evidence of attachment both to the Constitution and to the Union, since it is only by maintaining the different governments and departments within their respective limits, that the blessings of either can be perpetuated.

The extensive view of the subject thus taken by the committee, has led them to report to the House, as the result of the whole, the following resolution:

> *Resolved*, That the General Assembly, having carefully and respectfully attended to the proceedings of a number of the states, in answer to its resolutions of December 21, 1798, and having accurately and fully re-examined and reconsidered the latter, finds it to be its indispensable duty to adhere to the same, as founded in truth, as consonant with the Constitution, and as conducive to its preservation; and more

especially to be its duty to renew, as it does hereby renew, its protest against "the alien and sedition-acts," as palpable and alarming infractions of the Constitution.

VI.

The States Are the Protecting Shield

Speech of Connecticut Governor Jonathan Trumbull Opening of the Special Session of the Legislature February 23, 1809

Governor Trumbull addresses the legislature of Connecticut on the subject of the embargo enacted by President Jefferson. The significance of his remarks is obvious. In addition to opposing the embargo and endorsing the principle of state interposition, he expressly declares it to be "useful for the general good, if the State Legislatures were often to cast a watchful eye towards the general government, with a view, candidly to consider, and judiciously discern, whether the powers delegated to the United States are not exceeded, or are so exercised as not to interfere with or counteract those which are reserved by the people for their own management."

Gentlemen of the Council, Mr. Speaker, and Gentlemen of the House of Representatives:

Impressed with the importance of the communications which I have now to lay before you—prompted also by the concurrent petitions of a number of the citizens of this State, conveyed to me with their resolutions adopted in their several town meetings, convoked for the purpose; and having had under my own consideration, the very alarming crisis of our national affairs, arising from a variety of measures adopted and contemplated by our national legislature, more especially from the permanency of the embargo, with the means resorted to for its more rigorous enforcement, and particularly the late law of Congress, passed on the 9th day of January last, containing many very extraordinary, not to say unconstitutional provisions for its execution: I have viewed the prospect so momentous and threatening, that I have not hesitated to convene the Legislature of the State, at this unusual time, in order that they may have an opportunity to consider and deliberate on the extraordinary situation into which our country seems about to be plunged, if not speedily prevented: and to devise such constitutional measures as in their wisdom may be judged proper to avert the threatening evil.

It will be useful for the legislature to take a view of the various measures of the national legislature, during their present and preceding sessions, not only those which have immediate relation to the embargo, but other acts which have been and are under their consideration, affecting the rights, interests, welfare, and even the peace of the Union. Indeed, it would be useful for the general good, if the State Legislatures were often to cast a watchful eye towards the general government, with a view, candidly to consider, and judiciously discern, whether the powers delegated to the United States are not exceeded, or are so exercised as not to interfere with or counteract those which are reserved by the people for their own management. When under the direction of a wise and prudent discernment, a temperate caution—not an over jealous disposition, such an examination will always prove a wholesome measure.

On the present occasion, it will be unnecessary for me to enter into any particular statement of our private sufferings, or the threatening aspect of our public situation, in relation to the unprecedented acts of our General Government which are accumulating upon us. The individual feelings and experience of the members of this Legislature, now convened from all parts of the State, will speak the private distresses which have been produced by these acts: and your general information will give you, gentlemen, a correct view of the dangers which impend our public interests, liberty, rights and property, arising from the same source. Despairing of substantial relief from any other quarter, the people are now looking with anxious solicitude and hope, to the wisdom and direction of the Legislature of their own choice; and seem confident that some mode may be devised to remove the pressure under which they are at present suffering. To your collected wisdom and prudence they submit the task. And may it not be hoped, that, with our united efforts under a temperate, discreet and firm consideration of our situation and circumstances, we may be able by the influence of divine aid, to fulfill the just and reasonable expectations of our fellow citizens? Whenever our national legislature is led to overleap the prescribed bounds of their constitutional powers, on the State Legislatures, in great emergencies, devolves the arduous task—it is their right—it becomes their duty, to interpose their protecting shield between the right and liberty of the people, and the assumed power of the General Government....

In all our deliberations on this momentous occasion, may the divine wisdom guide us into the path of duty, and lead us to the happiest results for the general good, the peace and security of the people.

VII.

We Resist

Resolutions of the General Assembly of Connecticut 1809

At a special session of Connecticut's General Assembly in February 1809, the following resolutions in support of Governor Jonathan Trumbull's position and policy were adopted. They urge all parties to abstain from cooperating in the enforcement of an embargo whose substance and execution the legislature describes as unconstitutional. (These resolutions make particular reference to the legislature of Massachusetts, where similar sentiments were to be found.)

This Assembly have attended with anxious concern, to the several acts of Congress interdicting foreign commerce, and more especially to an act, approved on the 9th day of January last, by the President of the United States, under the title of "An Act, to enforce and make more effectual an act laying an embargo on all ships and vessels in the ports and harbors of the United States." After solemn deliberation and advisement thereon, the General Assembly are decided in the opinion, and do Resolve, that the acts aforesaid are a permanent system of measures, abandoning undeniable rights; interdicting the exercise of constitutional privileges, and unprecedented in the annals of nations; and do contain provisions for exercising arbitrary powers, grievous to the good people of this State, dangerous to their common liberties, incompatible with the constitution of the United States, and encroaching upon the immunities of this State.

Resolved, That to preserve the Union, and support the constitution of the United States, it becomes the duty of the Legislatures of the States, in such a crisis of affairs, vigilantly to watch over, and vigorously to maintain, the powers not delegated to the United States, but reserved to the States respectively, or to the people; and that a due regard to this duty, will not permit this Assembly to assist, or concur in giving effect to the aforesaid unconstitutional act, passed, to enforce the Embargo.

Resolved, That this Assembly highly approve of the conduct of his Excellency the Governor, in declining to designate persons to carry into effect, by the aid of *military power*, the act of the United States, enforcing the Embargo, and that his letter addressed to the Secretary for the Department of War, containing his refusal to make such designation, be recorded in the public records of this State, as an example to persons, who may hold places of distinguished trust, in this free and independent republic.

Resolved, That the persons holding executive offices under this State, are restrained by the duties which they owe this State, from affording any official aid or co-operation in the execution of the act aforesaid; and that his Excellency the Governor be requested, as commander in chief of the military force of this State, to cause these resolutions to be published in general orders: And that the secretary of this State be and he is hereby directed to transmit copies of the same to the several sheriffs and town clerks.

Resolved, That his excellency the Governor be requested to communicate the foregoing resolutions to the President of the United States, with an assurance that this Assembly regret that they are thus obliged under a sense of paramount public duty to assert the unquestionable right of this State to abstain from any agency in the execution of measures, which are unconstitutional and despotic.

Resolved, That this Assembly accord in sentiment, with the Senate and House of Representatives, of the commonwealth of Massachusetts, that it is expedient to affect certain alterations in the constitution of the United States; and will zealously cooperate with that commonwealth and any other of the States, in all legal and constitutional measures for procuring such amendments to the constitution of the United States as shall be judged necessary to obtain more effectual protection and defence for commerce; and to give to the commercial States their fair and just consideration in the Union, and for affording permanent security, as well as present relief, from the oppressive measures, under which they now suffer.

Resolved, That his Excellency the Governor be requested to transmit copies of the foregoing resolutions to the President of the Senate, and Speaker of the House of Representatives, in the commonwealth of Massachusetts, and to the Legislatures of such of our sister States, as manifest a disposition to concur, in restoring to commerce its former activity, and preventing the repetition of measures which have a tendency, not only to destroy it, but to dissolve the Union, which ought to be inviolate.

General Assembly, special session, February, 1809.

JOHN COTTON SMITH,

Speaker of the House of Representatives.

JONATHAN TRUMBULL, *Governor.*

Attest, SAMUEL WYLLYS, *Secretary*.

VIII.

Federalism Cannot Last without Nullification

Fort Hill Address
John C. Calhoun
July 26, 1831

John C. Calhoun (1782–1850) represented South Carolina in the House and Senate and served as vice president under John Quincy Adams and Andrew Jackson. As we noted in chapter 3, he anonymously composed the South Carolina Exposition and Protest in 1828. His writings emphasized the importance of the right of state nullification in the preservation of a federal system.

What follows here is an excerpt from Calhoun's Fort Hill Address, in which the sitting vice president defends nullification against criticism. As vice president, he almost certainly restrained himself from the more radical statement on the subject he might have made, but the reader will nevertheless discover a rigorous argument in the excerpt below.

Calhoun has been demonized in our popular culture to the point that anyone so much as referring to him is smeared and condemned, but as we saw in chapter 3, abolitionists fighting against the constitutionally questionable aspects of the fugitive slave laws did not hesitate for a moment to appeal to Calhoun's arguments and to refer to him by name. We, too, are capable of assessing his arguments on their merits.

The question of the relation which the States and General Government bear to each other is not one of recent origin. From the commencement of our system, it has divided public sentiment. Even in the Convention, while the Constitution was struggling into existence, there were two parties as to what this relation should be, whose different sentiments constituted no small impediment in forming that instrument. After the General Government went into operation, experience soon proved that the question had not terminated with the labors of the Convention. The great struggle that preceded the political revolution of 1801, which brought Mr. Jefferson into power, turned essentially on it, and the doctrines and arguments on both sides were embodied and ably sustained;—on the one, in the Virginia and Kentucky Resolutions, and the Report to the Virginia Legislature;—and on the other, in the replies of the Legislature of Massachusetts and some of the other States. These Resolutions and this Report, with the decision of the Supreme Court of Pennsylvania about the same time (particularly in the case of Cobbett, delivered by Chief Justice M'Kean, and concurred in by the whole bench), contain what I believe to be the true doctrine on this important subject. I refer to them in order to avoid the necessity of presenting my views, with the reasons in support of them, in detail. . . .

The great and leading principle is, that the General Government emanated from the people of the several States, forming distinct political communities, and acting in their separate and sovereign capacity, and not from all of the people forming one aggregate political community; that the Constitution of the United States is, in fact, a compact, to which each State is a party, in the character already described; and that the several States, or parties, have a right to judge of its infractions; and in case of a deliberate, palpable, and dangerous exercise of power not delegated, they have the right, in the last resort, to use the language of the Virginia Resolutions, "*to interpose for arresting the progress of the evil, and for maintaining, within their respective limits, the authorities, rights, and liberties appertaining to them.*" This right of interposition, thus solemnly asserted by the State of Virginia, be it called what it may,—State-right, veto, nullification, or by any other name,—I conceive to be the fundamental principle of our system, resting on facts historically as certain as our revolution itself, and deductions as simple and demonstrative as that of any political or moral truth whatever; and I firmly believe that on its recognition depend the stability and safety of our political institutions.

I am not ignorant that those opposed to the doctrine have always, now and formerly, regarded it in a very different light, as anarchical and revolutionary. Could I believe such, in fact, to be its tendency, to me it would be no recommendation. I yield to none, I trust, in a deep and sincere attachment to our political institutions and the union of these States. I never breathed an opposite sentiment; but, on the contrary, I have ever considered them the great instruments of preserving our liberty, and promoting the happiness of ourselves and our posterity; and next to these I have ever held them most dear. Nearly half my life has been passed in the service of the Union, and whatever public reputation I have acquired is indissolubly identified with it. To be too national has, indeed, been considered by many, even of my friends, my greatest political fault. With these strong feelings of attachment, I have examined, with the utmost care, the bearing of the doctrine in question; and, so far from anarchical or revolutionary, I solemnly believe it to be the only solid foundation of our system, and of the Union itself; and that the opposite doctrine, which denies to the States the right of protecting their reserved powers, and which would vest in the General Government (it matters not through what department) the right of determining, exclusively and finally, the powers delegated to it, is incompatible with the sovereignty of the States, and of the Constitution itself, considered as the basis of a Federal Union. As strong as this language is, it is not stronger than that used by the illustrious Jefferson, who said, to give to the General Government the final and exclusive right to judge of its powers, is to make "*its discretion, and not the Constitution, the measure of its powers;*" and that, "*in all cases of compact between parties having no common judge, each party has an equal right to judge for itself, as well of the infraction as of the mode and measure of redress.*" Language cannot be more explicit, nor can higher authority be adduced.

That different opinions are entertained on this subject, I consider but as an additional evidence of the great diversity of the human intellect. Had not able, experienced, and patriotic individuals, for whom I have the highest respect, taken different views, I would have thought the right too clear to admit of doubt; but I am taught by this, as well as by many similar instances, to treat with deference opinions differing from my own. The error may, possibly, be with me; but if so, I can only say that, after the most mature and conscientious examination, I have not been able to detect it. But, with all proper deference, I must think that theirs is the error who deny what seems to be an essential attribute of the conceded sovereignty of the States, and who attribute to the General Government a right utterly incompatible with what all acknowledge to be its limited and restricted character: an error originating principally, as I must think, in not duly reflecting on the nature of our institutions, and on what constitutes the only rational object of all political constitutions.

It has been well said by one of the most sagacious men of antiquity, that the object of a constitution is, to *restrain the government, as that of laws is to restrain individuals*. The remark is correct; nor is it less true where the government is vested in a majority, than where it is in a single or a few individuals—in a republic, than a monarchy or aristocracy. No one can have a higher respect for the maxim that the majority ought to govern than I have, taken in its proper sense, subject to the restrictions imposed by the Constitution, and confined to objects in which every portion of the community have similar interests; but it is a great error to suppose, as many do, that the right of a majority to govern is a natural and not a conventional right, and therefore absolute and unlimited. By nature, every individual has the right to govern himself; and governments, whether founded on majorities or minorities, must derive their right from the assent, expressed or implied, of the governed, and be subject to such limitations as they may impose. Where the interests are the same, that is, where the laws that may benefit one will benefit all, or the reverse, it is just and proper to place them under the control of the majority; but where they are dissimilar, so that the law that may benefit one portion may be ruinous to another, it would be, on the contrary, unjust and absurd to subject them to its will; and such I conceive to be the theory on which our Constitution rests.

That such dissimilarity of interests may exist, it is impossible to doubt. They are to be found in every community, in a greater or less degree, however small or homogeneous; and they constitute every where the great difficulty of forming and preserving free institutions. To guard against the unequal action of the laws, when applied to dissimilar and opposing interests, is, in fact, what mainly renders a constitution indispensable; to overlook which, in reasoning on our Constitution, would be to omit the principal element by which to determine its character. Were there no contrariety of interests, nothing would be more simple and easy than to form and preserve free institutions. The right of suffrage alone would be a sufficient guarantee. It is the conflict of opposing interests which renders it the most difficult work of man.

Where the diversity of interests exists in separate and distinct classes of the community, as is the case in England, and was formerly the case in Sparta, Rome, and most of the free States of antiquity, the rational constitutional provision is, that each should be represented in the government, as a separate estate, with a distinct voice, and a negative on the acts of its co-estates, in order to check their encroachments. In England, the Constitution has assumed expressly this form, while in the governments of Sparta and Rome, the same thing was effected under different, but not much less efficacious forms. The perfection of their organization, in this particular, was that which gave to the constitutions of these renowned States all their celebrity, which secured their liberty for so many centuries, and raised them to so great a height of power and prosperity. Indeed, a constitutional provision giving to the great and separate interests of the community the right of self-protection, must appear, to those who will duly reflect on the subject, not less essential to the preservation of liberty than the right of suffrage itself. They, in fact, have a common object, to effect which the one is as necessary as the other to secure *responsibility; that is, that those who make and execute the laws should be accountable to those on whom the laws in reality operate—the only solid and durable foundation of liberty*. If, without the right of suffrage, our rulers would oppress us, so, without the right of self-protection, the major would equally oppress the minor interests of the community. The absence of the former would make the governed the slaves of the rulers; and of the latter, the feebler interests, the victim of the stronger.

Happily for us, we have no artificial and separate classes of society. We have wisely exploded all such distinctions; but we are not, on that account, exempt from all contrariety of interests, as the present distracted and dangerous condition of our country, unfortunately, but too clearly proves. With us they are almost exclusively geographical, resulting mainly from difference of climate, soil, situation, industry, and production; but are not, therefore, less necessary to be protected by an adequate constitutional provision, than where the distinct interests exist in separate classes. The necessity is, in truth, greater, as such separate and dissimilar geographical interests are more liable to come into conflict, and more dangerous, when in that state, than those of any other description: so much so, that *ours is the first instance on record where they have not formed, in an extensive territory, separate and independent communities, or subjected the whole to despotic sway*. That such may not be our unhappy fate also, must be the sincere prayer of every lover of his country.

So numerous and diversified are the interests of our country, that they could not be fairly represented in a single government, organized so as to give to each great and leading interest a separate and distinct voice, as in governments to which I have referred. A plan was adopted better suited to our situation, but perfectly novel in its character. The powers of government were divided, not, as heretofore, in reference to classes, but geographically. One General Government was formed for the whole, to which were delegated all the powers supposed to be necessary to regulate the interests common to all the States, leaving others subject to the separate control of the States, being, from their local and peculiar character, such that they could not be subject to the will of a majority of the whole Union, without the certain hazard of injustice and oppression. It was thus that the interests of the whole were subjected, as they ought to be, to the will of the whole, while the peculiar and local interests were left under the control of the States separately, to whose custody only they could be safely confided. This distribution of power, settled solemnly by a constitutional compact, to which all the States are parties, constitutes the peculiar character and excellence of our political system. It is truly and emphatically *American, without example or parallel.*

To realize its perfection, we must view the General Government and those of the States as a whole, each in its proper sphere independent; each perfectly adapted to its respective objects; the States acting separately, representing and protecting the local and peculiar interests; and acting jointly through one General Government, with the weight respectively assigned to each by the Constitution, representing and protecting the interest of the whole; and thus perfecting, by an admirable but simple arrangement, the great principle of representation and responsibility, without which no government can be free or just. To preserve this sacred distribution as originally settled, by coercing each to move in its prescribed orbit, is the great and difficult problem, on the solution of which the duration of our Constitution, of our Union, and, in all probability, our liberty depends. How is this to be effected?

The question is new, when applied to our peculiar political organization, where the separate and conflicting interests of society are represented by distinct but connected governments; but it is, in reality, an old question under a new form, long since perfectly solved. Whenever separate and dissimilar interests have been separately represented in any government; whenever the sovereign power has been divided in its exercise, the experience and wisdom of ages have devised but one mode by which such political organization can be preserved,—the mode adopted in England, and by all governments, ancient and modern, blessed with constitutions deserving to be called free,—to give to each co-estate the right to judge of its powers, with a negative or veto on the acts of the others, in order to protect against encroachments the interests it particularly represents: a principle which all of our constitutions recognize in the distribution of power among their respective departments, as essential to maintain the independence of each; but which, to all who will duly reflect on the subject, must appear far more essential, for the same object, in that great and fundamental distribution of powers between the General and State Governments. So essential is the principle, that, to withhold the right from either, where the sovereign power is divided, is, in fact, *to annul the division* itself, and to *consolidate*, in the one left in the exclusive possession of the right, *all* powers of government; for it is not possible to distinguish, practically, between a government having all power, and one having the right to take what powers it pleases. Nor does it in the least vary the principle, whether the distribution of power be between co-estates, as in England, or between distinctly organized but connected governments, as with us. The reason is the same in both cases, while the necessity is greater in our case, as the danger of conflict is greater where the interests of a society are divided geographically than in any other, as has already been shown.

These truths do seem to me to be incontrovertible; and I am at a loss to understand how any one, who has maturely reflected on the nature of our institutions, or who has read history or studied the principles of free government to any purpose, can call them in question. The explanation must, it appears to me, be sought in the fact that, in every free State there are those who look more to the necessity of maintaining power than guarding against its abuses. I do not intend reproach, but simply to state a fact apparently necessary to explain the contrariety of opinions among the intelligent, where the abstract consideration of the subject would seem scarcely to admit of doubt. If such be the true cause, I must think the fear of weakening the government too much, in this case, to be in a great measure unfounded, or, at least, that the danger is much less from that than the opposite side. I do not deny that a power of so high a nature may be abused by a State; but when I reflect that the States unanimously called the General Government into existence with all its powers, which they freely delegated on their part, under the conviction that their common peace, safety, and prosperity required it; that they are bound together by a common origin, and the recollection of common suffering and common triumph in the great and splendid achievement of their independence; and that the strongest feelings of our nature, and among them the love of national power and distinction, are on the side of the Union, it does seem to me that the fear which would strip the States of their sovereignty, and degrade them, in fact, to mere dependent corporations, lest they should abuse a right indispensable to the peaceable protection of those interests which they reserved under their own peculiar guardianship when they created the General Government, is unnatural and unreasonable. If those who voluntarily created the system cannot be trusted to preserve it, who can?

So far from extreme danger, I hold that there never was a free State in which this great conservative principle, indispensable to all, was ever so safely lodged. In others, when the co-estates representing the dissimilar and conflicting interests of the community came into contact, the only alternative was compromise, submission, or force. Not so in ours. Should the General Government and a State come into conflict, we have a higher remedy: the power which called the General Government into existence, which gave it all its authority, and can enlarge, contract, or abolish its powers at its pleasure, may be invoked. The States themselves may be appealed to,—three fourths of which, in fact, form a power, whose decrees are the Constitution itself, and whose voice can silence all discontent. The utmost extent, then, of the power is, that a State, acting in its sovereign capacity as one of the parties to the constitutional compact, may compel the Government, created by that compact, to submit a question touching its infraction, to the parties who created it; to avoid the supposed dangers of which, it is proposed to resort to the novel, the hazardous, and, I must add, fatal project of giving to the General Government the sole and final right of interpreting the Constitution;—thereby reversing the whole system, making that instrument the creature of its will, instead of a rule of action impressed on it at its creation, and annihilating, in fact, the authority which imposed it, and from which the Government itself derives its existence.

That such would be the result, were the right in question vested in the Legislative or Executive branch of the Government, is conceded by all. No one has been so hardy as to assert that Congress or the President ought to have the right, or deny that, if vested finally and exclusively in either, the consequences which I have stated would necessarily follow; but its advocates have been reconciled to the doctrine, on the supposition that there is one department of the General Government which, from its peculiar organization, affords an independent tribunal, through which the Government may exercise the high authority which is the subject of consideration, with perfect safety to all.

I yield, I trust, to few in my attachment to the Judiciary Department. I am fully sensible of its importance, and would maintain it, to the fullest extent, in its constitutional powers and independence; but it is impossible for me to believe it was ever intended by the Constitution that it should exercise the power in question, or that it is competent to do so; and, if it were, that it would be a safe depository of the power.

Its powers are judicial, and not political; and are expressly confined by the Constitution "to all *cases* in law and equity arising under this Constitution, the laws of the United States, and the treaties made, or which shall be made, under its authority;" and which I have high authority in asserting excludes political questions, and comprehends those only where there are parties amenable to the process of the court. Nor is its incompetency less clear than its want of constitutional authority. There may be many, and the most dangerous infractions on the part of Congress, of which, it is conceded by all, the court, as a judicial tribunal, cannot, from its nature, take cognizance. The Tariff itself is a strong case in point; and the reason applies equally *to all others where Congress perverts a power from an object intended, to one not intended, the most insidious and dangerous of all infractions; and which may be extended to all of its powers, more especially to the taxing and appropriating*. But, supposing it competent to take cognizance of all infractions of every description, the insuperable objection still remains, that it would not be a safe tribunal to exercise the power in question.

It is a universal and fundamental political principle, that the power to protect can safely be confided only to those interested in protecting, or their responsible agents,—a maxim not less true in private than in public affairs. The danger in our system is, that the General Government, which represents the interests of the whole, may encroach on the States, which represent the peculiar and local interests, or that the latter may encroach on the former.

In examining this point, we ought not to forget that the Government, through all its departments, judicial as well as others, is administered by delegated and responsible agents; and that the *power which really controls, ultimately, all the movements, is not in the agents, but those who elect or appoint them*. To understand, then, its real character, and what would be the action of the system in any supposable case, we must raise our view from the mere agents to this high controlling power, which finally impels every movement of the machine. By doing so, we shall find all under the control of the will of a majority, compounded of the majority of the States, taken as political bodies, and the majority of the people of the States, estimated in federal numbers. These, united, constitute the real and final power which impels and directs the movements of the General Government. The majority of the States elect the majority of the Senate; of the people of the States, that of the House of Representatives; the two united, the President; and the President and a majority of the Senate appoint the judges: a majority of whom, and a majority of the Senate and House, with the President, really exercise all the powers of the Government, with the exception of the cases where the Constitution requires a greater number than a majority. The judges are, in fact, as truly the judicial representatives of this united majority, as the majority of Congress itself, or the President, is its legislative or executive representative; and to confide the power to the Judiciary to determine finally and conclusively what powers are delegated and what reserved, would be, in reality, to confide it to the majority, whose agents they are, and by whom they can be controlled in various ways; and, of course, to subject (against the fundamental principle of our system and all sound political reasoning) the reserved powers of the States, with all the local and peculiar interests they were intended to protect, to the will of the very majority against which the protection was intended. Nor will the tenure by which the judges hold their office, however valuable the provision in many other respects, materially vary the case. Its highest possible effect would be to *retard*, and not *finally to resist*, the will of a dominant majority.

But it is useless to multiply arguments. Were it possible that reason could settle a question where the passions and interests of men are concerned, this point would have been long since settled for ever by the State of Virginia. The report of her Legislature, to which I have already referred, has really, in my opinion, placed it beyond controversy. Speaking in reference to this subject, it says: "It has been objected" (to the right of a State to interpose for the protection of her reserved rights)

> that the judicial authority is to be regarded as the sole expositor of the Constitution. On this objection it might be observed, first, that there may be instances of usurped powers which the forms of the Constitution could never draw within the control of the Judicial Department; secondly, that, if the decision of the judiciary be raised above the sovereign parties to the Constitution, the decisions of the other departments, not carried by the forms of the Constitution before the Judiciary, must be equally authoritative and final with the decision of that department. But the proper answer to the objection is, that the resolution of the General Assembly relates to those great and extraordinary cases, in which all the forms of the Constitution may prove ineffectual against infractions dangerous to the essential rights of the parties to it. The resolution supposes that dangerous powers, not delegated, may not only be usurped and executed by the other departments, but that the Judicial Department may also exercise or sanction dangerous powers, beyond the grant of the Constitution, and, consequently, that the ultimate right

> of the parties to the Constitution to judge whether the compact has been dangerously violated, must extend to violations by one delegated authority, as well as by another,—by the judiciary, as well as by the executive or legislative.

Against these conclusive arguments, as they seem to me, it is objected that, if one of the parties has the right to judge of infractions of the Constitution, so has the other; and that, consequently, in cases of contested powers between a State and the General Government, each would have a right to maintain its opinion, as is the case when sovereign powers differ in the construction of treaties or compacts; and that, of course, it would come to be a mere question of force. The error is in the assumption that the General Government is a party to the constitutional compact. The States, as has been shown, formed the compact, acting as sovereign and independent communities. The General Government is but its creature; and though, in reality, a government, with all the rights and authority which belong to any other government, within the orbit of its powers, it is, nevertheless, a government emanating from a compact between sovereigns, and partaking, in its nature and object, of the character of a joint commission, appointed to superintend and administer the interests in which all are jointly concerned; but having, beyond its proper sphere, no more power than if it did not exist. To deny this would be to deny the most incontestable facts and the clearest conclusions; while to acknowledge its truth is, to destroy utterly the objection that the appeal would be to force, in the case supposed. For, if each party has a right to judge, then, under our system of government, the final cognizance of a question of contested power would be in the States, and not in the General Government. It would be the duty of the latter, as in all similar cases of a contest between one or more of the principals and a joint commission or agency, to refer the contest to the principals themselves. Such are the plain dictates of both reason and analogy. On no sound principle can the agents have a right to final cognizance, as against the principals, much less to use force against them to maintain their construction of their powers. Such a right would be monstrous, and has never, heretofore, been claimed in similar cases.

That the doctrine is applicable to the case of a contested power between the States and the General Government, we have the authority, not only of reason and analogy, but of the distinguished statesman already referred to. Mr. Jefferson, at a late period of his life, after long experience and mature reflection, says,

> With respect to our State and Federal Governments, I do not think their relations are correctly understood by foreigners. They suppose the former are subordinate to the latter. This is not the case. They are co-ordinate departments of one simple and integral whole. But you may ask, "If the two departments should claim each the same subject of power, where is the umpire to decide between them?" In cases of little urgency or importance, the prudence of both parties will keep them aloof from the questionable ground; but, if it can neither be avoided nor compromised, a convention of the States must be called to ascribe the doubtful power to that department which they may think best.

It is thus that our Constitution, by authorizing amendments, and by prescribing the authority and mode of making them, has, by a simple contrivance, with its characteristic wisdom, provided a power which, in the last resort, supersedes effectually the necessity, and even the pretext for force: a power to which none can fairly object; with which the interests of all are safe; which can definitively close all controversies in the only effectual mode, by freeing the compact of every defect and uncertainty, by an amendment of the instrument itself. It is impossible for human wisdom, in a system like ours, to devise another mode which shall be safe and effectual, and, at the same time, consistent with what are the relations and acknowledged powers of the two great departments of our Government. It gives a beauty and security peculiar to our system, which, if duly appreciated, will transmit its blessings to the remotest generations; but, if not, our splendid anticipations of the future will prove but an empty dream. Stripped of all its covering, the naked question is, whether ours is a federal or a consolidated government; a constitutional or absolute one; a government resting ultimately on the solid basis of the sovereignty of the States or on the unrestrained will of a majority; a form of government, as in all other unlimited ones, in which injustice, and violence, and force must finally prevail. *Let it never be forgotten that, where the majority rules without restriction, the minority is the subject*; and that, if we should absurdly attribute to the former the exclusive right of construing the Constitution, there would be, in fact, between the sovereign and subject, under such a government, no Constitution, or, at least, nothing deserving the name, or serving the legitimate object of so sacred an instrument.

How the States are to exercise this high power of interposition, which constitutes so essential a portion of their reserved rights that it *cannot be delegated without an entire surrender of their sovereignty*, and converting our system from a *federal* into a *consolidated* Government, is a question that the States only are competent to determine. The arguments which prove that they possess the power, equally prove that they are, in the language of Jefferson, "*the rightful judges of the mode and measure of redress*." But the spirit of forbearance, as well as the nature of the right itself, forbids a recourse to it, except in cases of dangerous infractions of the Constitution; and then only in the last resort, when all reasonable hope of relief from the ordinary action of the Government has failed; when, if the right to interpose did not exist, the alternative would be submission and oppression on one side, or resistance by force on the other. That our system should afford, in such extreme cases, an intermediate point between these dire alternatives, by which the Government may be brought to a pause, and thereby an interval obtained to compromise differences, or, if impracticable, be compelled to submit the question to a constitutional adjustment, through an appeal to the States themselves, is an evidence of its high wisdom: an element not, as is supposed by some, of weakness, but of strength; not of anarchy or revolution, but of peace and safety. *Its general recognition would of itself, in a great measure, if not altogether, supersede the necessity of its exercise, by impressing on the movements of the Government that moderation and justice so essential to harmony and peace, in a country of such vast extent and diversity of interests as ours*; and would, if controversy should come, turn the resentment of the aggrieved from the system to those who had abused its powers (a point all-important), and cause them to seek redress, *not in revolution or overthrow, but in reformation*. It is, in fact, properly understood, *a substitute,—where the alternative would be force,—tending to prevent, and, if that fails, to correct peaceably the aberrations to which all systems are liable, and which, if permitted to accumulate without correction, must finally end in a general catastrophe*. . . .

With every caution on my part, I dare not hope, in taking the step I have, to escape the imputation of improper motives; though I have, without reserve, freely expressed my opinions, not regarding whether they might or might not be popular. I have no reason to believe that they are such as will conciliate public favor, but the opposite, which I greatly regret, as I have ever placed a high estimate on the good opinion of my fellow-citizens. But, be that as it may, I shall, at least, be sustained by feelings of conscious rectitude. I have formed my opinions after the most careful and deliberate examination, with all the aids which my reason and experience could furnish; I have expressed them honestly and fearlessly, regardless of their effects personally, which, however interesting to me individually, are of too little importance to be taken into the estimate, where the liberty and happiness of our country are so vitally involved.

IX.

Nullification: Why the Critics Are All Wrong

An Exposition of the Virginia Resolutions of 1798
Judge Abel P. Upshur
1833

The full title of the pamphlet from which this selection is excerpted is An Exposition of the Virginia Resolutions of 1798; in a Series of Essays, Addressed to Thomas Ritchie, by a Distinguished Citizen of Virginia, Under the Signature of "Locke." *This pseudonymous series of essays is attributed to Judge Abel P. Upshur (1790–1844), whose career, as we noted in chapter 4, included service in the Virginia legislature, as a judge of the General Court of Virginia, and, in the early 1840s, as U.S. Secretary of State and Secretary of the Navy. Upshur's important 1840 book,* A Brief Enquiry into the True Nature and Character of Our Federal Government, *is a refutation of Joseph Story's nationalistic* Commentaries on the Constitution of the United States (1833).

Here Upshur is at pains to demonstrate that, whatever special pleading might be advanced to the contrary, nullification is the only means by which the principles set forth in the

Virginia Resolutions of 1798 can be enforced. Any lesser form of interposition is simply inadequate to their purpose. When he describes nullification as a constitutional remedy and contrasts it with revolution, he means that a nullifying state is not in fact overthrowing the constitutional order but operating within it. If anyone is overthrowing the constitutional order, it is a federal government that attempts to impose unconstitutional measures on the states.

The essays that follow, collected into a pamphlet, are addressed to Thomas Ritchie, who was Spencer Roane's cousin and the editor of the Richmond Enquirer. *To my knowledge, this pamphlet is appearing in print for the first time since its original publication in Philadelphia in 1833 (and subsequent periodical reprint in 1835). It is one of the most vigorous defenses of nullification, and among the most spirited replies to critics of the idea, ever written.*

NO. I.

. . . Permit me, then, as a citizen neither very young nor wholly unconnected; as one who considers every thing which he cherishes in our institutions in the most imminent peril; as one who sincerely believes that you can form the public mind of Virginia, and that Virginia can control the destinies of this once happy Union, to entreat you to answer explicitly the following interrogatories. They are propounded, not in the spirit of a controversialist, but with a deep conviction that they involve the only principles upon which the rights of the States can be maintained, and of course the only security against a consolidated and essentially monarchical government:

1. Is there, or is there not, any principle in the Constitution of the United States, by which the States may resist the usurpations of the Federal Government; or are such usurpations to be resisted only by revolution?
2. If there be no such principle, is not the Federal Government as unlimited in its powers as any other Government, whatever be its form, whose encroachments upon the rights of the citizen can be repelled only by rebellion, or other application of physical force?

If you believe, as I am sure you do believe, that there *is* such conservative principle in the Constitution, then I beg the favour of you to point it out, and tell us in what manner we may render it available. In doing this, be pleased to answer—

3. Is not the passing a law by Congress which the Constitution does not authorise, a usurpation on the part of that body? And is not every such unconstitutional law absolutely void, as passed by a delegated authority, beyond the limits of that authority?
4. Are the States bound to submit to laws which are unconstitutional, and therefore void?
5. If the States are not so bound to submit, is not the particular State which refuses to submit, right in so doing?
6. If the recreant State be right in her refusal to submit, are not the other States wrong in compelling her to submit? Is it not oppression of the worst sort, to coerce obedience to usurped power?

The above questions are propounded upon the hypothesis that Congress may have actually passed a law *palpably* and *dangerously* violating the Constitution. And now be pleased to tell us in what manner the fact of such palpable and dangerous violation is to be ascertained? In doing this, be also pleased to answer—

7. Is there any common umpire established by the Constitution, to whom may be referred questions touching a breach thereof?

If there be such common umpire, be pleased to point it out.

8. If there be no such common umpire, does it not result from the necessity of the case, that each State must judge thereof for itself?
9. If a State, in the actual exercise of this right, should decide that any given act of Congress *is* a palpable and dangerous violation of the Constitution, is there any right of appeal from that decision?
10. If there be, does the appeal lie to any other authority than the other parties to the Constitution?
11. Who are these "other parties"? The States or the people?

Upon this last question, you are already so fully committed, that it is impossible to doubt your answer. I have, therefore, to ask you—

12. Is not the decision of every inferior tribunal of competent jurisdiction, obligatory and conclusive, until it is reversed? And if so, is not the decision of a State upon a constitutional question on which it has a *right* to decide, conclusive as to such State, until it is reversed by the other States,

acting as such?

13. If it be thus conclusive, has the State a right to *act* upon its decision or not?
14. If it has no such right of action, is its right of judgment any thing more than a mere liberty of speech and of opinion, and, therefore, no *available* right at all?
15. If it *has* such right of action, is it to act by *submitting* to the usurped power, or by opposing it?

A man of your spirit, can give but one answer to this question. Then be good enough to tell us in *what manner* this opposition is to be made? In doing this, be pleased to answer—

16. Are petition, remonstrance and protest, any thing more than appeals to the oppressor, and therefore in no sense, to be called *opposition* to him? Or if it be opposition, and these petitions, remonstrances and appeals, should all be disregarded, is the matter to rest there?
17. If not, and farther resistance is to be made, ought not that resistance to be made in such form as to *redress the wrong*?
18. If so, can the wrong be redressed by the injured State going out of the Union? Does not this, on the contrary, *increase* the wrong as to her, by compelling her to relinquish all the advantages of the Union, to which she is fairly entitled, and at the same time, *encourage* the aggressors to persevere in the wrong, by withdrawing all opposition to them? Is not the "redress," in this mode of seeking it, merely an additional wrong done to the injured party?
19. If so, what do you propose to substitute for it?

You perceive, sir, that I have, in all these questions, followed very closely, the Virginia Resolutions and Madison's Report. They are the text upon which my future commentaries will be offered. I have done so on purpose, for you have always been an advocate of those documents, as being clearly orthodox; and as I entertain the same opinion of them myself, I am unfeignedly desirous to see by what process of reasoning, any two men of tolerable intellect, can be led to different conclusions from such principles. I confess that it seems to me exceedingly clear, that our Constitution is most worthless and tyrannical, if the usurpations of those who administer it, cannot be resisted by any means short of revolution. I have always considered the reserved powers of the States, as the only real check upon the powers of the Federal Government; and I have always considered it, not only the *right*, but the *imperious duty* of the States, so to apply that check, as *not to dissolve the Union*. And I have never been able to discover any mode of doing this, except by the positive refusal of the States to submit to usurpations, whilst, at the same time, remaining in the Union. They force the Federal Government back within the charter of its power. This seems to me an irresistible influence, from the principles indicated in the preceding interrogatories. Perhaps you can show me that these principles do not lead to Nullification? I shall be happy to be undeceived; but at present, I entertain no doubt, that *that* doctrine is the only one upon which the States can safely repose. It is easy to show that this is the legitimate result of the Resolutions of 1798. I shall endeavour to show this in a second letter, with which you will be shortly troubled. In the mean time, you will not only gratify me, but hundreds of others, by answering the foregoing interrogatories, distinctly, plainly, and directly. The views which

I now indicate, have already been substantially presented to the public; but, as I consider them of vital importance, I shall continue to press them under all the forms of which they are susceptible, until some one will condescend to prove them wrong....

NO. II.

In the letter which I addressed to you on the 2nd inst., I propounded to you within interrogatories, touching the great principles involved in the present measures of the Federal Government. I could not wait for your reply, even if there were better reasons than any which I can now discern, for expecting a reply at all. I do not expect it, and yet I venture to hope for it. You owe it to your own character, to your numerous patrons, and to the great cause in which you have professed to be a zealous labourer, to be no longer silent or mysterious, upon these important topics. Come out, I pray you, in a manner at once so distinct and unequivocal, as to leave no pretence, either to friend or foe, for accusing you of duplicity or timidity.

I live in a very retired corner of the country, sir, and seldom get the news until it is news no longer, in other places. Hence, at the date of my last letter, I had only *heard* of the President's late message to Congress. That most weak and sophistical, yet most dangerous document, was never read by me, until this morning. It has sunk into a still deeper depth of depression, the few lingering hopes which I was permitted to cherish, that the constitution and public liberty, would survive the administration of Andrew Jackson. I shall have something to say to you upon that subject hereafter. I proceed now to redeem my promise, in proving, or at least endeavouring to prove, that the Virginia resolutions of 1798, cannot be carried out in any other manner than by nullification. In doing this, I shall go back no farther than to the resolutions themselves. I shall give to the language employed, no other construction than that which every man of plain common sense will be compelled to give it. This is the only fair course of proceeding, for the resolutions were intended for the great body of the people, and must have been designed to be comprehensible by the meanest capacity. I will not do the Legislature the injustice of supposing, that they intended to wrap up in mystery, which none but the statesman or the man of learning could penetrate, principles which they deemed essential to the preservation of constitutional liberty. So much of those resolutions as relates to the present subject, as in the following words:—

> "That this Assembly doth explicitly and peremptorily declare, that it views the powers of the Federal Government as resulting from the compact to which the states are parties, as limited by the plain sense and intention of the instrument constituting that compact, as no farther valid than they are authorized by the grants enumerated in that compact; and that in case of a deliberate, palpable, and dangerous exercise of other powers, not granted by the said compact, the States who are parties thereto, have the right, and are in duty bound, to interpose for arresting the progress of the evil, and for maintaining within their respective limits, the authorities, rights and liberties appertaining to them."
>
> "That the good people of this Commonwealth, having ever felt, and continuing to feel, the most sincere affection

> for their brethren of the other States; the truest anxiety for establishing and perpetuating the union of all; and the most scrupulous fidelity to that constitution which is the pledge of natural friendship, the instrument of mutual happiness; the General Assembly doth solemnly appeal to the like dispositions in the other States, in confidence that they will concur with this Commonwealth in declaring, as it does hereby declare, that the acts aforesaid, [the alien and sedition laws,] are unconstitutional; and that the necessary and proper measures will be taken by each, for co-operating with this State, in maintaining unimpaired, the authorities, rights and liberties, reserved to the States respectively, or to the people."

In these resolutions, the following principles are distinctly affirmed:

1. That the Constitution of the United States is a Compact between the States, as such.
2. That the Government established by that Compact, possesses no power whatever, except what "the plain sense and intention" of that Compact gives to it.
3. That every act done by that Government, not plainly within the limits of its powers, is void.
4. That each State has a right to say whether an act done by that Government is plainly within the limits of its powers or not.
5. That the States are not bound to submit to, but may resist, any act of that Government which it shall so decide to be beyond the limits of its powers.

All this is plain enough, and is, as I understand, fully admitted by yourself. The only difficulty is, to discover *in what mode* the Resolutions contemplated that resistance should be applied. On this subject, I have to remark, *in limine*, that the Resolutions contemplate that "the necessary and proper measures will be taken by each State" *for itself*. No uniform mode of resisting the encroachments of the Federal Government is pointed out or suggested. Having affirmed the right, each State is left to its own mode of asserting it in practice. Taking the terms of the Resolutions in their utmost latitude, they authorize *any means of resistance whatever*. Such, however, is clearly not their meaning. A very slight analysis will force upon us the conviction that no mode of resistance is contemplated, except such as will *preserve the Union unimpaired, while it will effectually put down the usurped power*. This is shown—

1. By the profession of "sincere affection" for the people of the other States; of "anxiety for establishing and perpetuating the union of all;" and of "the most scrupulous fidelity to the Constitution." It is upon the strength of these feelings, and with a view to these objects, that the co-operation of the other States is invited.
2. The interposition of the States must be in such mode as *to "arrest the progress of the evil."*
3. It must at the same time be such as *"to maintain within their respective limits, the authorities, rights and liberties appertaining to them."*
4. It is to be remarked, that we have here a distinct declaration that there is within the Constitution of the United States, some principle, by which the encroachments and

> usurpations of the Federal Government may be resisted. I say *within the Constitution*, and not extra-constitutional and revolutionary.

And now, Sir, will you be good enough to tell me in what manner that principle is to be applied? Permit me to examine all the modes of resistance which occur to my own mind, and to see which of them is within the principles thus asserted.

1. Petition, remonstrance, protest.—It cannot, I think, be sincerely asserted, that these are any means of *resistance* at all. It is such a resistance as your slave may make, when you chastise him for an imputed fault. If all right of farther resistance be disclaimed, this is an implied admission that the party to whom the appeal is addressed, may, if he chooses, persevere in the wrong. In point of fact, however, remonstrance and protest are founded in the idea that there *is* such right of farther resistance. Petition is a simple appeal for mercy or forbearance; protest and remonstrance, affirm a *right*, and *threaten* the enforcement of it. *But they do not in themselves enforce* it, and therefore are not resistance.
2. An appeal to arms.—This is utterly against all notions of constitutional remedy. Our Government is founded in free choice, and is supposed by public opinion alone. A resort to arms, therefore, would at once change the whole genius of the Constitution. A case might certainly arise, in which a State might rightfully resort to arms for the purpose of putting down or resisting the usurpations of the Federal Government. Suppose, for instance, that the

President should send a regiment of his standing army, to turn our Legislature out of doors, and pull down the capitol, I presume that Governor Floyd would be clearly right in calling upon the militia to put every soldier of them to the sword, if the civil authority should prove unable to "arrest the progress of the evil." At all events, the Legislature might authorize him to do so. This, however, is an extreme case, and such as could not have been anticipated; for the Government could not exist a day, with an administration capable of such an outrage. An actual appeal to arms, therefore, is not to be thought of, as among the proposed modes of resistance.

3. A repeal of the unconstitutional law by Congress. This, I perceive, is one of the President's modes, but unfortunately, he is not very apt to discern the principles which his measures involve. This would, indeed, be a complete remedy for the evil, and an ample redress of the wrong.—You know, however, sir, that although you may "call spirits from the vasty deep," it is not certain that they will "come when you do call them." It is not likely that the usurper will either acknowledge his usurpation, or lay down his usurped power. You must remember too, that the usurper in the present case, is *a majority of the people, usurping upon the rights of the minority*, and the history of the tariff laws, ought to convince you how unapt such usurpers are to give way. This remedy, therefore, would be of little value in practice. Besides, it is in principle, a simple *appeal to the wrong doer*, and is therefore, no more a mode of resistance, than the right of petition. Every thing is left at last, to the will and discretion of the usurping power.

4. An amendment of the constitution. I certainly should not have mentioned this as a means of resistance, if it had not been mentioned by the President, as one of the modes in which the aggrieved States or people, might seek redress. No man, but one of his peculiar intellect, would ever think *of an amendment of the Constitution*, as a means of resisting *a breach of that instrument*. It is not the object to amend the Constitution, but to *preserve it, unimpaired as it is*. I hope that the President's future labors, in the study of the Constitution, may show him this distinction.
5. Secession, or a withdrawal from the Union by the aggrieved State. This, sir, is your favourite mode, and as far as I can perceive, your *only* mode, of resisting the usurpations of the Federal Government. The President, however, in the plentitude of his merciful consideration of State Rights, does not even allow them this humble refuge from oppression.—Let us now see how you will carry out this mode of resistance, consistently with the resolutions of 1798.

In the first place, a State which withdraws from the Union, *breaks* the Union. This is true, *ex vi termini*, and therefore, need not be proved. But I have already shown that the resolutions of 1798, proceed upon the idea, that the Union is to be *preserved*; and indeed, that is the main object of resistance, as therein contemplated. In this respect, therefore, secession is not a means of resistance within those resolutions.

In the second place, the resistance therein contemplated, must be such as will "*arrest the progress of the evil*." Will you be so obliging as to tell me, sir, how a usurped power can be *resisted*, by *giving way to it*. In one way, indeed, the evil may be arrested by secession; the usurped power may be rendered nugatory, by withdrawing from its reach, all the subjects upon which it can exercise itself. I can scarcely imagine, however, that this tame and submissive idea, was entertained by the Statesmen of 1798. It appears to my humble understanding, that secession, so far from being a form of *resistance* to usurped power, is the precise reverse; it is neither more nor less than a *running away from the oppressor*. And so far from "arresting the progress of the evil," it encourages and invites the evil, by removing all restraint from the wrong-doer. In *this* view, therefore, it is not within the resolutions of 1798.

In the third place, the interposition of the States, must be such as to "*maintain within their respective limits, the authorities, rights and liberties, appertaining to them*." Now what are these "authorities, rights and liberties?" To you, sir, I need not say, that as sovereign and independent States, they are entitled to all the authorities, rights and liberties, which at any time, belonged to them as such, except such part thereof, as they plainly surrendered when they ratified the constitution. These they may, it is true, enjoy in a state of separation. But they are also entitled to all the authorities, rights and liberties, which the other States guarantied to them, by the terms of Union. Among these are to be remembered, their just weight in the measures of the common government; a share in the common property of the whole; protection by the common power; a Republican Government assured by that power, and all and every benefit and advantage which they could enjoy as *members of the Union*. It was in this character alone, that their co-operation was invoked in the resolution of 1798. And now, sir, be good enough to say how the authorities, rights, and liberties, which belong to the States, as members of the Union, can be "maintained," by their *going out of the Union*. If you cannot, you must feel yourself bound, in candor, to admit that in *this* respect also, secession is not within the resolutions of 1798. I know you will tell me that these resolutions have been much misunderstood. You have already said so, and much subtlety in reasoning, and refinement in language, have been resorted to by your correspondents to prove it. It is for this very reason, that I have taken such parts of the resolution only, as no man can misunderstand, and such as do not admit of but one construction. You may refine until doomsday, and you will not change the plain meaning and object of the plain language employed.

I have thus examined every mode of "arresting the progress of the evil, and maintaining within the respective limits of the States, the authorities, rights and liberties which appertain to them," which occur to my mind, except nullification. It appears, I think, clearly enough, that none of these will answer the purpose. If there be any other mode, you will confer a great benefit upon the country, by pointing it out. I promised to prove to you that Nullification is this other mode, but I must make that the business of another letter. I have already occupied quite as much space in the *Whig* as I am fairly entitled to, and would not willingly trespass too far upon the indulgence of its Editors. Besides, sir, although you may not consider these letters worthy of being *answered*, I am very desirous that they should be *read*, and, therefore, I will make them so short as not to deter any one from perusing them, and not to fatigue any one over-much, who shall venture upon that undertaking.

NO. III.

I am now to prove to you, sir, that Nullification is the only mode in which the usurpations of the Federal Government may be resisted by the States, in accordance with the principles of our resolutions of 1798. Daring as you may consider this enterprise, I do not enter upon it with any fear, although I approach without flourish of trumpets, or any other parade. I am a plain, practical man, and desire to state my opinions in a manner which other plain, practical men will understand. If such men are not the *ornaments* of the country, they are at least its strength and support, and the very people to whose capacity all reasoning upon political subjects ought to be addressed.

I beg you to bear in mind the principles which have already been stated as deducible from the resolutions of 1798. Perhaps our best course of proceeding will be to state them in detail, and see whether nullification does or does not conform to every one of them.

1. The resolutions assert that there is *some* mode *within* the Constitution by which the usurpations of the Federal Government may be resisted by the States. Now, it is true that nullification is denied to be a constitutional remedy; but the nullifiers assert that it *is* constitutional; and I mention the point only to show that they do not intend to assert any extra-constitutional or revolutionary remedy—and that so far, at least, they are within the resolutions of 1798. Whether their remedy is constitutional or not, supposing the principles of the resolutions to be so, must depend on its conformity with those principles in the subsequent

propositions. We remark, therefore, that

2. The remedy must be such as to "*arrest* the progress of the *evil.*"—Now, be pleased to bear in mind, that nullification does not proceed upon any supposed right of the State to *repeal a constitutional law*, but upon the right of a State to *declare that an unconstitutional law really is so, and to refuse obedience to it for that reason*. I beg you to bear this distinction in mind. If nullification proposes any thing more or less than this, I am no nullifier, and do not understand the doctrine. Now, sir, is not this right of a State (to decide on the constitutionality of an act of Congress) distinctly asserted in the resolutions of 1798? Nay, has not Virginia asserted it in *practice*, both in regard to the Alien and Sedition Laws, and in regard to these very Tariff Laws themselves? We all know that such is the fact. And was not resistance to such unconstitutional laws distinctly contemplated in the resolutions of 1798? I have already shown that it was; and if any farther proof is necessary, it will be found, in all abundance, in the address to the people which accompanied those resolutions. It appears, then, that the *principles* upon which nullification proceeds, are (in the abstract) in strict conformity with those of the resolutions of 1798. But those principles, it is admitted, must be limited and qualified by the object in view. We are, then, to inquire whether nullification does, or does not, "arrest the progress of the evil." The evil is the exercise of an usurped power: nullification declares that the usurped power shall no longer be obeyed. Is not this the best of all possible modes, if not the *only* mode, in which it can be "arrested"? Perhaps it is not too great a refinement to say,

that the "arrest" here contemplated, is of the *usurpation* only, and not of the *usurping power*. In other words, it is not designed to put down the Federal Government—nor embarrass nor impede its legitimate operation; but simply to prevent it from exercising a power which does not belong to it. Hence, no resort is contemplated in the resolutions of 1798 to any measures which may submit the existence of that Government to the decision of arms. Its operations *within* the constitution must all go on as before, whilst its operations *beyond* the Constitution must be "arrested." Now, this is precisely and *peculiarly* the effect of nullification. And, strange to tell, it is on this very ground that you and others have most strongly assailed that doctrine. You all say, that it is absurd to pretend that a State can be *in* the Union and *out* of the Union at the same time; and that it is monstrous in a State to contend for all the advantages of the Union, as to certain laws, while she refuses to submit to the burthens imposed by other laws. Nothing in nature can be more perfectly self-evident than all this. It is not surprising that a man of General Jackson's measure of intellect and information should be deceived by such a superficial view of the subject; but we had a right to expect better things from a veteran in politics, like yourself. Remember, sir, that a law *beyond* the Constitution *is no law at all*, and there is no right any where to enforce it. A State which refuses to submit to such a pretended law, is strictly *within* the Union—because she is *in strict obedience to the Constitution*; and it is strange to say that she "refuses to submit to the burthens" imposed by any LAW which is NOT LAW AT ALL.

> There, then, you have a picture of Nullification. It secures to the State the right to remain in the Union, and to enjoy all the advantages which the Constitution and laws can afford—submitting, at the same time, to all which that Constitution and laws rightfully enjoin; while it "arrests the progress" of usurped power, by destroying the obligation of every pretended law which the Constitution does not authorise, and which, therefore, is NOT law. If this is not the meaning of the resolutions of 1798, I have much misunderstood them. It is precisely upon this point that the public mind of Virginia has been most strangely misled by the authority of the President's name, and the speciousness of your paragraphs. You owe the people a heavy debt of reparation, which I hope you will live to pay. This leads us to the second object of the resolutions of 1798, which is "to maintain within the limits of the respective States, the authorities, rights, and liberties appertaining to them." I have already shown, in my second letter, that these authorities, rights, and liberties are not merely those which belong to every sovereign State, and which may be enjoyed as well in a state of separation as in league with others, but also all the authorities, rights, and liberties which the States are entitled to, under the Constitution and *as members of the Union*. No State, therefore, can possibly effect this object of the resolutions of 1798, by any proceeding which *either withdraws her from the Union* or *weakens her just influence in it*.

The remarks offered under the preceding head, apply with equal force and propriety to this. You and the President both say, that it is arrogance and presumption in a State to insist on retaining her place and influence in the Union, while she refuses to submit to part of its laws. Admitting, again, that this is perfectly true, but re-asserting that it cannot apply to the refusal of a State to submit to what is NOT law, I have to ask you how it is possible for a State to "maintain her authorities, rights, and liberties," except by the check which she may apply *as a State, and as a member of the United States*, to the usurpations of the Federal Government, or by an appeal to arms? I pray you, sir, to enlighten my understanding upon this subject. If YOU cannot show me some other mode of proceeding, I take it for granted that no one else can. At all events, until it shall be done by some one or other, I shall be compelled to continue in my present heresy. If it was the meaning and object of the resolutions of 1798, that the States had the right, and were in duty bound, to resist the usurpations of the Federal Government, by some means, which, *at the same time that it arrested the evil, should preserve the Union unbroken*, I must be permitted to think that Nullification, if it does not attain these objects completely, comes much nearer to it than any other proceeding which has yet been proposed. I know, sir, that you, and hundreds of others, have said that the resolutions of 1798 have been misunderstood. Perhaps so. It is true their language has appeared to me, and to others like me, to be extremely plain—and it is our own construction of it alone which has formed our principles. Yet it is possible that it may hide some meaning deeper than we have been able to penetrate. I pray you to tell us what it is. Do not content yourself with the THEORY only, but but *[sic]* let us know the precise extent of our rights, and *the precise mode in which they may be constitutionally asserted, according to the resolutions of 1798.*

It has not escaped my attention that, according to those resolutions, the State interposition which they contemplate is not authorised, except in cases of "deliberate, palpable, and dangerous exercise of powers not granted." It will be obvious, however, to intellects less clear than your own, that this does not affect, in any degree, the principle upon which State resistance is justified, nor even the mode in which it may be exerted. It merely points out the *proper occasion* for the *application* of the principle. And it will be sufficient here to remark, that according to your own theory, which in this respect agrees with the resolutions, *each State is the exclusive judge for itself, whether the usurpation is deliberate, palpable, and dangerous, or not.* It follows, of course, that no objection to Nullification can be derived from this view of the subject.

I have now, sir, to present to you a dilemma, connected with this part of our inquiries, and to ask you in what manner you propose to escape its horns?

South Carolina says that an unconstitutional law is void, and so say the Virginia Resolutions—South Carolina says that each State has a right to decide for itself whether a law is constitutional or not, and so say the Virginia Resolutions—South Carolina, in the exercise of this right, has declared that the Tariff Laws ARE unconstitutional, and so say the Virginia Resolutions of 1828 and 1829 (I have forgotten the date) and so, Mr. Ritchie, SAY YOU. How, then, can you countenance the President, *in subjecting the citizens of South Carolina to the sword, for not submitting to what you yourself believe to be a sheer usurpation on the part of the Federal Government?* Do, sir, in pity to our oppressed spirits, answer this question. You will not answer it, sir—because you CANNOT answer it without convicting yourself of inconsistency. THIS I

WILL PROVE—for I do not mean to allow you any refuge from this dilemma. South Carolina is either right in her proceedings, (principles and all,) or else she is wrong. If she is RIGHT, then there can be no pretence whatever for making war upon her: if she is WRONG, *how does that fact appear?* It is admitted that the other States, co-parties with her to the Constitution, have not said so. Congress alone, and the President, or rather the *Federal Government, has said it.* Do you, sir, acknowledge any such right in the Federal Government? Is it not perfectly clear, that if such right exists, the Federal Government *is an appellate tribunal,* WITH POWER TO DECIDE, IN THE LAST RESORT, UPON THE CONSTITUTIONALITY OF ITS OWN ACTS? Of what avail is the right of a State to pronounce that an unconstitutional act of Congress is *really so,* if Congress may overrule that decision? Is not this, sir, the very essence of that consolidation against which the Virginia Resolutions, Madison's Report, and your own valuable labours, have so long contended? It is impossible, then, for you to justify Congress and the President, except by asserting, either that Congress may overrule the decision of South Carolina, upon a question touching their own powers, and, by the same rule, may overrule the decision of every other State, and thus become the *sole judges of the extent of their own powers*; or by asserting that they may *constitutionally enforce an unconstitutional law.* Can you, sir, escape this difficulty, without abandoning every principle for which you have professed to contend for thirty years? I am exceedingly anxious to know in what manner you will do it. For myself, I can discover but one possible loop-hole of retreat, and even that I will endeavour to close upon you.—I reserve this, however, for a succeeding letter.

NO. IV.

In my last letter, sir, I submitted for your solution, a proposition which appears to me to place you in considerable difficulty. A lion in the toils might, in perfect consistency with his character, decline all means of escape, through fear of committing his dignity upon an unsuccessful effort. In order that I may reconcile you to this course, (believing that you are already determined on pursuing it,) I proceed to show you that you *could not* escape, if you *would*.

You will perhaps say, that although a State has a right to pronounce on the constitutionality of an act of Congress; yet it is, nevertheless, bound to submit to an act so pronounced to be unconstitutional, *until the other States shall have sanctioned its decision*. This, if it were true, might perhaps afford some ground of apology for the President and Congress. It is this which I have already alluded to, as presenting the only possible chance of escape from the horns of my dilemma. Indeed, sir, it may be useful for you to know, that a great many of the most vociferous denouncers of Nullification go with it, in perfect fellowship, until it reaches this point. I will endeavour now to show that there is no sort of reason for separating here; and if I should succeed in this effort, you may rely upon it, that a vast number who are now in your ranks will desert to mine. I affirm, therefore, that the Resolutions of 1798, *so far from countenancing the idea that a State which has pronounced an act of Congress to be unconstitutional; is bound to obey that law, until the other States shall sanction its decision, do distinctly assert the precise reverse*. This, I doubt not, I shall prove.

I presume it will readily be admitted, that Madison's Report, which was made expressly to sustain those Resolutions, is a fair interpreter of their meaning. That Report, after stating the proposition, that "where resort can be had to no tribunal superior to the authority of the parties, the parties themselves must be the judges in the last resort, whether the bargain made has been pursued or violated," proceeds thus: "The States, then, being the parties to the Constitutional Compact, and in their sovereign capacity, it follows, of necessity, that there can be no tribunal above their authority, to decide, *in the last resort*, whether the Compact made by them be violated; and, consequently, that, as the parties to it, they must decide, *in the last resort*, such questions as may be of sufficient magnitude to require their interposition. From this view of the Resolution, it would seem inconceivable that it can incur any just disapprobation from those who, laying aside all momentary impressions, and recollecting the genuine source and object of the Federal Constitution, shall candidly and accurately interpret the meaning of the General Assembly. If the deliberate exercise of dangerous powers, palpably withheld by the Constitution, could not justify *the parties to it*, in interposing, even so far as to avert the progress of the evil, and thereby to preserve the Constitution itself, as well as to *provide for the safety of the parties to it*, there would be an end of all relief from usurped power, and a direct subversion of the rights *specified or recognized under all the State Constitutions, as well as a plain denial of the fundamental principle on which our independence itself was declared*."

This language appears to me to be plain enough for any common understanding. It even goes a bow-shot beyond the Nullification of South Carolina. That State admits that the other States, acting as such, may overrule her decision; but the Resolutions, as explained by the Report, contemplate such decision as "*in the last resort*," and therefore, *final and conclusive*. This must be the correct interpretation, unless the Report, by the term "States" and "parties," intended to limit itself to the *plural number*, and of course, not to include a *single State, acting by itself*. This is, at least, a mere quibble, altogether unworthy of the dignity of the subject; but as there appears to be a determination to get rid of our old principles in some way or other, their friends must not neglect their defence, even at those points which would seem to be impregnably intrenched. If, then, the Resolutions do not contemplate the interposition of *each* State for itself, they must contemplate such interposition either by *all* the States, or by a *majority of the States*, or by a plural number, *less than a majority of the States*. If the first was meant, it was a most useless and ridiculous parade of argument, to prove what is altogether self-evident. Certainly those who *made the Government* have a right not only to check and control it, but even to *unmake* it, whenever *all* of them concur in that wish. If, therefore, *this* be the meaning of the Resolutions, they only affirm what no one would ever think of denying, and what is equally true of other Governments as of ours. Do the Resolutions, then, refer to *a majority of the States?* The same remark applies here. The right of a majority to rule, is a fundamental principle in *all* Representative Governments, supposing always, that they exercise that right consistently with the rights of the minority. It follows, *a fortiori*, that they have a right to interpose to prevent the *minority* from usurping upon *their* rights. If, then, *this* be the meaning of the Resolutions, they employ a very useless solemnity in affirming a mere truism. Besides, it is idle to suppose, that the interposition either of *all* the States, or of *a majority of them*, is intended to be asserted as a *right*, when the object is *to correct the usurpations of that very majority itself*. Certainly those who do the wrong, not only have a *right* to redress it, but are in *duty bound* to do so. Do the Resolutions, then, contemplate a plural number *less* than a majority? If so, a single State may act for itself, upon the same principle; for there is no rule, either in ethics or politics, which measure the rights of a minority, by the mere number who may happen to compose it. Indeed, that the action by a single State, for itself, was contemplated, is manifest enough, from other considerations. In the first place, the *language imports* it, and will be so understood by every reader, who is not prone to look for refinement and sublimity in every thing. Moreover, it is the particular object of the written Constitutions to define and limit the powers of the Government; to guard against usurpations; *to protect the weak against the strong; to guard the rights of the minority against the encroachments of the majority*. The States, when they formed the Compact, brought to that work, their entire sovereignty, and all their rights. If they did not then surrender that sovereignty and those rights altogether, they must have designed to reserve to *themselves*, the task of protecting them. A case may very well arise, in which an unconstitutional law may affect the rights of a single State only; and it would be a mocking of the very name of State Rights, to say that in such case, she may not protect herself. In what other course can her "safety" be "provided" for? If twenty-three States should unite in cutting up every right which appertains to the twenty-fourth, has that State no redress except what a "majority" of her oppressors may choose to grant? If this be the meaning of the Resolutions, so far from affirming and protecting State Rights, they affirm that no *single* State has any rights at all. Besides, the Resolutions speak only of the *reserved rights* of the States; among which reserved rights, is that which authorises State interposition, to arrest the usurpations of the Federal Government. Now, how are these rights "reserved"? Does one State "reserve" its own rights to another State, or any number of other States? This seems to me, to be a grant, and not a *reservation* of a right. Each State, then, reserves its own rights to *itself*, and the Resolutions affirm, that the right to refuse obedience to an unconstitutional law, is among those reserved rights. Again: If the State may not act upon its own decision, until the majority have sanctioned it, the *right so* to decide, is, as to all practical results, *in that majority*, and not in the State. The State has only the right *to express its opinion*; which opinion, although involving her "safety," and her very existence, goes for nothing, until *approved by others*. This is, indeed, a meagre State Right, Mr. Ritchie. Besides, sir, is there not some contradiction in the positions that a State may declare a law to be unconstitutional, and yet that it is bound to submit to that law, for some given time? What difference is there, in principle, between an obligation to submit to an unconstitutional law for one day, and an obligation to submit to it for one year, or for ever? I confess that I can see none at all. Finally, sir—for the subject was really not worthy of even these few practical and popular views of it—suppose that the other States should refuse to say whether the particular State which undertakes to pronounce a law unconstitutional, is right or wrong? There are no means of *compelling* them to decide, and of course, a majority of the States, upon your supposition, (if it be yours,) have only to *stand mute*, in order to deprive all the other States, and *constitutionally too*, of every right which appertains to them. Nay, even if the other States should be disposed to act upon the subject in good faith, the right which the individual State interposes to protect, may be such as to be *lost for ever, unless it be promptly asserted*. Our slave population will at once suggest to you such a case. The very delay, therefore, of this previous appeal, may be fatal to the very existence of the right. I can scarcely think that it was the intention of the Resolutions of 1798, to produce any such result as this.

And now, sir, let me bring you back to my dilemma. The Resolutions of 1798, approved by you, acknowledge the right of South Carolina, to pronounce the Tariff Laws unconstitutional; and *do not* require that she shall forbear to act on that decision, until it shall be affirmed by a majority of the other States. South Carolina *has* pronounced those laws unconstitutional, and you have over and over again declared, that *she is right* in that respect. *How then can you countenance the President and Congress, in subjecting her people to the sword, for not obeying those laws?* I would, if a regard to decorum did not forbid it, *defy* you to the answer. You ought to give it, and plainly and satisfactorily too, or else you ought to change your course. You are encouraging the President in making war upon South Carolina. It is war, sir, however you may disguise it—*civil war*—with all its unnumbered train of sufferings, tears and sorrows. A husband and a father who contemplates this result, must have a nature more callous than I take yours to be, if he can admit into his calculations, either the "feelings" of a political favourite, the success of party objects, or the poor pride of opinion. You can, if you choose, arrest the wide spreading desolation with which our whole country is threatened. I beseech you to reflect that it is at least possible, that you are permitting innocent blood to be shed, when it is in your power to prevent it. Shall it not, hereafter, be required at your hands?

...The President has profited by your suggestions, and has founded his proposed measures of violence and carnage, upon reasons with which you have furnished him. The history of that man's past life, affords full and terrible proof, that he never wants [i.e., lacks] excuses, good or bad, for any outrage which he may propose to perpetrate upon the Laws and Constitution of his country. Posterity will do him justice, although this age seems determined to be blind to his real character. I cannot close these letters without an attempt to show, that there is no reason whatever, which can justify or extenuate the sanguinary purpose which he now entertains. I have not yet, however, quite done with the subject of Nullification. It will be continued in my next letter.

NO. V.

...It is perfectly true, as the President contends, that if a State may declare *one* law to be unconstitutional, it may declare any and every *other* law to be so; and by the same rule, each State may, in the exercise of the same right, select a particular law or laws as unconstitutional, and thus utterly destroy the uniform operation of the system. But while this is certainly *possible*, it is in no degree *probable*, and cannot possibly occur, except in such a state of public feeling in regard to the Union, as would at all events, dissolve it by other means. If the States no longer wish to remain in Union, they will of course separate. But if they are really desirous to *preserve* the Union, *their own interest* affords a sufficient pledge that they will not endanger it, by throwing themselves upon their reserved rights, except in extreme cases, which require it. If one State or two States, should be mad enough to do so, it cannot be imagined that such a number of them will do so as to afford any ground for the President's fears, or any application for the argument which he derives from them. The Government of the United States, is the mere agent of the States, for specified purposes, and it is inconceivable that the States who appointed that agent for their own use and advantage, would without cause, so embarrass its action, as to render its agency of no value. In practice therefore, this argument of the President is not entitled to any consideration. And even if it were otherwise, is it more consistent with principle, that the agent should control the constituent, or that the constituent should control the agent? These views of the subject, however, are worth nothing. We cannot judge for the practical operation of the Government, by any such extreme case. Human sagacity cannot foresee, nor human prudence provide for all possible contingencies; nor can human language define and limit every possible modification of social rights. Although Governments are primarily founded in distrust, yet there is, of necessity, some degree of confidence in all of them. The wisest statesmen can do no more than repose that confidence in the safest hands, while at the same time, he surrounds it with all practicable guards against abuse. If the States may abuse their reserved rights in the manner contemplated by the President, the Federal Government, on the other hand, may abuse its *delegated* rights. There is danger from *both* sides, and as we are compelled to confide in the one or the other, we have only to inquire, which is most worthy of our confidence. In the first place, as I have already remarked, the States cannot have *any interest* to abuse their reserved rights. Besides, the right for which they contend, is not a *right of action* at all, but merely a right to *check unauthorised action*, in the other party. The *abuse* of this right, can be found in nothing but in the interposition of the State to check its own agent, in doing what it expressly authorised its own agent to do, for its own advantage. The right itself is indispensable to self-preservation, while the abuse of it is not to be contemplated as sufficiently probable, to found any argument against the right itself. On the other hand, the Federal government has a direct interest to enlarge its own powers, by encroaching on the rights of the States. The constituent can rarely, if ever, have an interest in contracting the powers of his agent, but *prima facie*, the agent always has an interest in making them greater. And when we reflect on the strong love which most men feel, for patronage and power, the influence of this interest upon the *mere men* who wield the Federal Government, (and who as to this argument, must be identified with it) affords much cause for distrust and fear. It is therefore much more probable that the Federal Government will abuse its power, than that the States will abuse theirs. And if we suppose a case of *actual* abuse on either hand, it will not be difficult to decide which is the greater evil. If a State should abuse its rights of interposition by arresting the operation of a *constitutional* law, the worst that could come of it, would be to suspend the operation of the law for a time, as to that State, while it would have all its effects within the other States. This would certainly be unjust, but in most cases, would be attended with very little practical evil. In some cases, it is true, the consequences might be serious, such, for instance, as might arise in a time of war; but it is precisely in such cases that the State would have the *least motive* for coming into collision with her sister States. Besides, according to the doctrine for which I am contending, this evil would be temporary only; it must cease in some way or other, as soon as the other States act upon the subject. I acknowledge however, that it is at best an evil, but it is an evil inseparable from our system, and one which cannot be avoided except by submitting to a *greater* evil. It is perfectly evident that this right must exist in the States unless it be incompatible with the rights of the Federal Government. Supposing this incompatibility to exist, there must be a right in that Government to control the States in this respect, and to enforce a law which the States may have pronounced to be unconstitutional. Let us now suppose an *abuse* of this right. It would consist in an attempt by the Federal Government, to coerce obedience to an *unconstitutional* law.—This, sir, it seems to me, is *despotism in its very essence*. If the Federal Government may enforce *one* unconstitutional law, it may enforce *every* unconstitutional law, and thus all the rights of the States and the people may fall one by one, before the omnipotence of that Government. This consequence is too manifest to escape even the most superficial observation. The worst possible result of nullification, even in the opinion of its bitterest opponents, is to dissolve the Union—and this result does not legitimately flow from it; while the alternative which they propose, establishes an absolute despotism, which not only *dissolves the Union, but establishes the worst possible form of Government upon its ruins*. Thus it appears that nullification is much *less apt to* be abused, than the alternative remedy, and *when abused*, its consequences are infinitely less to be deprecated. Of the two evils, I choose the least. I prefer the remedy, which although in its extreme abuse, it may lead to disunion, may be peaceful in its results, to one which *necessarily dissolves the Union, and whose direct object* and tendency are to *violence and blood, and absolute power.*

And now Sir, you have a full view of nullification as I understand it. As I sincerely desire to be right in politics, as well as in morals and religion, I submit myself with all deference, to the correction of your great wisdom....

X.

Judges Are Human Beings, Not Gods

A Review of the Proclamation of President Jackson
Littleton Waller Tazewell
1833

Littleton Waller Tazewell (pronounced TAZ-well, 1774–1860) served in the U.S. House of Representatives and the United States Senate, and as the 26th governor of Virginia. His father, Henry Tazewell, had been a U.S. senator in the 1790s and served as a captain during the Revolutionary War.

Appalled at the arguments advanced in Andrew Jackson's Proclamation Regarding Nullification of December 10, 1832, a document he considered absurd in its logic and dangerous in its political tendency, Tazewell composed a systematic reply that took the form of articles in Virginia's Norfolk and Portsmouth Herald. *What follows is the twelfth chapter of these collected essays, as they later appeared in* A Review of the Proclamation of President Jackson *(Norfolk, VA: J.D. Ghiselin, 1888).*

In this essay, Tazewell considers the claim that the judicial branch is the appropriate arbiter of disputes over power that may arise between the federal government and the states. This may be the most challenging of the selections for many readers, but it repays careful study. Tazewell offers numerous arguments to demonstrate that the judicial branch of its very nature cannot perform this function. Even if it could, it cannot be seriously thought of as an impartial arbiter between the federal government and the states when it is itself a branch of the federal government, one of the contending parties.

This objection is, that no State may rightfully assume as a fact, that the Covenant has been broken by any of its co-States, or act upon such an assumption, without violating its own faith: because the covenant itself has provided an arbiter to decide all such questions, by whose decisions the faith of all the parties must be bound. This arbiter is said to be the Supreme Court of the United States. To this objection, which is founded upon the supposed existence of a common arbiter, authorized and capable to decide all infractions of the Constitution, of which any State may have cause to complain, many answers may be given, all equally conclusive to shew, that no such arbiter, clothed with such authority, either does, or ought to be expected to exist.

The first of these answers is, that according to no legal possibility, could the case supposed to exist, ever be presented to the Supreme Court for its decision, even if the sovereign parties were content to abide by that decision.—The Judges of the Supreme Court, like all other Judges, are appointed to decide "cases," and not to amuse themselves or to edify mankind (as the President seeks to do in this Proclamation), with *obiter dicta*, or with public Lectures, communicating the results of their lucubrations upon mere questions of law, of politics, or of any other art or Science. These cases, too, according to the very terms of the Constitution, must be "cases in law and equity," and we have the authority of this court itself, for saying that there cannot exist any case in law or equity, but one presented to a Court by the representations of parties. The law professor in every College, nay, the very undergraduates of his Class, may deliver theses and dissertations upon questions of Sovereignty, of Politics, or of law, and may amuse and improve themselves by imagining suits brought by John Doe versus Richard Roe, to try these questions. But it would be a high contempt of every court, to attempt to steal from it an opinion, upon any question presented in a case brought by such imaginary parties; and not a less contempt of public justice, if a judge should wander out of the case before him, to prejudge some other, or to determine any mere abstract proposition not necessary to the decision of the matter submitted by the parties to his determination.—Now, the case supposed to exist, is the case of a Covenant of Union, believed by one of the parties to be violated by the government of the United States, the agent of all the parties. In such a case, the act complained of being already done by the government, the United States would have no need to become actors, or to go before any court to assert the power that has been already exerted; and it would be difficult to find the authority under which any one, as an actor, may implead the United States in their own courts.

But here it may be said, perhaps, as is often said, that the government of the United States can only act by Individuals, and upon Individuals; and as the courts are always open to such parties, all questions of constitutional right may so readily be brought before the Supreme Court. To this commonplace assertion, I oppose a flat denial. The evil complained of, may not be the consequence of any act whatever, but of a wilful omission to act, on the part of the government. In such a case, it cannot be pretended, that there is any individual, to whom the aggrieved sufferer may resort for redress, by a suit in court—or the evil complained of, may be an act, which, although palpably wrong, may not require the agency of any individual; or although wantonly oppressive and cruelly unjust upon all the inhabitants of a State, may nevertheless, like every common nuisance, be injurious to no one of them in particular, and therefore would be an act not to be redressed in any private suit. Suppose for example, Congress should pass a law giving a preference to the ports of one State over those of another, which they are expressly forbidden to do in the very terms of the Constitution itself; what Individual could sue, or what Individual might he implead, for the perpetration of an act so ruinous to the injured State?

Even in cases where the Courts might take cognizance of the act done, because done by some Individual to some other Individual, the judgement in such a case could bind none but the parties to the suit. It would not repeal the unconstitutional act; and might not even furnish any compensation to the Individual injured.—Some agent of the law-makers in execution of their orders, which are in direct violation of the Constitution, does me a great injury. I sue him. The court agrees with me, that the act was lawless and unauthorized.

The jury awards an amount of damages to me as a just compensation for the wrong I have sustained. The Court gives me a judgement against him for that sum. But the agent is insolvent or runs away, and I cannot get the intended compensation. Will any one say, that the Court can compel those by whose orders the wicked deed was done, and to test whose authority for directing it to be done, the suit was brought, to pay me? Certainly not. I may petition them to do so, but if they reject my petition, the arm of the Judiciary is impotent to obtain for me the relief to which the Court itself has said I was entitled—even if the judgement proves efficacious in my case, that judgement cannot prevent the perpetration of a similar outrage upon me or my neighbour the next day, under the same usurped authority.

The judgement does not repeal the law, but declares simply, that it constitutes no defence to the defendant in the particular case brought before the Court by the parties then litigant therein. So that until the Legislature will be graciously pleased to repeal their law, every Individual of the State, may be compelled to go through the same tedious and expensive proceedings, and to incur the same hazards, in order to obtain relief against an act of the government which has been already decided by the supposed arbiter to be an unauthorized usurpation of lawless power. Now what a strange arbiter must he be, whose decision, if in favor of one of the parties, is binding and obligatory, but if made against that party, is of no avail to terminate the subject of difference.

The next answer to this objection is this: where a case in law or equity is properly brought before the Court, by actual suitors, if in the progress of this suit, it is found to involve a question of the mere discreet exercise of political power confessedly granted, the Judges themselves acknowledge, that this question they are incompetent to decide, but as to all such matter, they are bound *jurare per verba maistri;* and, to say, as Judges, that whatever is, is right, although as Individuals, every one of them may know it is not so. While doubt exists, whether the political power exercised is granted or not, the Court may give an opinion upon the subject. But let it be once conceded, that the power has been granted by the Constitution and the Court is then compelled to say, that it has nothing to do with the question of policy, nor is authorized to ask, why such power has been exerted.

If Congress declare a war, although for the most unrighteous purpose for which war ever was declared by the veriest tyrant that ever disgraced a throne, the Judiciary must apply the sanctions of the law, to all acts done contrary to the wicked will of the Legislature.

If the President and Senate make Treaties, sapping the very foundations of the Constitution, the Judiciary cannot declare them void, or prevent their execution by the executive. If Congress wantonly levy duties and imposts for any purpose whatever, the Judicial power is helpless to afford relief.

They cannot injoin the marching of armies, the sailing of fleets, the slaughter of innocent men, the levy of taxes, or the execution of Treaties.

Yet it is precisely in such cases, that the interposition of the Sovereign parties to the Covenant, will, probably, ever be necessary.

It is idle, then, to say, that they may not interpose even in these cases, at least for the reason given. For the very foundation of the objection to such interposition, is, that as there is a common arbiter appointed to decide the case, the parties may not rightfully assume to decide it, each for itself.

The next answer to this objection is, that the evil complained of may be the act of the Judiciary itself, the enforcement of the Sedition law for example, or the application of the common law of England, as a criminal code, to the Citizens of the United

States. Both these cases have occurred. Here, it would be monstrous, to refer to the Judiciary to decide whether the Judiciary itself had done right; and yet the objection applies equally to all cases.

Another answer is, that in this government, composed as it is of co-ordinate departments, there exists no reason why more respect should be paid to the acts of one of these departments, than to those of any other; and if it is admitted, that neither of these departments is bound by the act of its co-ordinate, it would be strange indeed to say, that the sovereign of all was bound by such an act. Now, the objection itself asserts, that the Judiciary is not bound by the acts of the Legislature or of the Executive; and no one, it is believed, will contend that either of the other departments is bound by the Judgements of the Judiciary, however obligatory these may be upon the parties.

I speak not of courtesy and respect, but of obligation merely. Should the Judiciary declare an act of the Legislature void, such a declaration, as I have already said, cannot repeal the law, although it may prevent its application to the particular case sub Judice. Congress may establish other Courts or other Judges to execute the law; or the President and Senate, in execution of such laws, may appoint additional Judges of the Supreme Court, who may differ from their associates and over-rule the past decision in the first new case, that comes before the Court. Nay the House of Representatives may impeach and the Senate condemn the Judges, for this very decision given in violation of the law enacted by them.

I do not mean to say, that any of these things would be right: but when reasoning upon the case of a violated Constitution, I have a right to suppose, that all legal means would be employed by the violators, to make their violation effectual; and so to prove, that the Judiciary cannot bind the Legislature.—We have the authority of the President himself for saying, that he feels himself as much bound by his oath to support the Constitution as any one else can do; and therefore, if his agency is required, whether by the Legislature or the Judiciary, to do any act which he believes unconstitutional, he will not be made to sin against his own conscience and to violate his oath. His new partisans used to censure him bitterly for this assertion: but yet he never made one more moral, legal, or constitutional than it is. This is a government of concurring powers, its departments are all co-ordinates, nor can any one of them move far in any direction, without encountering its fellow, by whose concurrence alone, it may proceed in that way.

Of all these departments, the Judiciary is the weakest, because, it cannot act until invited to do so, its sphere of action is very limited, nor can it do any positive act, without the permission of the Legislature, and the co-operation of the Executive.

But lastly, can the human mind conceive a more audacious proposition, than that which suggests, that in a controversy between the parties to a Covenant, by which covenant an agent is created, where the matter in dispute between the principals, regards the authority exerted by the agent, the decision of this controversy must be referred to the agent himself? The very exertion of the authority by the agent, is a decision that he believes he may rightfully do so; and after this, it is gravely proposed, to leave the matter to the final arbitrament of one who has already decided it, and who has decided it, too, with the approbation of the very persons who proposed such a reference.

In transactions between man and man, none could hesitate what name to bestow upon such a proposition: but where the Sovereignty of the States and the freedom of their people is concerned, a gross fraud is metamorphosed into a political theory only. Nor will the case be changed materially if the nominated arbiter has never yet decided the question, provided that arbiter be the Supreme Court; this arbiter is not even given by lot. It is appointed by the supposed wrong doer, paid by him, accountable to him, subject at any moment to be punished and cashiered by him, and this too, for giving the very decision its conscience might prompt. Thus, matters which would constitute valid and legal objections, to witnesses, to Jurors, and to the Judges themselves, in the most trifling controversy between man and man, are to be overlooked and disregarded, in the support of a new theory, which seeks to constitute the Federal government the sole Judge of its own power.

I have great respect for the Judiciary of every country, but no lawyer or historian can tell, in what age or in what country, the Judiciary have ever been able, even where it was willing, to protect the rights of the people against the usurpations of Government. England has long been blessed with a Judiciary, composed of men, whose intelligence, whose integrity, and whose firmness, would not suffer in comparison with that of any others who have ever been or are now on earth. But when or who of these Judges have ever been able to save the privileges of the people from the prerogatives of the crown, unless the Judiciary was sustained by another branch of the government? And how many examples are there, of acts of Parliament made for the special purpose of saving the people from the Judiciary? For the Judiciary of the United States, I entertain at least as much respect as I do for any other Judiciary. I will not say more; and I cannot say less. With the individual Judges, I have nothing to do. They shall all be, if any one thinks so, what some of them certainly are, "like Mansfield wise, and as old Foster just." But all must know that the robes of office do not cover angels, but mere men, as prone to err, as any other men of equal intelligence, of equal purity, and of equal constancy. We all know, too, that some of the supreme Judges of the United States, have not thought it unbecoming their high places, to accept Foreign Missions, to present themselves as candidates for other offices, and to enter into newspaper disquisitions upon party topics. I do not mean to blame them for such things, but merely to shew from such facts, that the rights of sovereign States, when assailed by the government of the United States, could not be safely confided to a forum so constituted, even if it was possible that it could take cognizance of the subject. Nor can he be considered as a discreet friend to the Judiciary I should think, who desired to embark it in this fearful strife.

I have answered this first objection, founded upon the suggestion, that the Supreme Court of the United States is the common arbiter appointed to decide all questions that may arise between a State and its co-States, touching the violation of their mutual covenant. My answer to the remaining objections I must postpone to another number.

XI.

Nullification vs. Slavery

Joint Resolution of the Legislature of Wisconsin
March 19, 1859

Chapter 3 of this book described the matter of Sherman Booth, the Wisconsin abolitionist whose agitation in behalf of the alleged fugitive slave Joshua Glover found him several times brought up on charges by federal authorities. What follows are the resolutions passed by the state legislature, some six decades after the publication of the Virginia and Kentucky Resolutions, regarding this affair. The last two paragraphs are drawn very substantially from the Kentucky Resolutions of 1798 and 1799.

Whereas, the Supreme Court of the United States has assumed appellate jurisdiction in the matter of the petition of Sherman M. Booth for a writ of habeas corpus, presented and prosecuted to final judgment in the supreme court of this state, and has, without process, or any of the forms recognized by law, assumed the power to reverse that judgment, in a matter involving the personal liberty of the citizen, asserted by and adjusted to him by the regular course of judicial proceedings upon the great writ of liberty secured to the people of each state by the constitution of the United States:

And whereas, such assumption of power and authority by the supreme court of the United States, to become the final arbiter of the liberty of the citizen, and to override and nullify the judgments of the state courts' declaration thereof, is in direct conflict with that provision of the constitution of the United States which secures to the people the benefits of the writ of habeas corpus:

Therefore,

Resolved, the Senate concurring, That we regard the action of the supreme court of the United States, in assuming jurisdiction in the case before mentioned, as an arbitrary act of power, unauthorized by the constitution, and virtually superseding the benefit of the writ of habeas corpus, and prostrating the rights and liberties of the people at the foot of unlimited power.

Resolved, That this assumption of jurisdiction by the federal judiciary, in the said case, and without process, is an act of undelegated power, and therefore without authority, void, and of no force.

Resolved, That the government formed by the Constitution of the United States was not the exclusive or final judge of the extent of the powers delegated to itself; but that, as in all other cases of compact among parties having no common judge, each party has an equal right to judge for itself, as well of infractions as of the mode and measure of redress.

Resolved, that the principle and construction contended for by the party which now rules in the councils of the nation, that the general government is the exclusive judge of the extent of the powers delegated to it, stop nothing short of despotism, since the *discretion* of those who administer the government, and not the *Constitution*, would be the measure of their powers; that the several States which formed that instrument, being sovereign and independent, have the unquestionable right to judge of its infractions; and that a *positive defiance* of those sovereignties, of all unauthorized acts done or attempted to be done under color of that instrument, is the rightful remedy.

Acknowledgments

ONE NICE THING ABOUT TRAVELING AND SPEAKING SO MUCH is that I have managed to make friends with experts on just about everything. For discussing some of the issues in this book with me, I am grateful to Michael Boldin, Donald Livingston, Jon Roland, Phillip Magness, Clyde Wilson, Brion McClanahan, Kevin Gutzman, and Stephan Kinsella. For helping me out with various clerical tasks, I wish to thank Eric William Smith, Jennifer Lewis, Brian Ramsdell, and Allison Harnack. Thanks also to Laurence Vance for allowing me the use of a portion of the foreword I wrote to Vance Publications' edition of Abel Upshur's *Brief Enquiry into the True Nature and Character of Our Federal Government*, and to *Taki's Magazine* for the use of a portion of my article "Is There Sovereignty Beyond the State?" Stephen Carson graciously performed critical copyediting services. My editor, Anneke Green, provided invaluable assistance; her suggestions regarding the organization of the argument made this a much better book. And thanks to Regnery Publishing for its usual efficiency, for bringing this book out so quickly, and for not needing to be badgered into appreciating the significance of the topic. As always, I am grateful to the Ludwig von Mises Institute for its support of my work.

Thanks to my wife, as usual, for her unflagging support. I wasn't as frantic as usual this time, I'm happy to say, even though this was a very time-sensitive project. Once again my mother helped out with babysitting services that yielded me several crucial and productive Saturdays. And thanks to our four daughters, to whom this book is dedicated. In all my projects, the one non-negotiable block of time in which I do not work extends from the end of my working day until the moment they go to bed. They always put a smile on my face, and every day I want to return the favor.

APPENDIX

The Constitution of the United States

We the People of the United States, in Order to form a more perfect Union, establish Justice, insure domestic Tranquility, provide for the common defence, promote the general Welfare, and secure the Blessings of Liberty to ourselves and our Posterity, do ordain and establish this Constitution for the United States of America.

ARTICLE I

Section 1

All legislative Powers herein granted shall be vested in a Congress of the United States, which shall consist of a Senate and House of Representatives.

Section 2

The House of Representatives shall be composed of Members chosen every second Year by the People of the several States, and the Electors in each State shall have the Qualifications requisite for Electors of the most numerous Branch of the State Legislature.

No Person shall be a Representative who shall not have attained to the Age of twenty five Years, and been seven Years a Citizen of the United States, and who shall not, when elected, be an Inhabitant of that State in which he shall be chosen.

Representatives and direct Taxes shall be apportioned among the several States which may be included within this Union, according to their respective Numbers, which shall be determined by adding to the whole Number of free Persons, including those bound to Service for a Term of Years, and excluding Indians not taxed, three fifths of all other Persons. The actual Enumeration shall be made within three Years after the first Meeting of the Congress of the United States, and within every subsequent Term of ten Years, in such Manner as they shall by Law direct. The Number of Representatives shall not exceed one for every thirty Thousand, but each State shall have at Least one Representative; and until such enumeration shall be made, the State of New Hampshire shall be entitled to chuse three, Massachusetts eight, Rhode-Island and Providence Plantations one, Connecticut five, New-York six, New Jersey four, Pennsylvania eight, Delaware one, Maryland six, Virginia ten, North Carolina five, South Carolina five, and Georgia three.

When vacancies happen in the Representation from any State, the Executive Authority thereof shall issue Writs of Election to fill such Vacancies.

The House of Representatives shall chuse their Speaker and other Officers; and shall have the sole Power of Impeachment.

Section 3

The Senate of the United States shall be composed of two Senators from each State, chosen by the Legislature thereof for six Years; and each Senator shall have one Vote.

Immediately after they shall be assembled in Consequence of the first Election, they shall be divided as equally as may be into three Classes. The Seats of the Senators of the first Class shall be vacated at the Expiration of the second Year, of the second Class at the Expiration of the fourth Year, and of the third Class at the Expiration of the sixth Year, so that one third may be chosen every second Year; and if Vacancies happen by Resignation, or otherwise, during the Recess of the Legislature of any State, the Executive thereof may make temporary Appointments until the next Meeting of the Legislature, which shall then fill such Vacancies.

No Person shall be a Senator who shall not have attained to the Age of thirty Years, and been nine Years a Citizen of the United States, and who shall not, when elected, be an Inhabitant of that State for which he shall be chosen.

The Vice President of the United States shall be President of the Senate, but shall have no Vote, unless they be equally divided.

The Senate shall chuse their other Officers, and also a President pro tempore, in the Absence of the Vice President, or when he shall exercise the Office of President of the United States.

The Senate shall have the sole Power to try all Impeachments. When sitting for that Purpose, they shall be on Oath or Affirmation. When the President of the United States is tried, the Chief Justice shall preside: And no Person shall be convicted without the Concurrence of two thirds of the Members present.

Judgment in Cases of Impeachment shall not extend further than to removal from Office, and disqualification to hold and enjoy any Office of honor, Trust or Profit under the United States: but the Party convicted shall nevertheless be liable and subject to Indictment, Trial, Judgment and Punishment, according to Law.

Section 4

The Times, Places and Manner of holding Elections for Senators and Representatives, shall be prescribed in each State by the Legislature thereof; but the Congress may at any time by Law make or alter such Regulations, except as to the Places of chusing Senators.

The Congress shall assemble at least once in every Year, and such Meeting shall be on the first Monday in December, unless they shall by Law appoint a different Day.

Section 5

Each House shall be the Judge of the Elections, Returns and Qualifications of its own Members, and a Majority of each shall constitute a Quorum to do Business; but a smaller Number may adjourn from day to day, and may be authorized to compel the Attendance of absent Members, in such Manner, and under such Penalties as each House may provide.

Each House may determine the Rules of its Proceedings, punish its Members for disorderly Behaviour, and, with the Concurrence of two thirds, expel a Member.

Each House shall keep a Journal of its Proceedings, and from time to time publish the same, excepting such Parts as may in their Judgment require Secrecy; and the Yeas and Nays of the Members of either House on any question shall, at the Desire of one fifth of those Present, be entered on the Journal.

Neither House, during the Session of Congress, shall, without the Consent of the other, adjourn for more than three days, nor to any other Place than that in which the two Houses shall be sitting.

Section 6

The Senators and Representatives shall receive a Compensation for their Services, to be ascertained by Law, and paid out of the Treasury of the United States. They shall in all Cases, except Treason, Felony and Breach of the Peace, be privileged from Arrest during their Attendance at the Session of their respective Houses, and in going to and returning from the same; and for any Speech or Debate in either House, they shall not be questioned in any other Place.

No Senator or Representative shall, during the Time for which he was elected, be appointed to any civil Office under the Authority of the United States, which shall have been created, or the Emoluments whereof shall have been encreased during such time; and no Person holding any Office under the United States, shall be a Member of either House during his Continuance in Office.

Section 7

All Bills for raising Revenue shall originate in the House of Representatives; but the Senate may propose or concur with Amendments as on other Bills.

Every Bill which shall have passed the House of Representatives and the Senate, shall, before it become a Law, be presented to the President of the United States: If he approve he shall sign it, but if not he shall return it, with his Objections to that House in which it shall have originated, who shall enter the Objections at large on their Journal, and proceed to reconsider it. If after such Reconsideration two thirds of that House shall agree to pass the Bill, it shall be sent, together with the Objections, to the other House, by which it shall likewise be reconsidered, and if approved by two thirds of that House, it shall become a Law. But in all such Cases the Votes of both Houses shall be determined by yeas and Nays, and the Names of the Persons voting for and against the Bill shall be entered on the Journal of each House respectively. If any Bill shall not be returned by the President within ten Days (Sundays excepted) after it shall have been presented to him, the Same shall be a Law, in like Manner as if he had signed it, unless the Congress by their Adjournment prevent its Return, in which Case it shall not be a Law.

Every Order, Resolution, or Vote to which the Concurrence of the Senate and House of Representatives may be necessary (except on a question of Adjournment) shall be presented to the President of the United States; and before the Same shall take Effect, shall be approved by him, or being disapproved by him, shall be repassed by two thirds of the Senate and House of Representatives, according to the Rules and Limitations prescribed in the Case of a Bill.

Section 8

The Congress shall have Power To lay and collect Taxes, Duties, Imposts and Excises, to pay the Debts and provide for the common Defence and general Welfare of the United States; but all Duties, Imposts and Excises shall be uniform throughout the United States;

To borrow Money on the credit of the United States;

To regulate Commerce with foreign Nations, and among the several States, and with the Indian Tribes;

To establish an uniform Rule of Naturalization, and uniform Laws on the subject of Bankruptcies throughout the United States;

To coin Money, regulate the Value thereof, and of foreign Coin, and fix the Standard of Weights and Measures;

To provide for the Punishment of counterfeiting the Securities and current Coin of the United States;

To establish Post Offices and Post Roads;

To promote the Progress of Science and useful Arts, by securing for limited Times to Authors and Inventors the exclusive Right to their respective Writings and Discoveries;

To constitute Tribunals inferior to the supreme Court;

To define and punish Piracies and Felonies committed on the high Seas, and Offences against the Law of Nations;

To declare War, grant Letters of Marque and Reprisal, and make Rules concerning Captures on Land and Water;

To raise and support Armies, but no Appropriation of Money to that Use shall be for a longer Term than two Years;

To provide and maintain a Navy;

To make Rules for the Government and Regulation of the land and naval Forces;

To provide for calling forth the Militia to execute the Laws of the Union, suppress Insurrections and repel Invasions;

To provide for organizing, arming, and disciplining, the Militia, and for governing such Part of them as may be employed in the Service of the United States, reserving to the States respectively, the Appointment of the Officers, and the Authority of training the Militia according to the discipline prescribed by Congress;

To exercise exclusive Legislation in all Cases whatsoever, over such District (not exceeding ten Miles square) as may, by Cession of particular States, and the Acceptance of Congress, become the Seat of the Government of the United States, and to exercise like Authority over all Places purchased by the Consent of the Legislature of the State in which the Same shall be, for the Erection of Forts, Magazines, Arsenals, dock-Yards, and other needful Buildings;—And

To make all Laws which shall be necessary and proper for carrying into Execution the foregoing Powers, and all other Powers vested by this Constitution in the Government of the United States, or in any Department or Officer thereof.

Section 9

The Migration or Importation of such Persons as any of the States now existing shall think proper to admit, shall not be prohibited by the Congress prior to the Year one thousand eight hundred and eight, but a Tax or duty may be imposed on such Importation, not exceeding ten dollars for each Person.

The Privilege of the Writ of Habeas Corpus shall not be suspended, unless when in Cases of Rebellion or Invasion the public Safety may require it.

No Bill of Attainder or ex post facto Law shall be passed.

No Capitation, or other direct, Tax shall be laid, unless in Proportion to the Census or enumeration herein before directed to be taken.

No Tax or Duty shall be laid on Articles exported from any State.

No Preference shall be given by any Regulation of Commerce or Revenue to the Ports of one State over those of another; nor shall Vessels bound to, or from, one State, be obliged to enter, clear, or pay Duties in another.

No Money shall be drawn from the Treasury, but in Consequence of Appropriations made by Law; and a regular Statement and Account of the Receipts and Expenditures of all public Money shall be published from time to time.

No Title of Nobility shall be granted by the United States: And no Person holding any Office of Profit or Trust under them, shall, without the Consent of the Congress, accept of any present, Emolument, Office, or Title, of any kind whatever, from any King, Prince, or foreign State.

Section 10

No State shall enter into any Treaty, Alliance, or Confederation; grant Letters of Marque and Reprisal; coin Money; emit Bills of Credit; make any Thing but gold and silver Coin a Tender in Payment of Debts; pass any Bill of Attainder, ex post facto Law, or Law impairing the Obligation of Contracts, or grant any Title of Nobility.

No State shall, without the Consent of the Congress, lay any Imposts or Duties on Imports or Exports, except what may be absolutely necessary for executing it's inspection Laws: and the net Produce of all Duties and Imposts, laid by any State on Imports or Exports, shall be for the Use of the Treasury of the United States; and all such Laws shall be subject to the Revision and Controul of the Congress.

No State shall, without the Consent of Congress, lay any Duty of Tonnage, keep Troops, or Ships of War in time of Peace, enter into any Agreement or Compact with another State, or with a foreign Power, or engage in War, unless actually invaded, or in such imminent Danger as will not admit of delay.

ARTICLE II

Section 1

The executive Power shall be vested in a President of the United States of America. He shall hold his Office during the Term of four Years, and, together with the Vice President, chosen for the same Term, be elected, as follows:

Each State shall appoint, in such Manner as the Legislature thereof may direct, a Number of Electors, equal to the whole Number of Senators and Representatives to which the State may be entitled in the Congress: but no Senator or Representative, or Person holding an Office of Trust or Profit under the United States, shall be appointed an Elector.

The Electors shall meet in their respective States, and vote by Ballot for two Persons, of whom one at least shall not be an Inhabitant of the same State with themselves. And they shall make a List of all the Persons voted for, and of the Number of Votes for each; which List they shall sign and certify, and transmit sealed to the Seat of the Government of the United States, directed to the President of the Senate. The President of the Senate shall, in the Presence of the Senate and House of Representatives, open all the Certificates, and the Votes shall then be counted. The Person having the greatest Number of Votes shall be the President, if such Number be a Majority of the whole Number of Electors appointed; and if there be more than one who have such Majority, and have an equal Number of Votes, then the House of Representatives shall immediately chuse by Ballot one of them for President; and if no Person have a Majority, then from the five highest on the List the said House shall in like Manner chuse the President. But in chusing the President, the Votes shall be taken by States, the Representation from each State having one Vote; A quorum for this purpose shall consist of a Member or Members from two thirds of the States, and a Majority of all the States shall be necessary to a Choice. In every Case, after the Choice of the President, the Person having the greatest Number of Votes of the Electors shall be the Vice President. But if there should remain two or more who have equal Votes, the Senate shall chuse from them by Ballot the Vice President.

The Congress may determine the Time of chusing the Electors, and the Day on which they shall give their Votes; which Day shall be the same throughout the United States.

No Person except a natural born Citizen, or a Citizen of the United States, at the time of the Adoption of this Constitution, shall be eligible to the Office of President; neither shall any Person be eligible to that Office who shall not have attained to the Age of thirty five Years, and been fourteen Years a Resident within the United States.

In Case of the Removal of the President from Office, or of his Death, Resignation, or Inability to discharge the Powers and Duties of the said Office, the Same shall devolve on the Vice President, and the Congress may by Law provide for the Case of Removal, Death, Resignation or Inability, both of the President and Vice President, declaring what Officer shall then act as President, and such Officer shall act accordingly, until the Disability be removed, or a President shall be elected.

The President shall, at stated Times, receive for his Services, a Compensation, which shall neither be increased nor diminished during the Period for which he shall have been elected, and he shall not receive within that Period any other Emolument from the United States, or any of them.

Before he enter on the Execution of his Office, he shall take the following Oath or Affirmation:—"I do solemnly swear (or affirm) that I will faithfully execute the Office of President of the United States, and will to the best of my Ability, preserve, protect and defend the Constitution of the United States."

Section 2

The President shall be Commander in Chief of the Army and Navy of the United States, and of the Militia of the several States, when called into the actual Service of the United States; he may require the Opinion, in writing, of the principal Officer in each of the executive Departments, upon any Subject relating to the Duties of their respective Offices, and he shall have Power to grant Reprieves and Pardons for Offences against the United States, except in Cases of Impeachment.

He shall have Power, by and with the Advice and Consent of the Senate, to make Treaties, provided two thirds of the Senators present concur; and he shall nominate, and by and with the Advice and Consent of the Senate, shall appoint Ambassadors, other public Ministers and Consuls, Judges of the supreme Court, and all other Officers of the United States, whose Appointments are not herein otherwise provided for, and which shall be established by Law: but the Congress may by Law vest the Appointment of such inferior Officers, as they think proper, in the President alone, in the Courts of Law, or in the Heads of Departments.

The President shall have Power to fill up all Vacancies that may happen during the Recess of the Senate, by granting Commissions which shall expire at the End of their next Session.

Section 3

He shall from time to time give to the Congress Information of the State of the Union, and recommend to their Consideration such Measures as he shall judge necessary and expedient; he may, on extraordinary Occasions, convene both Houses, or either of them, and in Case of Disagreement between them, with Respect to the Time of Adjournment, he may adjourn them to such Time as he shall think proper; he shall receive Ambassadors and other public Ministers; he shall take Care that the Laws be faithfully executed, and shall Commission all the Officers of the United States.

Section 4

The President, Vice President and all civil Officers of the United States, shall be removed from Office on Impeachment for, and Conviction of, Treason, Bribery, or other high Crimes and Misdemeanors.

Article III

Section 1

The judicial Power of the United States shall be vested in one supreme Court, and in such inferior Courts as the Congress may from time to time ordain and establish. The Judges, both of the supreme and inferior Courts, shall hold their Offices during good Behaviour, and shall, at stated Times, receive for their Services a Compensation, which shall not be diminished during their Continuance in Office.

Section 2

The judicial Power shall extend to all Cases, in Law and Equity, arising under this Constitution, the Laws of the United States, and Treaties made, or which shall be made, under their Authority;—to all Cases affecting Ambassadors, other public Ministers and Consuls;—to all Cases of admiralty and maritime Jurisdiction;—to Controversies to which the United States shall be a Party;—

to Controversies between two or more States;—between a State and Citizens of another State;—between Citizens of different States;—between Citizens of the same State claiming Lands under Grants of different States, and between a State, or the Citizens thereof, and foreign States, Citizens or Subjects.

In all Cases affecting Ambassadors, other public Ministers and Consuls, and those in which a State shall be Party, the supreme Court shall have original Jurisdiction. In all the other Cases before mentioned, the supreme Court shall have appellate Jurisdiction, both as to Law and Fact, with such Exceptions, and under such Regulations as the Congress shall make.

The Trial of all Crimes, except in Cases of Impeachment, shall be by Jury; and such Trial shall be held in the State where the said Crimes shall have been committed; but when not committed within any State, the Trial shall be at such Place or Places as the Congress may by Law have directed.

Section 3

Treason against the United States, shall consist only in levying War against them, or in adhering to their Enemies, giving them Aid and Comfort. No Person shall be convicted of Treason unless on the Testimony of two Witnesses to the same overt Act, or on Confession in open Court.

The Congress shall have Power to declare the Punishment of Treason, but no Attainder of Treason shall work Corruption of Blood, or Forfeiture except during the Life of the Person attainted.

ARTICLE IV

Section 1

Full Faith and Credit shall be given in each State to the public Acts, Records, and judicial Proceedings of every other State. And the Congress may by general Laws prescribe the Manner in which such Acts, Records and Proceedings shall be proved, and the Effect thereof.

Section 2

The Citizens of each State shall be entitled to all Privileges and Immunities of Citizens in the several States.

A Person charged in any State with Treason, Felony, or other Crime, who shall flee from Justice, and be found in another State, shall on Demand of the executive Authority of the State from which he fled, be delivered up, to be removed to the State having Jurisdiction of the Crime.

No Person held to Service or Labour in one State, under the Laws thereof, escaping into another, shall, in Consequence of any Law or Regulation therein, be discharged from such Service or Labour, but shall be delivered up on Claim of the Party to whom such Service or Labour may be due.

Section 3

New States may be admitted by the Congress into this Union; but no new State shall be formed or erected within the Jurisdiction of any other State; nor any State be formed by the Junction of two or more States, or Parts of States, without the Consent of the Legislatures of the States concerned as well as of the Congress.

The Congress shall have Power to dispose of and make all needful Rules and Regulations respecting the Territory or other Property belonging to the United States; and nothing in this Constitution shall be so construed as to Prejudice any Claims of the United States, or of any particular State.

Section 4

The United States shall guarantee to every State in this Union a Republican Form of Government, and shall protect each of them against Invasion; and on Application of the Legislature, or of the Executive (when the Legislature cannot be convened), against domestic Violence.

ARTICLE V

The Congress, whenever two thirds of both Houses shall deem it necessary, shall propose Amendments to this Constitution, or, on the Application of the Legislatures of two thirds of the several States, shall call a Convention for proposing Amendments, which, in either Case, shall be valid to all Intents and Purposes, as Part of this Constitution, when ratified by the Legislatures of three fourths of the several States, or by Conventions in three fourths thereof, as the one or the other Mode of Ratification may be proposed by the Congress; Provided that no Amendment which may be made prior to the Year One thousand eight hundred and eight shall in any Manner affect the first and fourth Clauses in the Ninth Section of the first Article; and that no State, without its Consent, shall be deprived of its equal Suffrage in the Senate.

ARTICLE VI

All Debts contracted and Engagements entered into, before the Adoption of this Constitution, shall be as valid against the United States under this Constitution, as under the Confederation.

This Constitution, and the Laws of the United States which shall be made in Pursuance thereof; and all Treaties made, or which shall be made, under the Authority of the United States, shall be the supreme Law of the Land; and the Judges in every State shall be bound thereby, any Thing in the Constitution or Laws of any State to the Contrary notwithstanding.

The Senators and Representatives before mentioned, and the Members of the several State Legislatures, and all executive and judicial Officers, both of the United States and of the several States, shall be bound by Oath or Affirmation, to support this Constitution; but no religious Test shall ever be required as a Qualification to any Office or public Trust under the United States.

ARTICLE VII

The Ratification of the Conventions of nine States, shall be sufficient for the Establishment of this Constitution between the States so ratifying the Same.

The Word, "the," being interlined between the seventh and eighth Lines of the first Page, the Word "Thirty" being partly written on an Erazure in the fifteenth Line of the first Page, The Words "is tried" being interlined between the thirty second and thirty third Lines of the first Page and the Word "the" being interlined between the forty third and forty fourth Lines of the second Page.

Attest William Jackson Secretary

Done in Convention by the Unanimous Consent of the States present the Seventeenth Day of September in the Year of our Lord one thousand seven hundred and Eighty seven and of the Independence of the United States of America the Twelfth In witness whereof We have hereunto subscribed our Names,

G°. Washington
Presidt and deputy from Virginia

Delaware
Geo: Read
Gunning Bedford jun
John Dickinson
Richard Bassett
Jaco: Broom

Maryland
James McHenry
Dan of St Thos. Jenifer
Danl. Carroll

Virginia
John Blair
James Madison Jr.

North Carolina
Wm. Blount
Richd. Dobbs Spaight
Hu Williamson

South Carolina
J. Rutledge
Charles Cotesworth Pinckney
Charles Pinckney
Pierce Butler

Georgia
William Few
Abr Baldwin

New Hampshire
John Langdon
Nicholas Gilman

Massachusetts
Nathaniel Gorham
Rufus King

Connecticut
Wm. Saml. Johnson
Roger Sherman

New York
Alexander Hamilton

New Jersey
Wil: Livingston
David Brearley
Wm. Paterson
Jona: Dayton

Pennsylvania
B Franklin
Thomas Mifflin
Robt. Morris
Geo. Clymer
Thos. FitzSimons
Jared Ingersoll
James Wilson
Gouv Morris

AMENDMENT I

Congress shall make no law respecting an establishment of religion, or prohibiting the free exercise thereof; or abridging the freedom of speech, or of the press; or the right of the people peaceably to assemble, and to petition the Government for a redress of grievances.

AMENDMENT II

A well regulated Militia, being necessary to the security of a free State, the right of the people to keep and bear Arms, shall not be infringed.

AMENDMENT III

No Soldier shall, in time of peace be quartered in any house, without the consent of the Owner, nor in time of war, but in a manner to be prescribed by law.

AMENDMENT IV

The right of the people to be secure in their persons, houses, papers, and effects, against unreasonable searches and seizures, shall not be violated, and no Warrants shall issue, but upon probable cause, supported by Oath or affirmation, and particularly describing the place to be searched, and the persons or things to be seized.

AMENDMENT V

No person shall be held to answer for a capital, or otherwise infamous crime, unless on a presentment or indictment of a Grand Jury, except in cases arising in the land or naval forces, or in the Militia, when in actual service in time of War or public danger; nor shall any person be subject for the same offence to be twice put in jeopardy of life or limb; nor shall be compelled in any criminal case to be a witness against himself, nor be deprived of life, liberty, or property, without due process of law; nor shall private property be taken for public use, without just compensation.

AMENDMENT VI

In all criminal prosecutions, the accused shall enjoy the right to a speedy and public trial, by an impartial jury of the State and district wherein the crime shall have been committed, which district shall have been previously ascertained by law, and to be informed of the nature and cause of the accusation; to be confronted with the witnesses against him; to have compulsory process for obtaining witnesses in his favor, and to have the Assistance of Counsel for his defence.

AMENDMENT VII

In Suits at common law, where the value in controversy shall exceed twenty dollars, the right of trial by jury shall be preserved, and no fact tried by a jury, shall be otherwise re-examined in any Court of the United States, than according to the rules of the common law.

AMENDMENT VIII

Excessive bail shall not be required, nor excessive fines imposed, nor cruel and unusual punishments inflicted.

AMENDMENT IX

The enumeration in the Constitution, of certain rights, shall not be construed to deny or disparage others retained by the people.

AMENDMENT X

The powers not delegated to the United States by the Constitution, nor prohibited by it to the States, are reserved to the States respectively, or to the people.

AMENDMENT XI

Passed by Congress March 4, 1794. Ratified February 7, 1795.

The Judicial power of the United States shall not be construed to extend to any suit in law or equity, commenced or prosecuted against one of the United States by Citizens of another State, or by Citizens or Subjects of any Foreign State.

AMENDMENT XII

Passed by Congress December 9, 1803. Ratified June 15, 1804.

The Electors shall meet in their respective states and vote by ballot for President and Vice-President, one of whom, at least, shall not be an inhabitant of the same state with themselves; they shall name in their ballots the person voted for as President, and in distinct ballots the person voted for as Vice-President, and they shall make distinct lists of all persons voted for as President, and of all persons voted for as Vice-President, and of the number of votes for each, which lists they shall sign and certify, and transmit sealed to the seat of the government of the United States, directed to the President of the Senate;—the President of the Senate shall, in the presence of the Senate and House of Representatives, open all the certificates and the votes shall then be counted;—The person having the greatest number of votes for President, shall be the President, if such number be a majority of the whole number of Electors appointed; and if no person have such majority, then from the persons having the highest numbers not exceeding three on the list of those voted for as President, the House of Representatives shall choose immediately, by ballot, the President. But in choosing the President, the votes shall be taken by states, the representation from each state having one vote; a quorum for this purpose shall consist of a member or members from two-thirds of the states, and a majority of all the states shall be necessary to a choice. [And if the House of Representatives shall not choose a President whenever the right of choice shall devolve upon them, before the fourth day of March next following, then the Vice-President shall act as President, as in case of the death or other constitutional disability of the President.] The person having the greatest number of votes as Vice-President, shall be the Vice-President, if such number be a majority of the whole number of Electors appointed, and if no person have a majority, then from the two highest numbers on the list, the Senate shall choose the Vice-President; a quorum for the purpose shall consist of two-thirds of the whole number of Senators, and a majority of the whole number shall be necessary to a choice. But no person constitutionally ineligible to the office of President shall be eligible to that of Vice-President of the United States.

AMENDMENT XIII

Passed by Congress January 31, 1865. Ratified December 6, 1865.

Section 1

Neither slavery nor involuntary servitude, except as a punishment for crime whereof the party shall have been duly convicted, shall exist within the United States, or any place subject to their jurisdiction.

Section 2

Congress shall have power to enforce this article by appropriate legislation.

AMENDMENT XIV

Passed by Congress June 13, 1866. Ratified July 9, 1868.

Section 1

All persons born or naturalized in the United States, and subject to the jurisdiction thereof, are citizens of the United States and of the State wherein they reside. No State shall make or enforce any law which shall abridge the privileges or immunities of citizens of the United States; nor shall any State deprive any person of life, liberty, or property, without due process of law; nor deny to any person within its jurisdiction the equal protection of the laws.

Section 2

Representatives shall be apportioned among the several States according to their respective numbers, counting the whole number of persons in each State, excluding Indians not taxed. But when the right to vote at any election for the choice of electors for President and Vice-President of the United States, Representatives in Congress, the Executive and Judicial officers of a State, or the members of the Legislature thereof, is denied to any of the male inhabitants of such State, being twenty-one years of age, and citizens of the United States, or in any way abridged, except for participation in rebellion, or other crime, the basis of representation therein shall be reduced in the proportion which the number of such male citizens shall bear to the whole number of male citizens twenty-one years of age in such State.

Section 3

No person shall be a Senator or Representative in Congress, or elector of President and Vice-President, or hold any office, civil or military, under the United States, or under any State, who, having previously taken an oath, as a member of Congress, or as an officer of the United States, or as a member of any State legislature, or as an executive or judicial officer of any State, to support the Constitution of the United States, shall have engaged in insurrection or rebellion against the same, or given aid or comfort to the enemies thereof. But Congress may by a vote of two-thirds of each House, remove such disability.

Section 4

The validity of the public debt of the United States, authorized by law, including debts incurred for payment of pensions and bounties for services in suppressing insurrection or rebellion, shall not be questioned. But neither the United States nor any State shall assume or pay any debt or obligation incurred in aid of insurrection or rebellion against the United States, or any claim for the loss or emancipation of any slave; but all such debts, obligations and claims shall be held illegal and void.

Section 5

The Congress shall have the power to enforce, by appropriate legislation, the provisions of this article.

AMENDMENT XV

Passed by Congress February 26, 1869. Ratified February 3, 1870.

Section 1

The right of citizens of the United States to vote shall not be denied or abridged by the United States or by any State on account of race, color, or previous condition of servitude.

Section 2

The Congress shall have the power to enforce this article by appropriate legislation.

AMENDMENT XVI

Passed by Congress July 2, 1909. Ratified February 3, 1913.

The Congress shall have power to lay and collect taxes on incomes, from whatever source derived, without apportionment among the several States, and without regard to any census or enumeration.

AMENDMENT XVII

Passed by Congress May 13, 1912. Ratified April 8, 1913.

The Senate of the United States shall be composed of two Senators from each State, elected by the people thereof, for six years; and each Senator shall have one vote. The electors in each State shall have the qualifications requisite for electors of the most numerous branch of the State legislatures.

When vacancies happen in the representation of any State in the Senate, the executive authority of such State shall issue writs of election to fill such vacancies: Provided, That the legislature of any State may empower the executive thereof to make temporary appointments until the people fill the vacancies by election as the legislature may direct.

This amendment shall not be so construed as to affect the election or term of any Senator chosen before it becomes valid as part of the Constitution.

AMENDMENT XVIII

Passed by Congress December 18, 1917. Ratified January 16, 1919.

Section 1

After one year from the ratification of this article the manufacture, sale, or transportation of intoxicating liquors within, the importation thereof into, or the exportation thereof from the United States and all territory subject to the jurisdiction thereof for beverage purposes is hereby prohibited.

Section 2

The Congress and the several States shall have concurrent power to enforce this article by appropriate legislation.

Section 3

This article shall be inoperative unless it shall have been ratified as an amendment to the Constitution by the legislatures of the several States, as provided in the Constitution, within seven years from the date of the submission hereof to the States by the Congress.

AMENDMENT XIX

Passed by Congress June 4, 1919. Ratified August 18, 1920.

The right of citizens of the United States to vote shall not be denied or abridged by the United States or by any State on account of sex.

Congress shall have power to enforce this article by appropriate legislation.

AMENDMENT XX

Passed by Congress March 2, 1932. Ratified January 23, 1933.

Section 1

The terms of the President and the Vice President shall end at noon on the 20th day of January, and the terms of Senators and Representatives at noon on the 3d day of January, of the years in which such terms would have ended if this article had not been ratified; and the terms of their successors shall then begin.

Section 2

The Congress shall assemble at least once in every year, and such meeting shall begin at noon on the 3d day of January, unless they shall by law appoint a different day.

Section 3

If, at the time fixed for the beginning of the term of the President, the President elect shall have died, the Vice President elect shall become President. If a President shall not have been chosen before the time fixed for the beginning of his term, or if the President elect shall have failed to qualify, then the Vice President elect shall act as President until a President shall have qualified; and the Congress may by law provide for the case wherein neither a President elect nor a Vice President shall have qualified, declaring who shall then act as President, or the manner in which one who is to act shall be selected, and such person shall act accordingly until a President or Vice President shall have qualified.

Section 4

The Congress may by law provide for the case of the death of any of the persons from whom the House of Representatives may choose a President whenever the right of choice shall have devolved upon them, and for the case of the death of any of the persons from whom the Senate may choose a Vice President whenever the right of choice shall have devolved upon them.

Section 5

Sections 1 and 2 shall take effect on the 15th day of October following the ratification of this article.

Section 6

This article shall be inoperative unless it shall have been ratified as an amendment to the Constitution by the legislatures of three-fourths of the several States within seven years from the date of its submission.

AMENDMENT XXI

Passed by Congress February 20, 1933. Ratified December 5, 1933.

Section 1

The eighteenth article of amendment to the Constitution of the United States is hereby repealed.

Section 2

The transportation or importation into any State, Territory, or Possession of the United States for delivery or use therein of intoxicating liquors, in violation of the laws thereof, is hereby prohibited.

Section 3

This article shall be inoperative unless it shall have been ratified as an amendment to the Constitution by conventions in the several States, as provided in the Constitution, within seven years from the date of the submission hereof to the States by the Congress.

AMENDMENT XXII

Passed by Congress March 21, 1947. Ratified February 27, 1951.

Section 1

No person shall be elected to the office of the President more than twice, and no person who has held the office of President, or acted as President, for more than two years of a term to which some other person was elected President shall be elected to the office of President more than once. But this Article shall not apply to any person holding the office of President when this Article was proposed by Congress, and shall not prevent any person who may be holding the office of President, or acting as President, during the term within which this Article becomes operative from holding the office of President or acting as President during the remainder of such term.

Section 2

This article shall be inoperative unless it shall have been ratified as an amendment to the Constitution by the legislatures of three-fourths of the several States within seven years from the date of its submission to the States by the Congress.

AMENDMENT XXIII

Passed by Congress June 16, 1960. Ratified March 29, 1961.

Section 1

The District constituting the seat of Government of the United States shall appoint in such manner as Congress may direct:

A number of electors of President and Vice President equal to the whole number of Senators and Representatives in Congress to which the District would be entitled if it were a State, but in no event more than the least populous State; they shall be in addition to those appointed by the States, but they shall be considered, for the purposes of the election of President and Vice President, to be electors appointed by a State; and they shall meet in the District and perform such duties as provided by the twelfth article of amendment.

Section 2

The Congress shall have power to enforce this article by appropriate legislation.

AMENDMENT XXIV

Passed by Congress August 27, 1962. Ratified January 23, 1964.

Section 1

The right of citizens of the United States to vote in any primary or other election for President or Vice President, for electors for President or Vice President, or for Senator or Representative in Congress, shall not be denied or abridged by the United States or any State by reason of failure to pay poll tax or other tax.

Section 2

The Congress shall have power to enforce this article by appropriate legislation.

AMENDMENT XXV

Passed by Congress July 6, 1965. Ratified February 10, 1967.

Section 1

In case of the removal of the President from office or of his death or resignation, the Vice President shall become President.

Section 2

Whenever there is a vacancy in the office of the Vice President, the President shall nominate a Vice President who shall take office upon confirmation by a majority vote of both Houses of Congress.

Section 3

Whenever the President transmits to the President pro tempore of the Senate and the Speaker of the House of Representatives his written declaration that he is unable to discharge the powers and duties of his office, and until he transmits to them a written declaration to the contrary, such powers and duties shall be discharged by the Vice President as Acting President.

Section 4

Whenever the Vice President and a majority of either the principal officers of the executive departments or of such other body as Congress may by law provide, transmit to the President pro tempore of the Senate and the Speaker of the House of Representatives their written declaration that the President is unable to discharge the powers and duties of his office, the Vice President shall immediately assume the powers and duties of the office as Acting President.

Thereafter, when the President transmits to the President pro tempore of the Senate and the Speaker of the House of Representatives his written declaration that no inability exists, he shall resume the powers and duties of his office unless the Vice President and a majority of either the principal officers of the executive department or of such other body as Congress may by law provide, transmit within four days to the President pro tempore of the Senate and the Speaker of the House of Representatives their written declaration that the President is unable to discharge the powers and duties of his office. Thereupon Congress shall decide the issue, assembling within forty-eight hours for that purpose if not in session. If the Congress, within twenty-one days after receipt of the latter written declaration, or, if Congress is not in session, within twenty-one days after Congress is required to assemble, determines by two-thirds vote of both Houses that the President is unable to discharge the powers and duties of his office, the Vice President shall continue to discharge the same as Acting President; otherwise, the President shall resume the powers and duties of his office.

AMENDMENT XXVI

Passed by Congress March 23, 1971. Ratified July 1, 1971.

Section 1

The right of citizens of the United States, who are eighteen years of age or older, to vote shall not be denied or abridged by the United States or by any State on account of age.

Section 2

The Congress shall have power to enforce this article by appropriate legislation.

AMENDMENT XXVII

Originally proposed Sept. 25, 1789. Ratified May 7, 1992.

No law, varying the compensation for the services of the Senators and Representatives, shall take effect, until an election of representatives shall have intervened.

NOTES

CHAPTER 1

1. Matt Cover, "When Asked Where the Constitution Authorizes Congress to Order Americans to Buy Health Insurance, Pelosi Says, 'Are You Serious?'" CNSNews.com, October 23, 2009; available at http://www.cnsnews.com/news/print/55971.
2. "A Message from Congress: No One Questions Our Authority," CNSNews.com, February 3, 2010; available at http://www.cnsnews.com/news/print/60932.
3. Ibid.
4. Stephen Moore, "The Unconstitutional Congress," *Policy Review*, Spring 1995, 22.
5. See Larry Schwab, *The Illusion of a Conservative Reagan Revolution* (New Brunswick, NJ: Transaction, 1991).
6. Thomas Jefferson to William Branch Giles, December 26, 1825, in *The Writings of Thomas Jefferson*, vol. X, ed. Paul Leicester Ford (New York: G.P. Putnam's Sons, 1899), 355.
7. James J. Kilpatrick, *The Sovereign States: Notes of a Citizen of Virginia* (Chicago: Henry Regnery, 1957), 156. Emphasis added.
8. *State Documents on Federal Relations: The States and the United States*, ed. Herman V. Ames (New York: Longmans, Green, 1911), 113.
9. The pseudonymous author of *The Genuine Book of Nullification* (1831): "Thus would the entire operation of this remedy be peaceful and systematic. And this course would not (as it has been said) intimate

or involve a compulsion of other States of this Union to coincide with us in our construction of the Federal Constitution, nor that we refused to them the right of construing for themselves. So far from this being the case, we declare the fundamental principle of all State Rights' Doctrines to be that in case of an aggression upon the Sovereign Rights of the States, *each and every* State which is so aggrieved has the inherent right 'to judge for herself of the Infraction as well as of the mode and measure of redress,' and to *interpose her Sovereign shield to protect her own citizens* and to *maintain within her own limits* her rights and authorities, without interfering in any manner with the citizens, or the Rights and Authorities of her sister States. We should not go beyond the Boundaries of our own State—whilst we left to every other State of this Union the right and power in like manner to protect her own citizens from tyrannical oppression." Hampden (pseud.), *The Genuine Book of Nullification* (Charleston, SC: E.J. Van Brunt, 1831), 52. Emphasis in original. The phrase "to judge for herself of the Infraction as well as of the mode and measure of redress" is derived from the Kentucky Resolutions of 1798, composed by Thomas Jefferson and discussed in chapter 2 of the present volume.

10. Information available at http://www.SheriffsFirst.com.
11. For a full overview and critique of the Court's arguments, see Thomas E. Woods, Jr. and Kevin R. C. Gutzman, *Who Killed the Constitution?: The Fate of American Liberty from World War I to George W. Bush* (New York: Crown Forum, 2008), ch. 9.
12. See an interesting appreciation, from a left-wing perspective, of Thomas' strict-constructionist dissent: Fred Gardner, "The *Raich* Decision: All Power to the Federal Government," CounterPunch.org, June 14, 2005; available at http://www.counterpunch.org/gardner06142005.html.
13. Louisiana allows the use of medical marijuana in extremely rare instances.
14. Woods and Gutzman, *Who Killed the Constitution?*, 146.
15. Randy E. Barnett, "Reefer Madness," *Wall Street Journal*, March 16, 2007.
16. Jennifer Steinhauer, "Los Angeles Marijuana Sellers Limited," *New York Times*, January 26, 2010; available at http://www.nytimes.com/2010/01/27/us/27pot.html.
17. Committee on Health and Human Services, House Bill No. 2610; available at http://www.kslegislature.org/bills/2010/2610.pdf. Emphasis added.
18. See Patrick Reagan, "Cannabis, Compassion, and the Tenth Amendment," February 15, 2010; available at http://www.campaignforliberty.com/article.php?view=611. Emphasis added.

19. Attorney Jeff Matthews correctly points out that if anything, these states are being too timid in confining their legislation to guns manufactured in their particular states. For one thing, a gun can cross state lines for reasons having nothing to do with commerce, as when a person moves from one state to another and brings his belongings. Just because a gun crosses state lines does not make it part of interstate commerce. For another, even if a gun were purchased from another state several decades ago, does that mean the federal government right now can regulate that product however it wishes? Surely the federal government's regulatory control does not enjoy an infinite time horizon. See Jeff Matthews, "Commerce, Jurisdiction, and Firearms Freedom Acts," TenthAmendmentCenter.com, April 20, 2010; available at http://www.tenthamendmentcenter.com/2010/04/20/commerce-jurisdiction-and-firearms-freedom-acts/.
20. Information available at http://www.bringtheguardhome.org.
21. See Ben Manski, "From Liberty to Empire: The Demise of American Defense"; available at http://www.bringtheguardhome.org/publications/manski_liberty_to_empire_demise_of_defense.
22. Bob Unruh, "States' Rights Rebellion over National Guard," WorldNetDaily, January 26, 2010; available at http://www.worldnetdaily.com/index.php?pageId=122689; and Bob Unruh, "Obama's New Pick: Gov. of State that Linked Christians, Violence," WorldNetDaily, February 7, 2010; available at http://www.worldnetdaily.com/index.php?pageId=124238.
23. Bob Unruh, "States' Rights Rebellion over National Guard."
24. Ibid.
25. See John C. Calhoun, "A Discourse on the Constitution and Government of the United States," in *Union and Liberty: The Political Philosophy of John C. Calhoun*, ed. Ross M. Lence (Indianapolis: Liberty Fund, 1992), 178ff.
26. Chancellor Harper, *The Remedy by State Interposition or Nullification* (Charleston, SC: State Rights and Free Trade Association, 1832), 7. Emphasis added. Harper's speech, of which this is the text, was delivered on September 20, 1830. U.S. Senator John Taylor of Caroline said the same thing: "The expression in the constitution, 'shall be the supreme law of the land,' is restricted by its limitations and reservation, and did not convey any species of supremacy to the government, going beyond the powers delegated or those reserved." John Taylor, *New Views of the Constitution of the United States* (Washington, D.C.: Way and Gideon, 1823), 78.
27. Kirkpatrick Sale, *Human Scale* (New York: Coward, McCann & Geoghegan, 1980).

28. "59% Favor Letting States Opt Out of Federal Programs," Rasmussen Reports, February 15, 2010; available at http://www.rasmussenreports.com/public_content/politics/general_politics/february_2010/59_favor_letting_states_opt_out_of_federal_programs.
29. I got the idea to calculate these figures from Donald W. Livingston, "Dismantling Leviathan," *Harper's*, May 2002, 14. I have updated Livingston's figures to reflect the 2010 U.S. population.
30. John C. Calhoun, "Rough Draft of What Is Called the South Carolina Exposition," in Lence, ed., *Union and Liberty*, 353. Emphasis added.
31. Thomas Jefferson to Archibald Stuart, December 23, 1791, in *The Life and Writings of Thomas Jefferson*, ed. S. E. Forman (Indianapolis: Bowen-Merrill, 1900), 397.
32. Donald W. Livingston, "The Founding and the Enlightenment: Two Theories of Sovereignty," in *Vital Remnants: America's Founding and the Western Tradition*, ed. Gary L. Gregg II (Wilmington, DE: ISI Books, 1999), 247.

CHAPTER 2

1. For additional discussion of these clauses, see Thomas E. Woods, Jr., *33 Questions About American History You're Not Supposed to Ask* (New York: Crown Forum, 2007), in addition to the sources in this book.
2. The appearance of the term "general welfare" in the preamble to the Constitution is widely understood to be purely rhetorical, since preambles are merely descriptive and not of a legally binding nature. See, among many other sources, Madison's Report of 1800, which describes it as "contrary to every acknowledged rule of construction, to set up this part of an instrument, in opposition to the plain meaning expressed in the body of the instrument. A preamble usually contains the general motives or reasons, for the particular regulations or measures which follow it; and is always understood to be explained and limited by them. In the present instance, a contrary interpretation would have the inadmissible effect, of rendering nugatory or improper every part of the Constitution which succeeds the preamble." See also Kevin R. C. Gutzman, *Virginia's American Revolution: From Dominion to Republic, 1776-1840* (Lanham, MD: Lexington, 2007), 169.
3. Adrienne Koch, *Jefferson and Madison: The Great Collaboration* (New York: Alfred A. Knopf, 1950), 129.
4. James Madison, Virginia Report of 1800, excerpted in Document V.
5. Raoul Berger, *Federalism: The Founders' Design* (Norman: University of Oklahoma Press, 1987), 105.
6. Ibid., 106–7.

7. Thomas Jefferson, "Opinion Against the Constitutionality of a National Bank," in *The American Republic: Primary Sources*, ed. Bruce Frohnen (Indianapolis: Liberty Fund, 2002), 501.
8. John C. Eastman, "Restoring the 'General' to the General Welfare Clause," *Chapman Law Review* 4 (2001): 72–87; Robert G. Natelson, "The General Welfare Clause and the Public Trust: An Essay in Original Understanding," *University of Kansas Law Review* 52 (2003): 29–30, 47ff.
9. The *Federalist* (referred to in some modern treatments as the *Federalist Papers*, after Clinton Rossiter's 1961 collection of these documents) were a series of eighty-five newspaper articles pseudonymously written by Alexander Hamilton, James Madison, and John Jay, in support of ratification of the Constitution. They were composed between 1787 and 1788, and had already been assembled in a single collection by 1788.
10. See Natelson, "The General Welfare Clause and the Public Trust," 46.
11. Randy E. Barnett, "The Original Meaning of the Commerce Clause," *University of Chicago Law Review* 68 (Winter 2001); available at http://www.bu.edu/rbarnett/Original.htm.
12. Raoul Berger, "Judicial Manipulation of the Commerce Clause," *Texas Law Review* 74 (March 1996): 704.
13. Ibid., 705. Emphasis in original.
14. Berger, *Federalism*, 89.
15. Ibid., 95–96.
16. Jefferson, "Opinion Against the Constitutionality of a National Bank," 475–76.
17. St. George Tucker, *View of the Constitution of the United States with Selected Writings*, ed. Clyde N. Wilson (Indianapolis: Liberty Fund, 1999), 227–28.
18. See the contributions by Roane in *John Marshall's Defense of McCulloch v. Maryland*, ed. Gerald Gunther (Stanford, CA: Stanford University Press, 1969); John Taylor, *Construction Construed and Constitutions Vindicated* (Richmond, VA: Shepherd & Pollard, 1820), 165, 166.
19. James Madison, Report of 1800, excerpted in Document V.
20. Kurt T. Lash, "The Original Meaning of an Omission: The Tenth Amendment, Popular Sovereignty, and 'Expressly' Delegated Power," *Notre Dame Law Review* (2008): 1907. Emphasis added.
21. H. Newcomb Morse, "The Foundations and Meaning of Secession," *Stetson Law Review* 15 (1986).
22. Berger, *Federalism*, 65. Emphasis added.
23. Lash, "Original Meaning of an Omission," 1907; Berger, *Federalism*, 64. Emphasis added.
24. Ibid., 1892. Emphasis added.

25. Berger, *Federalism*, 64.
26. Lash, "Original Meaning of an Omission," 1905. Emphasis added.
27. These Federalists should not be confused with the people, also known as Federalists, who supported ratification of the Constitution. Jefferson, for instance, was a Federalist when it came to the Constitution (he supported it, with a few misgivings) but did not belong to the post-ratification political party known as the Federalists.
28. Lash, "Original Meaning of an Omission," 1893. Emphasis in Chase's original.
29. Charles J. Bloch, *States' Rights the Law of the Land* (Atlanta: The Harrison Company, 1958), 17–18.
30. Lash, "Original Meaning of an Omission," 1916–17.
31. The Ninth Amendment reads, "The enumeration in the Constitution, of certain rights, shall not be construed to deny or disparage others retained by the people." It means that the rights singled out in the Bill of Rights, although perhaps among the most significant and the ones most likely to be abused by government, do not exhaust the rights to be enjoyed by the people.
32. Lash, "Original Meaning of an Omission," 1925.
33. This was what North Carolina's James Iredell meant when he said the Constitution "is a declaration of particular powers by the people to their representatives, for particular purposes. It may be considered as a great power of attorney, under which no power can be exercised but what is expressly given." St. George Tucker, in what became the early republic's predominant text on the Constitution, applied Vattel's arguments to the American case to make precisely these points. Ibid., 1908–1909, 1923 and *passim*. Tucker noted that the combined effect of the Ninth and Tenth Amendments "appears to be, that the powers delegated to the federal government are, in all cases, to receive the most strict construction that the instrument will bear, where the rights of a state or of the people, either collectively, or individually, may be drawn in question." Tucker, *View of the Constitution*, 154. References to Vattel may be found throughout Tucker's text, with particular application to popular sovereignty and the Tenth Amendment.
34. Lash, "Original Meaning of an Omission," 1928–30.
35. Ibid., 1919, 1920–24.
36. I owe this formulation to Kevin Gutzman.
37. Berger, *Federalism*, 11–12.
38. Ibid., 18n63 and 19n64.
39. "Britney Spears: 'Trust Our President in Every Decision,'" CNN.com, September 3, 2003; available at http://www.cnn.com/2003/SHOWBIZ/Music/09/03/cnna.spears.

40. Thomas Jefferson to William Cary Nicholas, September 7, 1803, *Thomas Jefferson: Writings*, ed. Merrill D. Peterson (New York: Library of America, 1984), 1140.
41. See the argument in Jack P. Greene, *Peripheries and Center: Constitutional Development in the Extended Polities of the British Empire and the United States, 1607–1788* (New York: W.W. Norton, 1986), 115–16, 120, and ch. 6; see also Woods, *33 Questions*, ch. 15.
42. Jefferson made this statement in his draft of the Kentucky Resolutions of 1798, which can be found in *The Papers of Thomas Jefferson*, vol. 30, *1 January 1798 to 31 January 1799*, ed. Barbara B. Oberg (Princeton, NJ: Princeton University Press, 2003), 536–43.
43. Thomas Jefferson to William Cary Nicholas, September 7, 1803, in Peterson, ed., *Thomas Jefferson: Writings*, 1140.
44. *South Dakota v. Dole* (1987), cited in William J. Watkins, Jr., *Reclaiming the American Revolution: The Kentucky and Virginia Resolutions and Their Legacy* (New York: Palgrave, 2004), 130. Emphasis added. Many other cases containing similar assertions could of course be cited.
45. "At present," Adams said, "there is no more prospect of seeing a French army here than there is in heaven." Marco Bassani, *Liberty, State and Union: The Political Theory of Thomas Jefferson* (Macon, GA: Mercer University Press, 2010), 168.
46. Bassani, *Liberty, State and Union*, 170.
47. Madison added, "The management of foreign relations appears to be the most susceptible of abuse of all the trusts committed to a Government, because they can be concealed or disclosed, or disclosed in such parts and at such times as will best suit particular views; and because the body of the people are less capable of judging, and are more under the influence of prejudices, on that branch of affairs, than of any other." James Madison to Thomas Jefferson, May 13, 1798, in *The Republic of Letters: The Correspondence between Thomas Jefferson and James Madison 1776–1826*, vol. 2: *1790–1804*, ed. James Morton Smith (New York: W.W. Norton, 1995), 1048.
48. Republicans argued that the Alien Friends Act violated the Fifth Amendment, and Jefferson also suggested that the Constitution's prohibition on federal government interference with the slave trade until 1808 also prevented it from legislating on the migration of aliens, which was therefore properly a state concern.
49. Bassani, *Liberty, State and Union*, 167.
50. Thomas Jefferson to Samuel Smith, August 22, 1798, in *The Writings of Thomas Jefferson*, vol. 7, ed. Paul Leicester Ford (New York: G.P. Putnam's Sons, 1892–99), 275–80.
51. Watkins, *Reclaiming the American Revolution*, 44–47.
52. Bassani, *Liberty, State and Union*, 167.

53. Ibid., 163.
54. Hampden, *Genuine Book of Nullification*, 110.
55. Thomas Jefferson to John Taylor, November 26, 1798, quoted in Smith, ed., *The Republic of Letters*, 1071.
56. Thomas Jefferson to Abigail Adams, July 22, 1804, in *The Adams-Jefferson Letters: The Complete Correspondence between Thomas Jefferson and Abigail and John Adams*, vol. 1, ed. Lester J. Cappon (Chapel Hill, NC: University of North Carolina Press, 1959), 275.
57. Smith, ed., *The Republic of Letters*, 1068.
58. Bassani, *Liberty, State and Union*, 161.
59. James J. Kilpatrick, *The Sovereign States: Notes of a Citizen of Virginia* (Chicago: Henry Regnery, 1957), 75.
60. Ibid.
61. Emphasis added. The full text of the Kentucky Resolutions of 1799 is reproduced in Document IV.
62. It has often been said that the Virginia Resolutions of Madison were more restrained than the Kentucky Resolutions of Jefferson. But this argument has been carried too far. "The distinction so often drawn between Jefferson's strident and Madison's moderate tone seems strained," writes historian Kevin Gutzman. "There is no difference between 'null, void, and of no force or effect' and 'invalidity,' between 'nullifying' a statute and 'interpos[ing]' to prevent its enforcement." Kevin R. Gutzman, "A Troublesome Legacy: James Madison and 'the Principles of '98,'" *Journal of the Early Republic* 15 (Winter 1995): 581. It is hard to credit the idea that in the midst of calls for nullification, and with secession on the lips of people like John Taylor of Caroline and William Branch Giles, a man as intelligent as Madison wouldn't have known how his words would be taken. "One of Madison's most notable 'tactical adjustments,'" Gutzman continues, was "his campaign, as a retired former president, to becloud the events of 1798 by denying they had meant what they plainly had meant." K. R. Constantine Gutzman, "'Oh, What a Tangled Web We Weave…': James Madison and the Compound Republic," *Continuity* 22 (Spring 1998): 22. That Madison indicated in 1830 that he had never meant to propose nullification in his work on the Constitution or in his Virginia Resolutions of 1798 is very difficult to credit. That is certainly how other state legislatures had understood his words at the time. Indeed, Madison's frequent change of positions throughout his career was well known. Albert Taylor Bledsoe was blunt: "The truth seems to be, that Mr. Madison was more solicitous to preserve the integrity of the Union, than the coherency of his own thoughts." Albert Taylor Bledsoe, *The War Between the States* (Lynchburg, VA: J. P. Bell, 1915), 158. (Bledsoe's book was originally published in 1866 under a different title.) Madison even tried denying

that Jefferson had included the word "nullification" in his draft of the Kentucky Resolutions of 1798, an assertion he knew was false since he had seen the draft himself. When a copy of the original Kentucky Resolutions in Jefferson's own handwriting turned up, Madison had to withdraw that claim. Watkins, *Reclaiming the American Revolution*, 114.

A widely read book on nullification, published in 1831, dealt a blow to Madison's efforts to explain away his earlier writing. Hampden, the pseudonymous author, noted that the other state legislatures clearly interpreted the Virginia Resolutions to mean that the states could interpose for the protection of their people against the unconstitutional encroachments of the federal government. "How were these replies and protests of the States met by Mr. Madison in his famous and elaborate report upon them in '99? Does he declare in his report that they had misapprehended, or in any way misrepresented his meaning in his resolutions of '98? No indeed! Nothing of the kind!... Indeed it is apparent from the whole political course of Mr. Madison that his fundamental principles in politics are those of consolidation and monarchy—he so openly declared them in his Speeches in the General Convention, and such were his known and commonly avowed opinions of that day. When however, under the superior and more republican mind of Mr. Jefferson the Doctrines of State Rights became universally prevalent, and those of Consolidation were most odious and unpopular, we find Mr. Madison supporting these Republican principles with all the vigor of his naturally fine intellect, under the mentorship of his illustrious friend. But alas, upon the demise of that great man we find Mr. Madison again relapsing into his original strong Federal and Consolidation tenets—giving to the words and sentiments of his early and vigorous manhood a construction totally repugnant to their obvious and universal acceptation and in opposition to the contemporaneous understanding of his friends and of the Legislatures of the day." Hampden (pseud.), *The Genuine Book of Nullification* (Charleston, SC: E. J. Van Brunt, 1831), 54, 55.

On the weakness of Madison's later efforts to show that the Virginia Resolutions did not mean what they clearly did mean and what everyone had taken them to mean, see Kevin R. C. Gutzman, "From Interposition to Nullification: Peripheries and Center in the Thought of James Madison," *Essays on History* 36 (1994). *Essays on History* is the University of Virginia's online journal. As of this printing the article is available online at http://www.constitution.org/jm/gutzman1.html. See also Bassani, *Liberty, State and Union*, 195–96. A small industry has developed in defense of the claim that in spite of appearances, and in spite of what partisan humor at the time joked about, Madison was in fact perfectly consistent throughout his political career. The classic statement of this position is Lance Banning, *The Sacred Fire of Liberty: James Madison and the Founding of the American Republic* (Ithaca, NY: Cornell University Press, 1995). For the other side, see Kevin R. C. Gutzman, *James Madison and the Making of America* (New York: St. Martin's, forthcoming 2011).

63. Kilpatrick, *The Sovereign States*, 315n28.
64. Gutzman, *Virginia's American Revolution*, 126, 127.
65. Kilpatrick, *The Sovereign States*, 82.
66. Speech of Edward Livingston on the Alien Bill, June 19, 1798, in *American Oratory, or Selections from the Speeches of Eminent Americans*, compiled by A Member of the Philadelphia Bar (Philadelphia: DeSilver, Thomas & Co., 1836), 128.
67. *The Virginia and Kentucky Resolutions of 1798 and '99; with Jefferson's Original Draught Thereof, and Madison's Report, Calhoun's Address, Resolutions of the Several States in Relation to State Rights, with Other Documents in Support of the Jeffersonian Doctrines of* '98, ed. Jonathan Elliot (Washington, D.C.: Jonathan Elliot, 1832), 9.
68. Ibid.
69. Ibid., 11, 13.
70. Bassani, *Liberty, State and Union*, 178.
71. James Madison, Report of 1800, excerpted in Document V.
72. Bassani, *Liberty, State and Union*, 161–62.
73. Eugene D. Genovese, *The Southern Tradition: The Achievement and Limitations of an American Conservatism* (Cambridge: Harvard University Press, 1994), 56–57.

CHAPTER 3

1. William J. Watkins, Jr., *Reclaiming the American Revolution: The Kentucky and Virginia Resolutions and Their Legacy* (New York: Palgrave, 2004), 116.
2. Kevin R. C. Gutzman, *Virginia's American Revolution: From Dominion to Republic, 1776–1840* (Lanham, MD: Lexington, 2007), 114.
3. *To His Excellency Thomas Jefferson: Letters to a President*, ed. Jack McLaughlin (New York: W.W. Norton, 1991), 19.
4. Ibid., 21.
5. Ibid., 27.
6. James J. Kilpatrick, *The Sovereign States: Notes of a Citizen of Virginia* (Chicago: Henry Regnery, 1957), 127.
7. *State Documents on Federal Relations: The States and the United States*, ed. Herman V. Ames (New York: Longmans, Green, 1911), 34.
8. Ibid., 40.

9. Ibid., 41–42.
10. Ibid., 43–44. Emphasis added.
11. Ibid., 58.
12. Edward Payson Powell, *Nullification and Secession in the United States: A History of the Six Attempts During the First Century of the Republic* (New York: G.P. Putnam's Sons, 1897), 211.
13. Ibid., 224.
14. Ames, ed., *State Documents on Federal Relations*, 71–72. Emphasis added.
15. Ibid., 75.
16. On the unconstitutionality of the draft, see Thomas E. Woods, Jr. and Kevin R. C. Gutzman, *Who Killed the Constitution?: The Fate of American Liberty from World War I to George W. Bush* (New York: Crown Forum, 2008), ch. 8.
17. Ames, ed., *State Documents on Federal Relations*, 76.
18. Ibid., 76–77.
19. Daniel Webster, speech before the House of Representatives, December 9, 1814, in *We Who Dared to Say No to War: American Antiwar Writing from 1812 to Now*, eds. Murray Polner and Thomas E. Woods, Jr. (New York: Basic Books, 2008), 5.
20. Clyde N. Wilson, "Q&A on Nullification and Interposition," LewRockwell.com, February 8, 2010; available at http://www.lewrockwell.com/wilson/wilson32.1.html.
21. Webster, speech before the House of Representatives, December 9, 1814, in Polner and Woods, eds., *We Who Dared to Say No to War*, 9. Emphasis added.
22. Ames, ed., *State Documents on Federal Relations*, 76.
23. Emphasis in original. The full text of both the resolutions and the report appears in *The Virginia and Kentucky Resolutions of 1798 and '99; with Jefferson's Original Draught Thereof, and Madison's Report, Calhoun's Address, Resolutions of the Several States in Relation to State Rights, with Other Documents in Support of the Jeffersonian Doctrines of '98*, ed. Jonathan Elliot (Washington, D.C.: Jonathan Elliot, 1832), 80–81.
24. Ames, ed., *State Documents on Federal Relations*, 53.
25. Ibid., 142.
26. Ibid., 149.
27. Watkins, *Reclaiming the American Revolution*, 98–99.
28. Moreover, when during the Mexican War some pro-slavery southerners contemplated the annexation of all of Mexico, Calhoun was strongly opposed.
29. See H. Robert Baker, *The Rescue of Joshua Glover: A Fugitive Slave, the Constitution, and the Coming of the Civil War* (Athens, OH: Ohio University Press, 2006), 122.

30. According to Clyde Wilson, the distinguished historian who edited *The Papers of John C. Calhoun*, the argument that the nullification controversy of 1832–1833 was "really" about slavery "became a popular theory for the first time in the 1960s. It had not occurred to anyone before.... The South Carolinians, and every other state, and every Northern free trader, and every tariff advocate said at the time it was about tariff protection—its actual results and its justice or injustice. Nobody said a word about slavery. The interpretation basically comes back to the belief that everything that Southerners do and say is a code word about race, and that what they said about the tariff was therefore not really sincere and not really valid." Clyde N. Wilson, personal correspondence with the author, February 23, 2010.
31. Ames, ed., *State Documents on Federal Relations*, 175–76.
32. For an overview of the constitutional case against the Fugitive Slave Act of 1850, see Stanley W. Campbell, *The Slave Catchers: Enforcement of the Fugitive Slave Law, 1850–1860* (Chapel Hill, NC: University of North Carolina Press, 1968), ch. 2.
33. Robert Wild, "The Spirit of Nullification and Secession in the Northern States," *Proceedings of the State Bar Association of Wisconsin* (Milwaukee: The Evening Wisconsin Printing Co., 1912), 135.
34. Baker, *The Rescue of Joshua Glover*, 10.
35. Kilpatrick, *The Sovereign States*, 215.
36. Baker, *The Rescue of Joshua Glover*, 93. Emphasis in original.
37. Ibid., 118, 120–21, 132.
38. *Lane County* v. *Oregon*, quoted in Kurt T. Lash, "The Original Meaning of an Omission: The Tenth Amendment, Popular Sovereignty, and 'Expressly' Delegated Power," *Notre Dame Law Review* (2008): 1950.
39. I owe this last point to Robert P. Murphy.

CHAPTER 4

1. Donald W. Livingston, "The Founding and the Enlightenment: Two Theories of Sovereignty," in *Vital Remnants: America's Founding and the Western Tradition*, ed. Gary L. Gregg II (Wilmington, DE: ISI Books, 1999), 261.
2. Not all compact theorists supported nullification; John Randolph of Roanoke, like numerous others, believed in the right of secession but not nullification.
3. Joseph Story, *Commentaries on the Constitution of the United States*, 4th ed., vol. 1 (Boston: Little, Brown, 1873), 124. The first edition was published in 1833.
4. *The Correspondence and Public Papers of John Jay*, vol. 3, 1782–1793, ed. Henry P. Johnston (New York: G.P. Putnam's Sons, 1891), 454.

Emphasis removed. Jay's remarks are drawn from his opinion in *Chisholm* v. *Georgia* (1793).

5. Abel P. Upshur, *A Brief Enquiry into the True Nature and Character of Our Federal Government* (Petersburg, VA: Edmund and Julian C. Ruffin, 1840), 11.
6. Ibid., 12.
7. Ibid., 14.
8. Jackson's Proclamation is available at http://avalon.law.yale.edu/19th_century/jack01.asp.
9. Littleton Waller Tazewell, *A Review of the Proclamation of President Jackson* (Norfolk: J.D. Ghiselin, 1888), 25. Tazewell's reply to Jackson originally appeared as a series of newspaper articles following the issuance of Jackson's Proclamation of December 10, 1832.
10. Upshur, *Brief Enquiry*, 15.
11. Alden T. Vaughn, *New England Frontier: Puritans and Indians 1620-1675*, 3rd ed. (Norman, OK: University of Oklahoma Press, 1995), 174–75, 176–77.
12. Alexis de Tocqueville, *Democracy in America*, vol. 2, trans. Henry Reeve (New York: D. Appleton, 1904), 426. Volume 1 of *Democracy in America* was originally published in 1835 and volume 2 in 1840.
13. Richard Cobden to W. Hargreaves, June 22, 1861, in *The Life of Richard Cobden*, vol. 2, ed. John Morley (London: Macmillan, 1908), 381–82.
14. Upshur, *Brief Enquiry*, 15.
15. Story, *Commentaries*, vol. 1, 158.
16. If the First Continental Congress had had the character Story ascribes to it, it would be more difficult to account for the lackluster response from such colonies as Georgia and New York. Georgia was not represented as a colony; one person from Georgia was admitted as a delegate from his parish but did not vote on issues that required a majority of colonies to pass, since he had not been sent as a delegate of a colony. New York's representation was even more confusing, with various people from different parts of the colony portraying themselves as delegates from New York but not being recognized as such by the colonial government. The Continental Congress, Upshur explains, was "a *deliberative and advisory* body, and nothing more; and, for this reason, it was not deemed important, or, at least, not indispensable, that all the colonies should be represented, since the resolutions of congress had no obligatory force whatever. It was appointed for the sole purpose of taking into consideration the general condition of the colonies, and of devising and recommending proper measures, for the security of their rights and interests. For these objects no precise powers and instructions were necessary, and *beyond* them none were given." Upshur, *Brief Enquiry*, 20.

17. Upshur, *Brief Enquiry*, 31.
18. Ibid., 33.
19. Emmerich de Vattel, *The Law of Nations*, trans. Joseph Chitty (Philadelphia: T. & J.W. Johnson, 1867 [1758]), 2.
20. Robert Wild, "The Spirit of Nullification and Secession in the Northern States," *Proceedings of the State Bar Association of Wisconsin* (Milwaukee: The Evening Wisconsin Printing Co., 1912), 125.
21. Thomas Jefferson to Edward Everett, April 8, 1826, in *The Writings of Thomas Jefferson*, vol. X, *1816–1826*, ed. Paul Leicester Ford (New York: G.P. Putnam's Sons, 1899), 385.
22. "The United States were states, and they had joined together. The fact that their union had no set end date, in part because the length of the war could not be foreseen, was denoted by calling it 'perpetual.' (In those days treaties between European states often purported to be 'perpetual.' This did not mean that neither side could bring a treaty agreement to an end, but that there was no built-in sunset provision.)" Kevin R. C. Gutzman, *The Politically Incorrect Guide to the Constitution* (Washington, D.C.: Regnery, 2007), 12. Do not let this book's playful title fool you; it is a very significant work, even if tailored to a popular audience.
23. See Max Farrand, *The Framing of the Constitution of the United States* (New Haven, CT: Yale University Press, 1913), 190-91.
24. Kevin R. C. Gutzman, *Virginia's American Revolution: From Dominion to Republic, 1776–1840* (Lanham, MD: Lexington, 2007), 11.
25. Ibid., 19.
26. Ibid., 22.
27. Ibid., 30.
28. Raoul Berger, *Federalism: The Founders' Design* (Norman, OK: University of Oklahoma Press, 1987), 65.
29. Kevin R. C. Gutzman, "Edmund Randolph and Virginia Constitutionalism," *Review of Politics* 66 (Summer 2004): 491.
30. Gutzman, *Virginia's American Revolution*, 86.
31. Ibid.
32. James Madison, who unlike Randolph and Nicholas was never an attorney general and was not even a lawyer, wrote to a friend at the time that these conditions would have no legal force. He was wrong. As Professor Gutzman puts it, "Charity compels one to blame this misstatement on [Madison's] ignorance of the law of contracts and of treaties." Kevin R. C. Gutzman, "On Constitutional Issues," *Modern Age* 42 (Fall 2000): 399.
33. For the text, see "A Memorial From the General Assembly of Virginia," December 16, 1790, in *Hamilton and the National Debt*, ed. George Rogers Taylor (Boston: D.C. Heath, 1950), 56–57. The General

Assembly argued not simply that the power to assume the debts had not been granted, but also that such power had been expressly foreclosed by Article VI of the Constitution, which read in relevant part: "All Debts contracted and Engagements entered into, before the Adoption of this Constitution, shall be as valid against the United States under this Constitution, as under the Confederation."

34. *Patrick Henry: Life, Correspondence and Speeches*, vol. 2, ed. William Wirt Henry (New York: Charles Scribner's Sons, 1891), 456.
35. Ibid., 457.
36. Thomas Jefferson to James Madison, August 23, 1799, in *The Republic of Letters: The Correspondence between Thomas Jefferson and James Madison 1776–1826*, vol. 2: *1790–1804*, ed. James Morton Smith (New York: W.W. Norton, 1995), 1119.
37. Gutzman, *Virginia's American Revolution*, 118.
38. Ibid., 120.
39. The classic exposition of this view is Adrienne Koch and Harry Ammon, "The Virginia and Kentucky Resolutions: An Episode in Jefferson's and Madison's Defense of Civil Liberties," *William and Mary Quarterly* 5 (April 1948): 145–76.
40. Gutzman, *Virginia's American Revolution*, 130.
41. Ford, ed., *The Writings of Thomas Jefferson*, vol. X, 349n1.

CHAPTER 5

1. Ralph Raico, "The Theory of Economic Development and the 'European Miracle': The Vindication of P.T. Bauer," manuscript in possession of the author; a shorter version appeared in *The Collapse of Development Planning*, ed. Peter J. Boettke (New York: New York University Press, 1993).
2. Jean Baechler, *The Origins of Capitalism* (New York: St. Martin's, 1976), ch. 7. See also Thomas E. Woods, Jr., "Cobden on Freedom, Peace, and Trade," *Human Rights Review* 5 (October-December 2003): 77–90.
3. Robert Nisbet, *The Quest for Community: A Study in the Ethics of Order and Freedom* (New York: Oxford University Press, 1953), 98.
4. For the discussion of federative polities and modern states I am deeply indebted to Donald W. Livingston, "The Founding and the Enlightenment: Two Theories of Sovereignty," in *Vital Remnants: America's Founding and the Western Tradition*, ed. Gary L. Gregg II (Wilmington, DE: ISI Books, 1999), 243–74.
5. According to the libertarian Benjamin Constant, "The interests and memories which spring from local customs contain a germ of resistance which is so distasteful to authority that it hastens to uproot it. *Authority*

finds private individuals easier game; its enormous weight can flatten them out effortlessly as if they were so much sand" [emphasis added]. Alexis de Tocqueville noted in horror, "The old localized authorities disappear without either revival or replacement, and everywhere the central government succeeds them in the direction of affairs." Livingston, "The Founding and the Enlightenment," 251–52.

6. Thomas E. Woods, Jr., *33 Questions About American History You're Not Supposed to Ask* (New York: Crown Forum, 2007), 78–79.
7. Thomas E. Woods, Jr., *Meltdown: A Free-Market Look at Why the Stock Market Collapsed, the Economy Tanked, and Government Bailouts Will Make Things Worse* (Washington, D.C.: Regnery, 2009).
8. Adolf Hitler, *Mein Kampf*, trans. Ralph Manheim (New York: Hutchinson, 1969 [1925–26]), 526.
9. Senate Bill No. 311; available at http://leg1.state.va.us/cgi-bin/legp504.exe?101+sum+SB311.
10. House Bill 391; available at http://www.legislature.idaho.gov/legislation/2010/H0391.pdf.
11. Jeff Matthews, "To Our State Legislators: Nullification Requires Protection of Citizens," March 29, 2010; available at http://www.tenthamendmentcenter.com/2010/03/29/to-our-state-legislators-nullification-requires-protection-of-citizens/.
12. H. Robert Baker, *The Rescue of Joshua Glover: A Fugitive Slave, the Constitution, and the Coming of the Civil War* (Athens, OH: Ohio University Press, 2006), 162. Emphasis added.
13. Thomas J. DiLorenzo, "The Lunatic Left Is Getting Desperate," LewRockwell.com, March 22, 2010; available at http://www.lewrockwell.com/dilorenzo/dilorenzo183.html.
14. Ibid.
15. These figures come from Richard Fisher, president of the Federal Reserve Bank of Dallas, cited in Charles Goyette, *The Dollar Meltdown* (New York: Portfolio, 2009), 34–35.
16. I realize that there are some constitutionalist circles in which the very words "constitutional convention" are enough to condemn someone forever. I used to hold the same view until it finally dawned on me: what exactly is the nightmare scenario we are supposed to fear? That an amendment may be proposed granting the Congress general (rather than limited and enumerated) legislative power? Even if three-fourths of the states could somehow be persuaded to adopt such a thing, that's in practice what we already have. That the president may have a free hand in foreign affairs and domestic surveillance? We already have that. That the federal government may borrow and tax without limit? We have that, too. That a Federal Reserve System may destroy our money? We're already there. It's getting worse all the time, in spite of

the enormous and ongoing educational efforts on the part of countless grassroots activists. This is partly because the system is stacked against us. It may need to be tipped back in the direction of the states and the people by means of structural change.

17. See Woods, *33 Questions*, ch. 28; Clay S. Conrad, *Jury Nullification: The Evolution of a Doctrine* (Durham, NC: Carolina Academic Press, 1998).
18. Hampden (pseud.), *The Genuine Book of Nullification* (Charleston, SC: E. J. Van Brunt, 1831), 1. Emphasis added.
19. Jeff Woods, "State Legislator Says She Plans to Introduce 'Nullification' Bill," *Nashville City Paper*, December 29, 2009; available at http://nashvillecitypaper.com/content/city-news/state-legislator-says-she-plans-introduce-nullification-bill.
20. Murray N. Rothbard, Libertarian Party Keynote Address, 1977; excerpted at http://www.lewrockwell.com/rothbard/rothbard137.html.
21. Sanford Levinson, "States Can't Nullify Federal Law," *Austin American-Statesman*, February 6, 2010; available at http://www.statesman.com/opinion/insight/commentary-states-cant-nullify-federal-law-217250.html.
22. Ibid.
23. F. M. Anderson, "Contemporary Opinion of the Virginia and Kentucky Resolutions," *American Historical Review* 5 (December 1899): 225–52.
24. *State Documents on Federal Relations: The States and the United States*, ed. Herman V. Ames (New York: Longmans, Green, 1911), 43–44. Emphasis added.
25. *The Virginia and Kentucky Resolutions of 1798 and '99; with Jefferson's Original Draught Thereof, and Madison's Report, Calhoun's Address, Resolutions of the Several States in Relation to State Rights, with Other Documents in Support of the Jeffersonian Doctrines of '98* (Washington, D.C.: Jonathan Elliot, 1832), 81.
26. William J. Watkins, Jr., *Reclaiming the American Revolution: The Kentucky and Virginia Resolutions and Their Legacy* (New York: Palgrave, 2004), 117.
27. Thomas Jefferson to Charles Hammond, August 18, 1821, *The Writings of Thomas Jefferson*, vol. XV, ed. Albert Ellery Bergh (Washington, D.C.: Thomas Jefferson Memorial Association, 1907), 331–32.
28. Jon Roland, "Nullification is a Serious Option," *Austin American-Statesman*, February 8, 2010; available at http://www.statesman.com/opinion/nullification-is-a-serious-option-221199.html. My summary of Roland's views also derives from personal correspondence dated January 24, 2010.

Index

Z

About the Author

THOMAS E. WOODS, JR. (B.A., Harvard; M.A., M.Phil., Ph.D., Columbia) is a senior fellow at the Ludwig von Mises Institute in Auburn, Alabama. He is the author of ten books, including *Who Killed the Constitution?: The Fate of American Liberty from World War I to George W. Bush* (with Kevin R. C. Gutzman), 33 *Questions About American History You're Not Supposed to Ask,* and the *New York Times* bestsellers *The Politically Incorrect Guide™ to American History* and *Meltdown.*

Woods won the $50,000 first prize in the 2006 Templeton Enterprise Awards for *The Church and the Market: A Catholic Defense of the Free Economy.* Columbia University Press released his critically acclaimed 2004 book *The Church Confronts Modernity* in paperback in 2007. Woods's books have been translated into Italian, Spanish, Polish, German, Portuguese, Croatian, Korean, Japanese, Czech, and Chinese.

Woods edited and wrote the introduction to four additional books: *The Political Writings of Rufus Choate*, Murray N. Rothbard's *The Betrayal of the American Right*, *We Who Dared to Say No to War: American Antiwar Writing from 1812 to Now* (with Murray Polner), and Orestes Brownson's 1875 classic *The American Republic.* He is also the author of *Beyond Distributism*, part of the Acton Institute's Christian Social Thought Series.

Woods's writing has appeared in dozens of popular and scholarly periodicals, including *Investor's Business Daily*, *American Historical Review*, *Christian Science Monitor*, *Quarterly Journal of Austrian Economics*, *Economic Affairs* (U.K.), *Modern Age*, *American Studies*, *Journal of Markets & Morality*, *New Oxford Review*, *University Bookman*, *Catholic Social Science Review*, *Independent Review*, *Human Rights Review*, and *Journal des Economistes et des Etudes Humaines.* A contributor to half a dozen encyclopedias, Woods is co-editor of *Exploring American History: From Colonial Times to 1877*, an 11-volume encyclopedia. He is also a contributing editor of *The American Conservative* magazine.

Woods has appeared on FOX News Channel, MSNBC, CNBC, Bloomberg Television, FOX Business Network, and

C-SPAN, among other outlets. He has been a guest on hundreds of radio programs, including the Dennis Miller Show, the Michael Reagan Show, the Michael Medved Show, and National Public Radio's *Morning Edition* and *On Point*.

Woods lives in Auburn, Alabama, with his wife and four daughters, and maintains a website at TomWoods.com.